Veronese's Drawings

RICHARD COCKE

Veronese's Drawings

A CATALOGUE RAISONNE

SOTHEBY PUBLICATIONS

© Richard Cocke 1984
First published 1984 for Sotheby Publications by
Philip Wilson Publishers Ltd,
Russell Chambers, Covent Garden,
London WC2E 8AA

ISBN 0 85667 167 3

Designed by Mary Osborne
Printed by Jolly & Barber Ltd, Rugby
and bound by the University Press, Oxford

For S, R, M and D

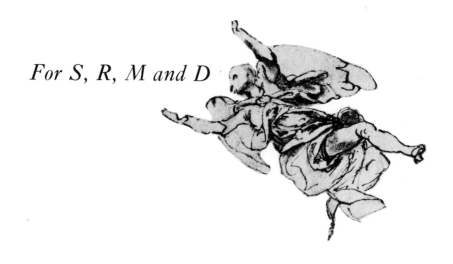

Contents

Acknowledgements

In the course of the long period of research which preceded the preparation of this book I incurred many debts. I am grateful to my colleagues at the University of East Anglia both for their encouragement and forebearance. Miss Alison Wardale typed and retyped the early drafts with extraordinary patience and Mrs Joan Awbery undertook the extensive correspondence and later revisions.

A grant from the British Academy enabled me to revisit the collections in Berlin and Dresden. The School of Fine Arts and Music contributed generously both to sabbatical leave and travel grants. I owe a very real debt to the staff of the many collections that I have consulted over the years. I am particularly grateful to those who have helped in the search for photographs, checked inscriptions and answered my queries: David Alston, Noel Annesley, Jacob Bean, Peter Day, Dr Peter Dreyer, Larissa Haskell, Carlos van Hasselt, Jürgen M. Lehmann, Oliver Logan, Agnes Mongan, Rudolfo Pallucchini, Felix Pryor, David Rosand, Jurriaan Poot and Janos Scholz.

I have benefited greatly from Professor Martindale's comments on the first draft of the introduction. That was ready for the press by the end of the summer of 1982, when it was delayed to allow for publication of the group of drawings purchased by the Louvre. I am grateful to Mlle Roseline Bacou for showing them to me, for allowing me to see the manuscript of her article before its publication and for her introduction to a private collection. Further travel to complete the revision of the catalogue was made possible by a grant from the British Academy.

From the outset Julien Stock took a keen interest in the project. His assistance has done much to improve the catalogue entries. I am especially grateful to him and to Philip Pouncey for their advice on attributional problems, although I alone am responsible for the selection of the material. At the publishers Joan A. Speers helped to remove many inconsistencies and obscurities in the manuscript. My greatest debt, however, is to my wife. Without her wise judgement it would not have been worth undertaking and without her enthusiasm it would not have been possible.

Chronology

1528
Birth of Veronese, Paolo Spezapreda, in Verona

16 April 1541
Paolo Spezapreda, still living in the parish of S. Paolo, Verona, is cited as a painter

1548
The date, inscribed in Roman numerals, of the *Christ preaching in the temple* in the Prado (Fig 1)

1551
The date of Veronese's frescoes in Villa Soranza

11 March 1553
Veronese, together with Battista del Moro, Domenico Brusacorci and Paolo Farinati, requests payment from Cardinal Ercole Gonzaga for the *Temptation of St Anthony* (Fig 18) painted for Mantua Cathedral

15 January 1555
Veronese is resident in Venice

1 December 1556
Contract for the ceiling of the nave of S. Sebastiano (Fig 5), for which Veronese is paid in the following year

1556
F. Sansovino, writing under the pseudonym Guisconi, in the *Tutte le cose notabili e belle che sono in Venetia*, refers to the work of: 'Paolo e compagni' in the rooms of the Consiglio dei Dieci in the Palazzo Ducale

1557
Payments to one of Vittoria's assistants for work at Palazzo Trevisan (Figs 6, 7, 8, 10)

31 March 1558
Veronese receives a payment of 105 ducats for his work on the frescoes in the upper nave of S. Sebastiano (Fig 11)

1559
A letter by Giulia da Ponte to Daniele Barbaro refers to Villa Maser, praising the fountain

1560–64
Series of accounts on the verso of the *Studies of the Virgin and Child, a horseman and a music-making angel* (53)

17 April 1566
Veronese marries Elena Badile in Verona

11 August 1568
The date of a letter to Veronese which forms the verso of the *Studies for a Mystic marriage of St Catherine and the Holy Family with Sts Anne, John the Baptist and Catherine* (56)

7 September 1568
Baptism of Veronese's eldest son, Gabriele

20 July 1570
Baptism of Veronese's second son, Carletto

6 July 1571
Publication of the Holy League to fight the Turks (*see* 61, 62)

29 April 1572
Payment for the *Feast of St Gregory the Great in Monte Berico*, Vicenza

18 July 1573
Veronese defends the *Feast in the house of the Levi* (Fig 35) before the Inquisition

1573
The date of the *Adoration of the Magi* from S. Silvestro, now in the National Gallery, London (Fig 34) and the *Madonna of the Rosary* (Fig 32)

1574
The date of the *Lamentation over the dead Christ* (Fig 40) in the church of SS. Annunziata, Ostuni

1575
Veronese is documented as working in Padua on the *Martyrdom of St Justina* (Fig 42) and the *Ascension of Christ* (Fig 43)

23 December 1575
First payment to Veronese for his work in the Sala del Collegio (Figs 54, 55)

1577
Destruction of the decoration of the Sala del Maggior Consiglio by fire

1577
Sebastiano Venier elected doge. He died in March 1578, (*see* Fig 56)

February 1578
The commission, under Giacomo Marcello and Giacomo Contarini, draws up the programme for the redecoration of the Sala del Maggior Consiglio. Veronese's canvases for the ceiling (Figs 57, 58) were completed by 1582

18 September 1582
Letter to Veronese from Marcantonio Gandini, on the verso of (99)

1583
Payment of Vittoria's workshop for the decoration of the chapel of the Sacrament in San Giuliano, for which Veronese designed the *Last Supper* (Fig 81)

1583 and 1584
A series of accounts, not by Veronese, which were used for the *Costume-studies for the Oedipus Tyrannus of Sophocles* (113, 114)

11 January 1584
Letter to Veronese on the verso of the *Studies for an Adoration of the shepherds* (116)

3 March 1585
Inaugural production of the *Oedipus Tyrannus* in the Teatro Olimpico with costumes sketched by Veronese (113, 114)

4 February 1588
Draft of an autograph letter on the verso of the *Studies for a Baptism of Christ* (125)

19 April 1588
Death of Paolo Veronese

Introduction

Introduction

The present catalogue of Veronese's drawings, which lists and describes over 150 autograph drawings, doubles the number included in the last complete catalogue: *Drawings of the Venetian Painters* by Hans Tietze and Erica Tietze-Conrat, published in 1944. Thus it underlines the justice of Mariette's appreciation written in 1741,[1] at a time when he knew only a comparatively limited number of drawings: 'Autant la plupart des Peintres Venitiens a paru negliger la partie du Dessein, autant Paul Véronèse s'est-il appliqué a la cultiver. Il n'a presque jamais peint aucun tableau, dont il n'ait fait auparavant un Dessein, arrêté et très-fini, et ce Dessein était suivi d'études en grand . . . On voit dans la collection de M.Crozat des Desseins qu'il a fait avec grand soin pour sa propre satisfaction [here catalogued as 19, 20, 21, 28 and 41]'. Yet the surviving drawings must represent only a small proportion of the original total: only one drawing for the frescoes at Villa Barbaro survives (14) together with one for the great *Feast in the house of Levi* (69) and there are none for the *Marriage feast at Cana* or for the organ case at S. Sebastiano.[2] That such drawings were made is suggested by the spread of the surviving drawings from the outset of Veronese's career (1, 2) down to the last year of his life (126, 127) and by their range from preparatory pen and ink sketches to detailed chalk studies.

While there is now general agreement on Veronese's importance as one of the outstanding Venetian draughtsmen, his drawings have been interpreted in two very different ways. Mariette, as quoted above, contrasted his use of drawings with that of other Venetian artists. The Tietzes, on the other hand, viewed drawings as an important aspect of Venetian practice from the Quattrocento onwards. They argued that the difference between the small graphic oeuvre of Titian and the comparatively large ones of Veronese, Bassano and Tintoretto was due to the accident

of survival attributable to the existence of an active family workshop which preserved the master's drawings as a part of their working stock in trade.

I believe that the evidence supports the view of Mariette, and that Veronese's use of drawings, like that of his contemporary Tintoretto, represented a deliberate rejection of Titian's working methods in favour of an older tradition which had been maintained in Florence. Accidents of survival make it impossible to give an account of Venetian draughtsmanship in the first half of the Quattrocento. Jacopo Bellini's great sketchbooks, in the British Museum and the Louvre, dating most probably from the 1450s, are the first major Venetian drawings known.[3] These highly worked out and finished drawings, often using both sides of the folio, document his new-found enthusiasm for perspective, for *all' antica* decoration on the fantastic buildings which dwarf the action and for a rather amateur antiquarianism. They bear no relationship to Jacopo's surviving paintings which are timid and conventional by contrast. His family's appreciation of his achievement is underlined by the care with which the sketchbooks were handed down within his workshop.[4] The medium in the Louvre sketchbook, of silverpoint supplemented by pen and ink and the unnatural settings with exaggerated foreshortening and schematic rocks must have seemed distant to Cinquecento artists and connoisseurs, but Jacopo's emphasis upon drawing as an end in its own right is echoed in Veronese's independent *chiaroscuro* drawings (here catalogued as 17–42).

The second half of the Quattrocento saw the development of a consistent use of drawings in the evolution of pictorial design in both Florence and Venice.[5] The process can be highlighted in the work of Ghirlandaio. The earliest stage in the preparation of the frescoes in S. Maria Novella is marked by rapidly annotated pen and ink sketches on white paper. Here the forms are suggested with great economy,[6] and in the next stage were elaborated with the addition of wash in more finished sketches.[7] Then the details of the drapery of a servant pouring water or of the head of an attendant were prepared either in pen and ink or chalk studies.[8] The final design was carefully executed in pen and ink and wash drawings which the contract specified had to be submitted to Ghirlandaio's patrons. The changes from the *modello* for the *Confirmation of the Franciscan order* in Berlin and the fresco itself show that in this case the patron must have exercised his rights and kept up with the latest papal fashion by demanding additional portraits of both people and buildings.[9]

The *modelli* were scaled up into cartoons from which the design was traced onto the freshly prepared plaster. Ghirlandaio's frescoes reveal his use of this technique, although no cartoons by him survive.[10] Venetian artists, by contrast with their Florentine contemporaries, omitted both this and the second stage and prepared their canvases directly from their drawings. They began with rapid pen and ink sketches generally drawn over red chalk suggesting the outline of the composition and giving a warmer tone to the white ground.[11] This richness of effect is also found in finished drawings made in preparation for the paintings, and is echoed in many of Veronese's drawings (43–50) as are the indications of size found on a number of Carpaccio's drawings (119).[12] Often artists like Carpaccio were more interested in defining the setting than the figures. This is true of the *St Augustine in his study* in the British Museum where a *pentimento* in the lintel of the doorway runs through the much sketchier head of the saint.[13] The wash in the *St Augustine* both works out the light effects of the canvas and achieves a richness of finish which is also found in the detailed studies of heads, drapery, etc.[14] These were made in grey and white washes on blue tinted paper whose pictorial character is richer than comparable Florentine drawings and anticipates some of Veronese's chalk studies (65, 112).

Although Venetian practice at the end of the Quattrocento differed from that in Florence it had enough in common for an artist trained in one school to feel at home in the other. Contemporaries were, however, already aware of the special character of Venetian art, its sense of *colorito*.

This can be seen in the happy outcome of Isabella' d'Este's often tortuous negotiations with Giovanni Bellini.[15] She had demanded an *istoria* for her studiolo but on learning of his reluctance to undertake a commission which would invite direct comparison with Mantegna, settled for a smaller *Nativity*. When, in 1504, after many delays and much diplomatic pressure the picture was ready in Venice, Lorenzo da Pavia wrote to Isabella, who had not yet seen it: 'Ma se io l'avese ordinato, averia volsuto le figure pù grande. Come scrise per l'altra, de invencione nesuno non pò arivare a messer Andrea Mantegna, che invero l'è ecelentisimo e el primo, ma Giovane Belino in colorir è ecelente, e tuti che à visto questo quadreto, ogneuono l'à comendato per una mirabile opera, et è ben finite quele cose è de vedere per sotile'.

The painting cannot now be identified but must have shared the poetic handling of landscape, light and drapery as well as the rich colours of the many masterpieces that Bellini created in the decade 1500–10.[16] The context within which Lorenzo da Pavia uses the term *colorito* is important for it demonstrates that it has nothing to do with the free almost sketchy exploitation of oil paint on coarsely woven canvas, which David Rosand identified as its main characteristic.[17] *Colorito* achieved some of its sense through the contrast with the *invencione* of Mantegna. Other contemporary theorists had linked Mantegna's *invencione* with his *disegno* and it was this contrast which was to dominate Cinquecento theory.[18]

That this is so reflects the special nature of Titian's rise to fame in Cinquecento Venice.[19] He retained Bellini's sensibility to light, colour and drapery but placed less emphasis upon drawings in the preparation of his many commissions and so gave a new meaning to the contrast between Venetian *colorito* and Florentine *disegno*. This becomes clear from the comparatively small number of drawings attributed to Titian, under fifty in the most recent catalogue by Konrad Oberhuber,[20] from which a number of previously accepted landscapes have to be removed since Peter Dreyer has shown them to be early forgeries.[21] This is a small number to set against the range of Titian's oeuvre and length of career. That this is not simply due to accidents of survival, as is often argued,[22] but reflects his working methods and approach to draughtsmanship should become clearer from a discussion of a number of his drawings. An older generation of critics rightly connected the pen and ink sketch in the Ecole des Beaux-Arts, Paris, with the fresco of the *Jealous husband killing his wife* of 1511 in the Scuola del Santo, Padua.[23] Their attribution to Titian has been replaced by one to Domenico Campagnola. The argument rests upon its similarity with the *David and Bathsheba* in the same collection, dated to 1517 through the sketches of the kneeling St Catherine on the verso which relate to Campagnola's engraving of the *Beheading of St Catherine* of that year.[24] Comparison of the two sheets, however, supports the older attribution of the *Jealous husband* to Titian. Its handling is freer and more direct than that of the *David and Bathsheba*, with a bold use of *pentimenti* in the wife's knees and a dramatic sense of form and movement not found in any certain Campagnola.

The graphic mode of the two sheets combining bold outlines with vigorous cross-hatching is unlike the comparable drawings of Gentile Bellini, Carpaccio or Mantegna. It strongly suggests the influence of the system of hatching developed in Dürer's mature prints. Titian would have been familiar with these as a result of Dürer's second visit to Venice in 1505–1507,[25] when they inspired his own great woodcut of the *Triumph of the Faith*.[26] The choice of graphic mode influenced the finished character of Titian's drawing, in contrast with the sketchier appearance of Carpaccio's comparable drawings, and the confusion between Titian and Campagnola is a testimony to the influence of Titian's drawings. The *Jealous husband*, although intended as a part of the preparatory process for a commissioned fresco, stood as a work of art in its own right after the artist had abandoned the design for one which, as Johannes Wilde demonstrated, reveals his awareness of the *Temptation* on the first half of Michelangelo's Sistine ceiling.[27]

Titian's subsequent preparatory drawings in pen and ink combine this decorative sense with a growing freedom and looseness in handling, which is echoed by the development of his chalk studies. In these he retained the coloured grounds of the older generation but substituted chalk for the use of the brush. This echoes the changes introduced in Florence around 1500 under the impact of Leonardo.[28] The great generation of Florentine artists who adapted Leonardo's new mastery of the chalk technique retained and perhaps refined the working procedure of the late

Quattrocento, in contrast with Titian whose chalk studies are extremely rare.

The masterful study for the sleeve of one of the apostles in the *Assuntà*, now in the British Museum, is by comparison to similar drawings by Raphael or Michelangelo, a work of art in its own right whose function in the design, where it was modified, was of secondary importance.[29] The precision and awareness of the textures of materials in this sketch is progressively abandoned in later chalk studies, the *Study of legs* in the Uffizi, for instance.[30] Titian also used chalk on coloured grounds for drawings which are squared for transfer and marked the final stage of the design. The forms in the *Sacrifice of Isaac* in the Ecole des Beaux-Arts and in the *Fallen horseman* in the Ashmolean Museum,[31] Oxford, are so generalised that they could only be used to indicate the figure's approximate position on the canvas. The face of the Abraham in the Paris sheet is suggested but not defined (he has at least two different noses) and this is also true of the foreshortening of Isaac's legs. Transferring such drawings to canvas would produce a mass of outlines, similar to those revealed by x-rays of Titian's canvases, which emphasise the often significant *pentimenti*. The creative freedom of this method reached its climax in Titian's late paintings, as described by Vasari who had visited Titian's studio on his second visit to Venice in the 1560s.[32] This approach stemmed from the working method of Giorgione who recast the *Tempesta* by replacing a seated nude woman with a standing shepherd.[33]

Vasari's disapproval of Titian's approach to painting ante-dates his knowledge of Titian's late style, although it was only in the second edition of the *Vite*, of 1568, that he voiced his hostility to Titian's dismissal of the standard Florentine procedure for preparing a design beginning with pen and ink sketches and ending with full-scale cartoons. Titian's surviving drawings invalidate any other interpretation of Michelangelo's famous comment on the *Danae* recorded by Vasari, with whom he had seen the painting in 1545:[34] 'it was a pity that in Venice painters did not learn how to draw'. The artist who had designed the *Leda* and the *Venus and Cupid* cannot have made this criticism out of prudery, as Charles Hope has suggested.[35] The weaknesses in the drawing of Danae's left leg, when combined with a working procedure which neglected life-studies, make this more than a theoretical defence of

1 Study for Christ preaching in the temple (actual size)

Florentine *disegno*, as Konrad Oberhuber has argued.[36]

In spite of Titian's prestige, his method of working directly onto the canvas was never universally accepted, even in Venice. Sebastiano del Piombo had been in close touch with Giorgione before his departure for Rome in 1511. His subsequent career and more especially his collaboration with Michelangelo, whose drawings he used as the basis for a number of major commissions, contrast strongly with the working method of Giorgione and Titian.[37] Pordenone, who had visited Rome most probably in 1516, studied the drawings of Andrea del Sarto, the outstanding draughtsman working in Florence. This influence has long been recognised in the detailed chalk studies for the Cremona fresco-cycle, but is also perceptible in the compositional chalk studies for the same cycle. These were established with a free flowing stroke[38] which he subsequently used in rapid pen and ink sketches revealing his appreciation of Titian's marvellous 1520 *Study of St Lawrence*, now in Berlin. Pordenone's only life-studies are related to the Cremona frescoes, and he appears to have abandoned the practice later in his career. Nevertheless, he retained an interest in other aspects of Sarto's draughtsmanship – an influence to be seen in his finished chalk and *chiaroscuro* drawings, which, like those of Sarto, were intended to enable him to visualise the design before its transfer to canvas.[39]

Although Pordenone did not work in Verona, his attitude (but not his drawing technique) appears to have been influential on the younger generation of artists both in Venice and Verona. They may also have known of Michelangelo's criticism of Titian, even though it only found its way into print in Vasari's *Vite*. The same views must underlie the schematic slogan formulated by Pino in his *Dialogo della Pittura* of 1548 that the outstanding painter would combine the *colorito* of Titian with the *disegno* of Michelangelo.[40]

The 1971 Verona exhibition, which was one of the first attempts to give an overall account of drawings in the city, revealed a break between the older artists (for whom drawing was relatively unimportant) and the younger generation, beginning with Battista del Moro, born just before Veronese in 1524. While Veronese's interest in drawing links with new developments in Verona, his graphic style looked beyond the confines of his native city. In the same way, his paintings achieved a unique combination of Central Italian *disegno* and Venetian *colorito*, with a palette reminiscent of that of Mantegna.

According to Ridolfi, Veronese had studied Dürer's woodcuts at the beginning of his training and then, later, Parmigianino's drawings. The bold hatching in the pen and ink *Study for the Christ preaching in the temple* of 1548 (1), clearly reveals his debt to Dürer, while the fluent graphic style with its liberal use of *pentimenti* finds its precedent in Parmigianino's drawings, even though the figures in the sketch are more Michelangelesque than those of the painting. Veronese's reliance on drawings as a means of preparing the design is further underlined by the chalk study for the man seated under Christ in the same painting (2, Fig 1). Here, however, the handling of the drapery with its painterly combination of chalk, white heightening

65   Study of a seated woman

It may have been supplemented by a finished *modello*, although the only surviving ones (75, 87, 88) date from later in his career. Until recently only a couple of chalk studies could be attributed to Veronese, since so few could be related to surviving paintings. The re-appearance of detailed studies like the *Study of the head and right arm of a man* (139), probably for the *Transfiguration* in Montagnana (Fig 98), and of the *Study of a seated woman* (65), for one of the servants in the background of the *Rape of Europa* (Fig 32), reveal the scope of Veronese's chalk studies and suggest that many more must still await recognition and publication.

This is further underlined by the identification of the first nude study for a painting, the *Study of a seated nude* (55), made in preparation for the cripple healed by St Barnabas in the *Miracle of St Barnabas* (Fig 25). The directness of vision in this life-study is echoed in the early *Study of legs* (2v) and underlines the extent of Veronese's dependence on drawing in the preparation of his paintings. The *Study of a seated nude* (55) is unusual in being drawn on buff paper. In most of his chalk studies Veronese contrasts the dark chalk with blue paper, echoing the pictorial effects introduced by Carpaccio and developed by Titian.

His handling of the chalk in a large and distinguished group of costume-studies echoes the generalised approach to form introduced by Titian (2, 60, 65, 67, 73, 77, 132, 140, 141, 147 and 152). The flexibility with which Veronese used chalk suggests a range of uses. The early *Study of Count Giuseppe Porto with his son Adriano* (4) was sketched in grey chalk, but was then reworked in the more precise medium of pen and ink and wash. Later Veronese used broad chalk strokes for the drawings in which he prepared the allegorical figures of the ceiling of the Sala del Collegio (70, 84, 85). The generalisation of the *Study of a standing lady* (81) suggests that it was not a costume-study for the portrait now in Lugano (Fig 52), but one of a series of pattern sheets submitted to the sitter before Veronese began the painting.

The generalised use of the chalk, which recurs in the *Study of an apostle* (76) and the *Study of the head of an old man looking down* (112), contrasts with that in another group of studies. These include the *Study of a Negro boy* (54) as well as (68), (128) and (143) where the realism

and coloured paper reveal his awareness of Titian's chalk studies. This is not surprising, for in a discussion of the early appreciation of drawings, Julius Held[41] drew attention to the important role played by Venetian amateurs of the early sixteenth century in the development of the taste for fine drawings. This has been further underlined by the early date suggested by Peter Dreyer for the group of landscapes forged as Titian's.[42]

The working procedure that Veronese adopted for *Christ preaching in the temple*, where the preparatory sketch was followed by detailed chalk studies (1, 2), marks a return to the traditional procedure which Titian had abandoned.

88 Modello for the Venice triumphant

matches that of the *Study of a seated Negro eating* (135), whose genre-like action has led to doubts about the attribution. Here the directness of vision matches that shown in the portraits of contemporaries which Veronese introduced into his religious paintings.[43]

The chalk studies must have helped to prepare the *modelli* which, like those of Pordenone, were intended to help Veronese visualise the composition and to execute its transfer to canvas (75, 87, 88). Only a comparatively few *modelli* survive, partially because of the use which was made of them by the workshop. One drawing, although not squared for transfer (16), was probably used as a *modello*, as it was spotted with paint while in the hands of the workshop. The *modelli* share the rich technique of the *chiaroscuro* drawings, which can probably be dated to the 1550s. This suggests that Veronese may well have prepared them from the outset of his career. The surviving *modelli* are squared for transfer but fulfil a variety of functions. The care with which the basic scheme of the architecture was first established in the *Modello for the Venice triumphant* (88) suggests that it was not intended to be submitted to the commission responsible for drawing up the programme, but was used to visualise the effect of the figures against the great setting which Veronese had devised. This is also suggested by the late addition of the heads of Agostino Barbarigo and St Justina behind the foreground group in the *Modello for Doge Sebastiano Venier's thanksgiving for the Battle of Lepanto* (87), which is intended to heighten the contrast between the earthly and heavenly spheres. The change led to a dramatic recasting of the iconography of the canvas (Fig 56), which must have been undertaken in consultation with the donor, but for which, as the drawing reveals, the initial impetus came from the artist.

The introduction of the view of the church of S. Giustina into the background of the canvas of the *Martyrdom of St Justina* (Fig 42), when it had not occurred in the *modello* (75), suggests that in this case the *modello* must have been submitted to the prior of S. Giustina, who called for this change. That the drawing is squared suggests that this was an additional function.

Cartoons, as already noted, had not played a part in Venetian drawing practice. None by Veronese survive, but the large *Study of a woman's head* in the Uffizi (14) is pricked for transfer and corresponds closely with one of the muses at Maser (Fig 13). It could be a fragment of a cartoon and suggests that Veronese made others especially for the large decorative works, both on canvas and in fresco, that he undertook at the end of the 1550s and the beginning of the 1560s. It is, however, possible that later in his career he abandoned the practice since the *Peter of Amiens exhorts Doge Vitale Michele* (Fig 63) was, according to Ridolfi, the cartoon for a tapestry intended for the Palazzo Ducale. The choice of oil on canvas could indicate that by this time, in the 1580s, Veronese no longer prepared large-scale cartoons as he had earlier in his career.

Veronese's working procedure was notable in one other respect; Ridolfi, who knew the collection of Veronese's heirs as well as that of Tintoretto's, was struck by the absence of small-scale wax models, in contrast with those left by Tintoretto.[44] The point seems to be confirmed by

the skill with which Veronese established the foreshortening of the ceiling at S. Sebastiano in the *Study for the
Triumph of Mordechai* (6) and the *Studies for the Triumph of
Mordechai and the Coronation of Esther* (5), which are not
based upon studio models. These may have been used for
the Fame in the early *Studies of Fame* (3), the foreshortened
man chastised by Cupid at the top of the later *Studies for
the four Allegories of Love* (78) for the St Sebastian in the
Studies of a Charity, Sts Justina and Sebastian (86), from
the Koenigs collection, which is based on a *modello* by his
friend Vittoria, and for the Ganymede in the *Studies for a
Last Supper and a Rape of Ganymede* (110). The famous
Roman bust of the so-called Vitellius from the Grimani
collection was drawn on the verso of the *Study for Liberality*
in the British Museum (70v) and formed the starting-point
for one of the less attractive guests in the *Feast in the house
of Levi* (Fig 36).

Just as Veronese's working procedure avoided the ex-
tremes found in Tintoretto's drawings, so his development
was gradual. Thus, although there is often no consensus on
the dates (and in some cases on the status) of undocumented
paintings, there are enough dated or datable works to
establish a framework within which to arrange his graphic
oeuvre. The arguments for the dating of individual sheets
are set out in the catalogue, but at a general level there is a
continuous but gradual growth in freedom of handling and
in the boldness with which figures are placed on the sheet.
Thus, in the period down to 1560, the pen and ink sketches
develop from the *Study for Christ preaching* of 1548 (1) to
the comparatively greater boldness of the *Study for the
Triumph of Mordechai* of 1556 (6) and the *Studies of Mercury*
from the following year (11); Veronese continued with this
mode of drawing but increasingly added white heightening
or more often a free wash applied with the brush.

The first drawing to show this combination is the *Studies
of Fame, Peace (?) and a cartouche* of 1551 (3). Fame's
drapery is modelled with a rather tentative brush-stroke
that only achieves its characteristic freedom with the 1557
sketches for Palazzo Trevisan (8, 9, 10 and 11). This
development is echoed in the white heightening which was
first applied in a rather schematic fashion in the 1548 *Study
of a seated man* (2) and develops greater assurance some six
years later in the *Count Giuseppe da Porto with his son
Adriano* (4), where it transforms the pen and ink under-

neath, and advances further in the *Study of twelve apostles*
at the beginning of the 1560s (16). The characteristic
blocks of white heightening with smaller snaking passages
are later broken up to suggest greater depth and fluency in
the *Study of a dead Christ and a skeleton* of 1573 (72) and
the 1575 *Modello for the Martyrdom of St Justina* (75).

This outline establishes a framework within which to
date the splendid series of finished *chiaroscuro* drawings
catalogued together (17–42) as independent works produced in the 1550s and early 1560s. These drawings have
long been among the best known and most sought after of
Veronese's drawings. There is also general agreement on
the links between different sheets, finding partial support
in (34) made in preparation for three different *chiaroscuro*
drawings (28, 29, 38). This consensus does not extend to
the questions of their date, which is either ignored or put at
the end of Veronese's career, or of the purpose for which
they were made. The handling of the white heightening
does not yet have the freedom of the later drawings and is
linked instead with the earlier ones. This appears to be
borne out by their, admittedly rather distant, relationship
with autograph paintings (one may ignore (19) and (28)
which were re-used for literal and unimaginative paintings
most likely produced by the workshop after Veronese's
death). Thus the undated *Rest on the Flight into Egypt* (Fig
16) and the *St Anthony Abbot enthroned* of 1570 (Fig 17)
were developed from the drawings (28) and (31), just as the
monumental Truth in the *Omnia Vanitas* in the Frick
collection of 1567 (Fig 22) evolves from the allegorical
ladies in a number of sheets (17, 22, 40). The theme of the
Triumph of Temperance over Vice (23) is similar to that of
the *Triumph of Patience over lack of self-restraint* (Fig 15) on
the ceiling of the Stanza del Tre Capi of the Consiglio dei
Dieci in the Palazzo Ducale, which was painted by the end
of the 1550s. It should be stressed that the painting has a
vividness and power, even allowing for the difference in
function, which makes it extremely unlikely that the drawing would come later. This early date is also reflected in the
experimental iconography of the drawings and in their
treatment of a wide range of modes – narrative in *The
supper at Emmaus* (35), *The angel appears to Zacharias* (24)
and the series of the *Rest on the Flight into Egypt* (25,
28–30), and the *sacre conversazioni* between saints (31 and
32) – together with the elaborate use of attributes and

25 Christ the Redeemer appears to Sts Peter and Anthony of Padua

accessories in both religious and mythological sheets (20, 22).

This description already offers an answer to the question of their function which elaborates Mariette's view that they were made 'avec grand soin pour sa propre satisfaction'. That satisfaction must have been sharpened by the criticism of Titian's attitude to drawing, already quoted, which stands in strong contrast to the first comment on Veronese's work in the rooms of the Consiglio dei Dieci (Fig 15) described by Francesco Sansovino, under the pseudonym of Guisconi[45] as: 'Opera veramente di disegno et gentile'.

This seems preferable to the alternative view[46] that they were intended as *modelli*, since none is squared for transfer and they are more highly finished than the surviving *modelli*. This is a matter of degree rather than kind, and has led to confusion. The *Temptation of St Anthony* (36) has been seen as the *modello* for the painting of the same subject of 1552 (Fig 18), but it differs so fundamentally that it seems more likely to be a later sketch intended to improve the design by making the saint more prominent.

The inscriptions which Veronese added to a number of the series (17–23), although couched in the first person, were not, as David Rosand first noted,[47] in his hand. In one case the inscription was written on a page which included a series of accounts (20v), another omits some details (19) and two more give misleading accounts of the allegories (17 and 23), as though Veronese had forgotten the original meaning. The inscription on the now lost *Pittura Sesta* (Fig 14), which was transcribed by Ridolfi, who is not always accurate: 'come meglio fine del libro sara dichiarito per intelligenza de' Pittori e per diletto degli amatori della Virtu', suggests that at the end of his career Veronese intended to collect the drawings together either to follow the example of Jacopo Bellini's sketchbooks or for publication. This might be connected with the plans for printing referred to on the verso of the Von Hirsch *Studies* of 1582 (99) and on the undated letter to Veronese, probably from Benedetto, and also from the 1580s which he re-used for the *Study for a Noli me Tangere* (115). It is possible that when Schiaminossi engraved the *Virgin and Child appear to Sts Thomas and Cecilia* (37 and Fig 19), in the early years of the seventeenth century, he was influenced by this unfulfilled plan. If this is so, the damage that he inflicted on the Berlin sheet should temper our disappointment that Veronese failed in his intention to have his drawings engraved, perhaps as a final tribute to Dürer.

Although relatively few drawings have survived from the 1560s, the outset of the most productive phase of Veronese's career, there are more from the 1570s when he began to design for the workshop starting with the *Studies for a Rape of Europa, the Madonna of the Rosary and a Pietà* (64). Here the studies for two school pictures are worked out with care and finish not found the hastier sketches for Veronese's own masterful *Rape of Europa*. On rare occasions Veronese repeated this degree of refinement in his pen and ink sketches for the workshop, the *Studies for a Baptism of Christ* in Düsseldorf (104), for instance. But it is generally impossible to tell from the drawing alone whether it was intended for use by Veronese or his workshop, as in the *Studies for a Visitation, St Nicholas in glory, Faith and Charity* (80).

Of the drawings that can be dated to the early 1560s, the series of Evangelists and Saints in the Hermitage (43–50) were framed for a function which cannot at present be reconstructed. The *Studies of a suit of armour* (51), whose handling is similar to that of the Hermitage drawings and with some of the finished *chiaroscuro* drawings, renders a type of armour which although it recurs in Veronese's paintings from the 1550s onwards, does not correspond with any painting and therefore appears to have been made for its own sake.

52   Study for the Martyrdom of St George

Veronese first demonstrates his mature style in the *Study for the Martyrdom of St George* of 1566 (52). Here we find the freedom of pen, the movement of figures and the rich wash which characterise the preparatory drawings in the period down to *circa* 1580. The energy of this sheet is found in the Kassel *Studies for the Feast in the house of Levi* (69), where what may well be the initial scheme with the Magdalen about to anoint Christ's feet is combined with vivid sketches of servants pouring out wine. A comparable style is to be found, too, in the *Study for the Feast in the house of Simon* (57) and the *Studies for a Marriage feast at Cana* (58), whose shared motifs (the stooping servant, the man sitting back in his chair and the curving table) are so changed in the paintings that their common ancestry is no longer apparent.

Equally radical changes are also illustrated in many of the drawings for the redecoration of the Palazzo Ducale after the fires of 1574 and 1577 (82–97). The studies for

the fresco of *Venice enthroned* in the Anticamera of the Sala del Collegio (Fig 54), which include a copy by Carletto after a lost drawing by his father (Fig 53), start with a centrally seated, passive Venice to whom homage is paid, and then move to an asymmetrical composition with a more active Venice (82 and 83). The differences between the *modello* and the painting of *Doge Sebastiano Venier's thanksgiving for the Battle of Lepanto* (87 and Fig 56), in the adjoining Sala del Collegio have received a detailed commentary from Professor Sinding-Larsen. His thesis that the changes were not planned by Veronese, is, as Sir Karl Parker had already indicated when first publishing the sheet, undermined by the *pentimenti* in the *modello*, most notably where Agostino Barbarigo is added over the flag together with St Justina.

The challenge of the scale on which Veronese had to work in the Sala del Maggior Consiglio, albeit often with the help of the workshop, led to an added concentration upon the settings in the drawings for the paintings for the walls (92 and 93). This is true of the cartoon for the unexecuted tapestry of *Peter of Amiens exhorts Doge Vitale Michele* (97) and it also shaped his approach to the *Modello for the Venice triumphant* (88) where the orthogonals were first established as a guide for the architecture over which the figures were then added. The *modello* must have brought together a number of earlier sketches for the figures, only one of which has survived, the *Studies of horsemen, a captive, a dog and a drum* (89). These may have been similar to the *Studies for a Coronation* (94–96), made after he had won the competition for this enormous undertaking with the *modello* in Lille (Fig 62), when he wanted to give the figures a clear identity through their attributes and also to link them together.

The 1580s marked the emergence of Veronese's late style in sombre masterpieces like the *Crucifixion* in Budapest (Fig 79) and the series of Old and New Testament canvases from the collection of the Duke of Buckingham (Fig 90); this was only one of the modes in which he worked, a point brought home by the small *Finding of Moses* in Washington (Fig 73) or, on a different scale, the *Venice triumphant* in the Sala del Maggior Consiglio (Fig 57). This duality is reflected in the contrast between the enormous simplification of the handling in the *Studies for groups of saints and a Coronation of the Virgin* (95) and the freedom of stroke in the *Study for*

119 Study for Christ washing the apostles' feet

Christ washing the apostles' feet (119). These two sheets, however, share the new sense of abstraction and concentration upon the graphic means. This is a common feature of the drawings from the 1580s where indeed Veronese achieves a more recognisable 'late style' than in his paintings. The individual strokes, whether part of a welter as in (119) or isolated as in (95) are more rapid, less connected, clumsier if taken out of context and more completely abstracted from the forms that they are intended to represent. There is a comparable development in Veronese's treatment of wash. This ranges from the convincing suggestion of form through the contrast between the white ground and the wash in the *Studies for a Last Supper and a Rape of Ganymede* (110) to the more broken handling of other drawings of this period (100, 116, 117),

where patches of wash of differing intensity are juxtaposed with a sense of abstraction. It matches, too, both Veronese's handling of pen and ink and his clumsier handwriting in the late 1570s (*compare* (53v) of 1560–64 with his letter to Gandini of 1578 (Fig 87)).

A surprisingly high proportion of pen and ink and wash studies have survived from this last phase of Veronese's career. Many of these rapid sketches were intended for commissions to be executed by the workshop (102, 110, 120, 124). These late drawings also reveal his contact with a wider non-Venetian clientele. The *Finding of Moses*, although carried out by the workshop, may well have been commissioned by the Dukes of Mantua in whose collection it was in 1627 (102), and the *Venus with a mirror* in the study in the British Museum (106) was made in preparation for the now lost painting which, according to Borghini, Veronese painted at the commission of Rudolf II. The *Studies for a Judith and Holofernes, David and Goliath and other compositions* (99), dated 1582 by the letter on the sheet, documents the moment at which Borghini collected information for the *Riposo* since it combines two of the subjects which he reported as having been painted for the newly elected Duke of Savoy, Charles Emanuel I.

The *Costume-studies for the Oedipus Tyrannus of Sophocles* (113 and 114) reveal Veronese's role in another important scheme, the inaugural presentation in Palladio's Teatro Olimpico, Vicenza. Contemporary sources indeed attribute the lavish costume designs to the Vicentine artist G.B.Maganza, four of whose drawings survive (Figs 83–85), but these turn out to be based upon a series of first ideas by Veronese, which needed to be worked up in greater detail for the seamstresses.

Maganza's faithful if uninspired versions of Veronese's drawings match the unimaginative way in which the workshop realised Veronese's rapid sketches (70, 72, 89, 94, Fig 69), although the *Study of the head of an old man looking down* (112) shows that Veronese also produced detailed studies to assist the process. The pictures produced after his death by his heirs claimed a link with the master's work through the signature 'EREDES PAULI CALIARI', but this is not borne out by examination of the drawings. The *Study for a Christ healing at the pool of Bethesda* (122) appears to have served as the starting-point for the now lost canvas engraved by Pietro Monaco (Fig 93) where the transformation of the design reveals the decisive role of the workshop.

For this reason, I do not follow the argument which has related the Fogg *Studies for a Baptism of Christ* (125), dated February 1588 by the letter on the verso, and the closely linked sheet now in Edinburgh (126) to the *Baptism* in the nave of the Redentore, signed by the Eredi. The canvas was probably commissioned only after Veronese's death on 19 April 1588. It reveals a superficial interest in Tintoretto alien to Veronese's more considered response which must be due to an elaboration of the project by the Eredi, who had the Fogg and Edinburgh sheets to hand. These seem to me to have been intended for the splendid canvas from S. Giovanni in Malta, now in Palazzo Pitti (Fig 95) the quality of which is brought out by comparison with a

school version (Fig 96) attempting to fuse motifs from the painting with others from the drawings.

In spite of his comparative youth, Carletto (b.1570) appears to have played the outstanding role in designing paintings for the Eredi, for whom he provided a number of preparatory drawings.[48] He had learned to draw by copying his father's drawings (Figs 53 and 103), and the handling of the drawing in which he recorded with evident pride his now destroyed fresco of *Cupid and Psyche* (Figs 99, 100) emulates the rich wash of Veronese's late drawings, the *Studies for a Last Supper and a Rape of Ganymede* (110), for instance, but is rather pedantic. This tendency is exaggerated in later drawings like the *Study for the Holy Family with Sts John the Baptist and Anne* (Fig 102) with its concern to match each fold with a precise stroke which loses the spontaneity of Veronese's work.

The *Study of a Venus seen from behind* (181) is a rare study from a model attributable to Carletto whose working procedure is further indicated by the *Study of hands* (168) and the *Study of the head of a woman* (217) which must have complemented the many preliminary studies to have survived. This makes him a dominant figure in the workshop and contrasts him with his uncle Benedetto. A small group of drawings can be attributed in part to the latter because the *Copy after a Rest on the Flight into Egypt* (212) after the canvas now in the Ringling Museum, Sarasota, is on the back of a series of accounts by Veronese which runs from June 1570 to October 1572. Unlike Carletto, Benedetto was deeply impressed by the freedom of his brother's pen and ink drawings and the richness of his handling of chalks, both of which are imitated in the chalk study after Martha in the *Feast in the house of Simon*, painted for the Servites and the pen sketch on the verso after Judas rising up from his chair (185v). They fail, however, to match the understanding of form of Veronese's contemporary drawings, the *Study of a kneeling magus* (67) and the *Study for a Lamentation over the dead Christ and a Supper at Emmaus* (74), for instance.

The attribution of the *Study of the Virgin and Child with Sts John the Baptist and Louis of Toulouse with unidentified donors* (165) remains controversial. I believe that its style cannot, as is often claimed, be reconciled with that of Veronese at the beginning of his career (see 1, 2 and 4). It is derived from the much later phase best represented by the

Modello for the Martyrdom of St Justina of 1575 (75), a date which fits both with the external history of the canvas and with the career of Alvise dal Friso to whom, together with the Bevilacqua-Lazise altar and the small replica in the Uffizi (Fig 104), it can be attributed. This is significant since the bold but clumsy handling of the St Louis recurs in the sketchier *Study of a kneeling woman* in a private collection, New York (Fig 109). The free handling with its bold use of *pentimenti* resembles that of a number of sheets, some of which had old attributions to Veronese and imitated his early style (196, 202, 205, 206 and Fig 106).

The freedom of Veronese's late style was the inspiration for many other artists, probably including Alessandro Maganza who may well have been responsible for (184) and (222). A wide range of drawings in the section of Rejected Attributions reveals other contemporary artists, few of whom can be identified (161, 164, 171, 174 and 180). By contrast, (97) may well be by Palma Giovane, and the magnificent chalk study in Haarlem (177) has recently been attributed to Domenichino.

Perhaps the most surprising sheet to be included in this section is the *Study of two palm trees* (157) which has long been admired as one of Veronese's outstanding *chiaroscuro* drawings. Although more detailed and finished than the sketch on the verso, the use of the white heightening on both is similar. This justifies the rejection since the verso is clearly related to a part of Mattia Preti's decoration in S. Giovanni in Valletta, Malta, of a century later. Comparison to the certain *chiaroscuro* drawings reveals an artist, although it is unlikely to be Preti, who had studied Veronese's achievement but preferred a more even, less subtly modulated approach. That the artist of the *Study of two palm trees* had seen the *chiaroscuro* drawings underlines the way in which Veronese's preoccupation with these drawings, suggested by the inscriptions which he dictated probably at the end of his career, influenced many of the most important collectors of drawings in the seventeenth century.

The taste for drawings, mentioned previously, led to the formation of outstanding collections in Italy, France and England. This began the dispersal of Veronese's drawings, now to be found in most of the major print-rooms of Europe and America but no longer in Verona or Venice. The *Rest on the Flight into Egypt* (28) copied by Van Dyck in the 1620s may have been in the family collection in Venice and four further *chiaroscuro* drawings were on display in Verona in the 1620s, when Ridolfi visited the city, in the Curtoni (41) and Muselli collections (19, 21). Those in the Muselli collection were show-pieces, which may have been displayed so that the inscriptions could be seen, since Ridolfi transcribed them. Together with the sheet from the Curtoni collection they formed a part of the great collection of Pierre Crozat in the next century. To them Crozat added a drawing from the Lely collection (28) and a group of less than typical preparatory sketches (161, 202 and 209).

This pattern of taste influenced Ridolfi who, in addition to the Curtoni and Muselli collections, mentioned the two *modelli* for the pictures on the walls of the Sala del Maggior Consiglio, as well as the *chiaroscuro* drawings in the Caliari collection. He omitted, however, the pen and chalk studies included, with no indication of author, in the 1682 inventory of the family's collection.[49] By this date they must have owned drawings by a wide range of followers but, even though nothing can be traced back to that collection, it seems reasonable to assume that there were still a number of autograph Veronese's. Crozat's collection echoed that of Everard Jabach, ceded in 1671 to the French Royal family. Jabach owned a number of finished drawings which he considered, not always correctly, to be by Veronese (4, 36, 187 and 188), and also the *Studies of Neptune with tritons and sea horses* (12), which remained among the anonymous drawings in his *rebut* until recognised as autograph some two centuries later by Albert Châtelet.

Sir Peter Lely's collection shared some of this bias since it included a notable series of finished drawings (17, 18, 22, 28, 35, 39 and 88). There was also, however, another class of drawing, the compositional sketch, which was to be important in subsequent English collecting (82, 117). Jonathan Richardson, Senior, for instance, owned only one finished *chiaroscuro* drawing, that engraved by Schiaminossi (37), and three preparatory drawings (1, 101, 102) from Lely's collection. His son owned one of each (18 and 57), while the greatest of all collectors, Sir Joshua Reynolds, owned one finished drawing (40) against thirteen preparatory drawings (8, 10, 11, 57, 59, 90, 101, 102, 115, 123, 126, 144), only one of which was misattributed (164). However, to judge from the summary catalogue of his collection drawn up when it was sold at Phillips, 5–26 March 1798, only a small proportion of his collection is now known.

Reynolds was influential both in the nature of his collection and also in his failure to discuss his drawings in the *Discourses*. Mariette's appreciation of Veronese's drawings, although based upon the limited range in the Crozat collection which he himself acquired, still remains, as shown above, the best account both of the role of drawings in the preparation of his paintings and of his use of white heightening.

The pattern set by Reynolds was followed by Marchese Jacopo Durazzo in Genoa, whose collection formed the basis for that now in Berlin. He owned a large number of rapid preliminary drawings (6, 21, 74, 79, 100, 119). Similar drawings were also included, often mislabelled, in an anonymous Italian collection, that is sometimes identified as the Borghese collection, although the appearance of the mark on a French drawing of the eighteenth century shows that it was only formed comparatively late (5, 71, 78, 99, 110, 127). It also included a large and distinguished group of chalk studies (60, 65, 73, 76, 81, 84, 128, 132, 133, 139, 143, 147, 185, 214).

The external history of the collection means that the attributions have to be treated with caution. They indicate the right area but cannot be relied upon as can be seen from the mistaken attributions of (76), (78), (128), (185) and (214). The trend to attribute to Veronese drawings by his studio becomes more pronounced in the nineteenth century. Only a small proportion of Sir Thomas Lawrence's collection, for instance, which passed to Samuel Woodburn and was sold at Christie's, 4–12 June 1860, has reappeared. It included notable autograph drawings (18, 29, 51, 59), but two others, which had been attributed to Veronese, were by his son Carletto.[50] These two sheets had passed to the Malcolm collection and thence to the British Museum in 1895. Two further drawings that can be attributed to Carletto (Figs 101 and 102) and one by an unidentifiable follower were thought to be by Veronese in Sir J. C. Robinson's 1876 catalogue of the Malcolm collection.[51]

In spite of these misattributions, distinguished drawings by Veronese have continued to reappear. By 1940 Franz Koenigs had a large group, most of which passed subsequently to the Museum Boymans-van Beuningen, Rotterdam. It included both preparatory sketches (53, 80,

84   Study for Moderation

86, 123, 212) as well as a number of chalk studies (67, 73, 213, 216). The Staatliche Kunstsammlungen in Kassel acquired a group of four outstanding drawings in 1939 (69, 83, 91 and 120). After the war the Kupferstichkabinett in Berlin-Dahlem acquired the group of drawings from the Durazzo collection already on deposit there. During this period the British Museum purchased two previously unknown drawings (24 and 70) and other important drawings went to Munich (93), the Metropolitan Museum in New York (18), which had disappeared since the mid-nineteenth century, and (78), and the National Gallery of Scotland, in Edinburgh (119). Important drawings continued to emerge in private collections (1, 20, 64, 76, 98, 110, 114, 147): most recently Roseline Bacou acquired a striking group of previously unknown drawings for the Louvre (5, 71, 81, 84, 127, 149, 150, 151, 152, 153, 203).

The scholarly neglect into which the study of the drawings fell in the period after Mariette ended in a rather cautious way with Von Hadeln's 1911 article in Thieme-Becker listing eleven drawings, four of which are accepted here.[52] Von Hadeln failed, however, to include any of the pen and ink sketches to which attention was later drawn by Borenius in 1921 when he published a group of ten such drawings. Borenius's lead was then followed by Von Hadeln in his *Venezianische Zeichnungen der Spätrenaissance* of 1926 where he reproduced thirty-six drawings and referred to another seven (mostly those published by Borenius), of which only five are not accepted here. That catalogue remains fundamental and was used by Professor Fiocco in his monograph two years later.[53] Fiocco concentrated upon the paintings but included a catalogue of the drawings based upon Von Hadeln's to which he added the two drawings in Bayonne (63 and 108), two in the Morgan Library as well as (86), which had previously been attributed to Tiziano Aspetti but whose connection with the Tribune of the Sala del Collegio in the Palazzo Ducale (Fig 56) he recognised.

Further drawings were published by Sir Karl Parker in 1930 (87), J. Meder in 1933 (124) and Byam Shaw in 1935 (82), which, in part at least, prepared for the expansion of the corpus by Hans Tietze and Erica Tietze-Conrat in 1944. They attributed about sixty-seven drawings to Veronese (of which six are rejected here),[54] listing another sixty-two rejected attributions and thirty-four school drawings; of these twelve are here returned to Veronese[55] following the lead of Jacob Bean (63), Sir Karl Parker (115), Philip Pouncey (4) and James Byam Shaw (62). This does not explain the enormous discrepancy between this present catalogue, with over 150 autograph drawings, and that of the Tietzes. In large measure the difference reflects the continued activity of scholars beginning with Hans Tietze himself who added (1) in 1948, the year in which A. E. Popham drew attention to the drawing in Holkham (39). This tradition of connoisseurship was continued by James Byam Shaw, associated with Colnaghi's where two new drawings appeared in 1952 and 1962 (30 and 137), John Gere at the British Museum, who was responsible for the attribution of (104) in Düsseldorf, while (118) at Princeton was discovered by his colleague, Philip Pouncey, now consultant to Sotheby's where a group of important drawings has emerged in recent years (2, 5, 86, 105, 126). The four drawings in Kassel were published by Dr Oehler in 1953 and two years later Bernard Degenhart

discussed the newly acquired sheet in Munich; Sir Karl Parker drew attention to another fine late drawing that had escaped attention in his 1956 catalogue of the Ashmolean (90) and Deusch published the *Studies for a Rape of Europa and the Madonna of the Rosary and a Pietà* in 1968 (64), while in 1971 Cocke related a chalk study (2) with a misleading attribution to Palma to the 1548 *Christ preaching in the temple*.

Other drawings which had been misattributed in both private and public collections were returned to Veronese by David Rosand in 1966 (36) and 1971 (34), by Roger Rearick in his 1976 Uffizi catalogue where he drew attention to a fine sheet at Chatsworth (16) and by Albert Châtelet in 1978 when he published two drawings in the Louvre that he had identified much earlier (12 and 107). This activity was matched by the exhibitions of Venetian drawings arranged by the Fondazione Giorgio Cini under the inspiration of Professor Giuseppe Fiocco and continued under Professor Rodolfo Pallucchini. The catalogues often serve as the best available reference works for many museums and collections and that of 1971 offered the first survey of Renaissance drawings in Verona. Although Professor Terisio Pignatti's monumental monograph in 1976 included a wider range of material than Professor Fiocco's of some fifty years earlier, it again concentrated upon the paintings, with only a small sample of the drawings, discussed without a catalogue. This omission I hope to have remedied in the present catalogue, in which I have aimed both to sum up the different strands of modern research and to present a personal view in my disagreement with a number of recent arguments and attributions. The work corresponds to another important trend in research on Venetian drawings. Art historians have now moved away from the general synthesis presented by the Tietzes in their 1944 study, towards a detailed discussion (often in the form of a monograph) of artists ranging from Jacopo Bellini[56] and Carpaccio,[57] through Titian,[58] Lotto,[59] Schiavone,[60] and Pordenone[61] down to Tintoretto.[62] The two notable absentees in that list are Veronese and Jacopo Bassano on whom both Alessandro Ballarin and Roger Rearick have published much new material. The absence of Veronese would count for little were he not so great a designer with a clear sense of function and, even in the slightest sketch, of decoration. Mariette's account of Veronese's drawings, quoted at the beginning of the introduction, remains valid even for the much larger corpus assembled here. Many drawings still await identification and recognition, but the time seems right for a book which will re-assert Veronese's place as one of the great Renaissance draughtsmen.

NOTES

Works cited only in an abbreviated form are given in full in the Bibliography: for a detailed account of individual drawings (with bibliographies) the reader is referred to the relevant catalogue entries

1 (Paris, 1741), p75

2 One is mentioned in the contract with the carpenter Domenico Marangone, dated 26 October 1558, Pignatti 252 doc 15

3 M. Röthlisberger in *Saggi e Memorie di Storia dell' Arte* 2 (1959), pp 41 ff; C. L. Joost-Gaugier in *Zeitschrift für Kunstgeschichte* 38 (1975), pp 1 ff; F. Saxl, 'Jacopo Bellini and Mantegna as Antiquarians' reprinted in *A Heritage of Images* (Harmondsworth, 1970), pp 57 ff

4 A. E. Popham and P. Pouncey, *Italian Drawings in the Department of Prints and Drawings in the British Museum, the Fourteenth and Fifteenth Centuries* (London, 1950), p 14 identifying the London sketchbook in the wills of Jacopo's widow Anna (d. 25 November 1471) and Gentile Bellini (d. 18 February 1507). It was subsequently in the collection of Gabriele Vendramin

5 F. Ames-Lewis, *Drawing in Early Renaissance Italy* (New Haven and London, 1981), pp 138 ff. I have supplemented and corrected the account in the light of Cinquecento procedure as described for Raphael by J. Shearman, 'Raphael's Unexecuted Projects for the Stanze' in *Walter Friedlaender zum 90. Geburtstag*, ed. G. Kauffmann and W. Sauerländer (Berlin, 1964), p 175

6 The *Birth of the Virgin* in the British Museum, for example, Popham and Pouncey p 45, Ames-Lewis p 149

7 I take this stage, which is clarified in the analysis of Shearman, to be represented by the Vienna *Annunciation to Zacharias*, which Ames-Lewis pp 146 and fig 145 describes as a contract drawing

8 Ames-Lewis pp 145 ff and figs 153 and 160

9 H. Glasser, *Artists' Contracts of the Early Renaissance* (New York and London, 1977), pp 140 ff for Ghirlandaio's contract with Giovanni Tornabuoni for the S. Maria Novella frescoes. I am not convinced that any such drawings for this cycle have survived. It is striking that no comparable drawings are called for in Venetian contracts, Ames-Lewis pp 146 ff. The smartest precedent filled with the most portraits was the cycle commissioned from a team of artists for the walls of the Sistine chapel, L. D. Ettlinger, *The Sistine Chapel before Michelangelo* (Oxford, 1965)

10 E. Borsook, *The Mural Painters of Tuscany* (London, 1960), pp 26 (the development of cartoons) and 31 (Ghirlandaio)

11 This can be seen in Carpaccio's drawings of the *English prince taking leave of his father* at Chatsworth and the *Fortified harbour with ships* in the British Museum, J. Lauts, *Carpaccio; Paintings and Drawings* (London, 1962), pls 24 and 25

12 The *Study for a Sacra Conversazione* in the Uffizi indicates the size, *see also* the Uffizi and Uppsala drawings for the cycle in the Scuola di San Giorgio degli Schiavone, Lauts pls 90, 96 and 111

13 Lauts pls 103 and 104, Ames-Lewis p 143

14 Lauts pls 88, 98 and 167

15 C. M. Brown, *Isabella d'Este and Lorenzo da Pavia* (Geneva, 1982), pp 84 for the letter and 153 note 3 for a summary of the modern literature

16 J. Wilde, *Venetian Art from Bellini to Titian* (Oxford, 1974), pp 42–57

17 'Giorgione, exploiting the physical qualities of the oil medium and the rough textures of canvas, had opened up new expressive possibilities' in the 'Crisis of the Venetian Renaissance tradition', *Arte* 11–12 (1970), pp 7 ff, reprinted in *Painting in Cinquecento Venice: Titian, Veronese, Tintoretto* (New Haven, 1982). Rosand rightly connects this critical discussion with the appearance of Franco's and Fialetti's drawing-books in the early years of the seventeenth century. While intended to educate Venetian artists in the practice of drawing, the extent and range of Veronese's drawings (fully revealed in the present catalogue) show that the same intention had been at work some sixty years earlier. This use of the term 'colorito' was introduced by Piero della Francesca in his *De Prospectiva Pingendi*, ed. G. N. Fasola (1942), p 63

18 Giovanni Santi in his rhymed poem on the life of the Duke of Urbino (written sometime before his death in 1494) praises Mantegna for his *disegno, inventione* and *colorito*, ed. and trans C. Gilbert, *Italian Art 1400–1500, Sources and Documents* (New Jersey, 1980), pp 95 ff; Cinquecento attitudes stem from Vasari 7 (1962), p 327. Pino, writing in 1548 (two years before the publication of the *Vite*), echoes Vasari's distinction in the passage cited under note 40 below. Titian is the supreme representative of *colorito* for L. Dolce, *Dialogo della pittura intitolato l'Aretino* of 1557, ed. and trans M. W. Roskill, *Dolce's 'Aretino' and Venetian Art Theory of the Cinquecento* (New York, 1968). The issue is also discussed by Rosand (1970), pp 6–12

19 As Mrs E. Tietze-Conrat observed, this has much to do with his use of the arch publicist, Aretino, to draft many of his letters, 'Titian as a letter-writer', *Art Bulletin* 26 (1944), pp 117 ff

20 K. Oberhuber, *Disegni di Tiziano e della sua cerchia* (Fondazione Giorgio Cini, Venice, 1976) and also W. R. Rearick, *Tiziano e il disegno Veneziano del suo Tempo* (Florence, 1976)

21 P. Dreyer, 'Tizianfalschungen des Sechzehnten Jahrhunderts', *Pantheon* 38 (1979), pp 365–75

22 Oberhuber pp 15–16

23 Oberhuber p 123, it is closely linked with the *Landscape* in Vienna and the *Apostles* in the Louvre, which must also probably be returned to Titian, Oberhuber pp 122 and 125. The drawing of the *Miracle of the new-born child* in the Fondazione Custodia is at best a copy, perhaps after a now lost drawing, but it does not stand comparison with the *Jealous husband*, Oberhuber p 23 and fig 5

24 Oberhuber pp 119–20

25 This possibility was suggested by Pat Rubin's paper, 'German prints and the formation of Raphael's graphic style', delivered at the March 1983 conference of the Association of Art Historians, held in London. Rubin suggested the influence of Schongauer on the development of Ghirlandaio's cross-hatching in the 1480s. For Dürer, consult E. Panofsky, *The life and art of Albrecht Dürer* (Princeton, 1955), pp 107 ff

26 C. Hope, *Titian* (London, 1980), pp 14–15

27 Wilde p 123

28 Ames-Lewis pp 169 ff

29 Oberhuber pp 77–78

30 Oberhuber fig 21

31 Oberhuber pp 93–96

32 Vasari 7 (1962), p 332 and Hope p 131

33 Wilde pp 63 ff

34 Vasari 7 (1962), p 327

35 Hope pp 89–91

36 Oberhuber p 16

37 This view, first argued by J. Wilde, *Italian Drawings in the British Museum: Michelangelo and his studio* (London, 1953), pp 27–31 is now widely accepted: M. Lucco, *L'Opera completa di Sebastiano del Piombo* (Milan, 1980), cats 52, 55 and 94 and M. Hirst, *Sebastiano del Piombo* (Oxford, 1981)

38 Cohen p 47

39   *Compare* Pordenone's red chalk study for *God the Father* at Cortemaggiore at Chatsworth, Cohen pl 52, with Sarto's chalk *modello* for the *Pietà* in Palazzo Pitti, J. Shearman, *Andrea del Sarto* (Oxford, 1965), pl 127b and the *chiaroscuro* drawing of *Prophets and sibyls* in the Ashmolean, Cohen pl 68, with Sarto's early *modello* for a *Madonna and four saints* in the Louvre, Shearman pl 4b

40   'e se Tiziano e Michiel Angelo fussero un corpo solo, over al disegno di Michiel Angelo aggiontovi il colore di Tiziano se gli potrebbe dir lo dio della pittura', Cocke *Master Drawings* (1977) p 259 citing P. Pino, *Dialogo della Pittura* (Venice, 1548), *ed. cit.* P. Barocchi, *Trattati d'arte del Cinquecento* I (Bari, 1960), pp 126–27

41   'The early appreciation of drawings', *Studies in Western Art; Acts of the International Congress of the History of Art* (Princeton, 1963), p 78

42   This implication of Dreyer's argument was emphasised to me by Dr Jaynie Anderson, *see* under note 21

43   *Compare* the portrait of Fra Bernardo Torlioni as St Francis in the main altar of S. Sebastiano, and that of Girolamo Scrocchetto in the *Marriage feast at Cana*, Pignatti pls 377 and 375, *see also* (34)

44   Ridolfi II p 14, for Tintoretto, *see also* P. Rossi, *I disegni di Jacopo Tintoretto* (Florence, 1975), p 2 and figs 1–35; Ridolfi p 346 for his account of Veronese, *see also* under (87)

45   Cocke *Master Drawings* (1977) p 259

46   Tentatively suggested by Tietze and Tietze-Conrat p 337 and under individual entries in their catalogue. It is argued with greater conviction by Malke 1980

47   Rosand 1971 p 208

48   *See* under (188)

49   Ridolfi p 345 refers to 'molti disegni a chiaroscuro in carte tinte' these would presumably have formed a part of no 784 'Vaseti di colori diversi – altre carte di disegni a chiari scuri no. 94' of the 1682 inventory, Gattinoni p 37; the rest of the same number included 126 chalk or pen drawings. No 753 on p 35 included 646 sheets and no 783 on p 36 a further 620. It is striking that they never adopted a mark for their collection. *See also* Tietze and Tietze-Conrat pp 336 ff

50   Inv. 1895–9–15–843; Robinson no 398. Inv. 1895–9–15–842; Robinson no 397

51   Inv. 1895–9–15–844; Robinson no 399

52   'Paolo Caliari' in *Allgemeines Lexikon der Bildenden Künstler*, Thieme-Becker 5 (Leipzig, 1911), p 397

53   *Paolo Veronese* (Bologna, 1928)

54   (157, 162, 163, 193, 214 and 215)

55   (4, 25, 31, 32, 38, 40, 54, 62, 68, 115, 121, 135)

56   *See* note 3 above

57   M. Muraro, *I Disegni di Vittore Carpaccio* (Florence, 1977)

58   Oberhuber *cit.* note 20 above

59   P. Pouncey, *Lotto Disegnature* (Vicenza, 1963)

60   F. L. Richardson, *Andrea Schiavone* (Oxford, 1980)

61   Cohen 1980

62   Rossi *cit.* note 44 above

Colour Plates

106   Studies of Venus with Cupid (actual size)

4   Study of Count Giuseppe da Porto with his son Adriano

131   Study of a seated woman seen from behind

28   Rest on the Flight into Egypt

19   Pittura Quarta: Virgin and Child surrounded by six angels

102   Study for a Finding of Moses

114   Costume-studies for the Oedipus Tyrannus of Sophocles

36   Temptation of St Anthony

75   Modello for the Martyrdom of St Justina

70   Study for Liberality

14   Study of a woman's head

12   Studies of Neptune with tritons and sea horses (actual size)

Catalogue

Early Drawings

The drawings included in this section range in date from the two surviving sketches (1, 2) for the *Christ preaching in the temple* (Fig 1) of 1548 to the *Study of twelve apostles* (16) for the nave of S. Sebastiano, probably decorated in the early 1560s. In the earliest preparatory sketch (1) Veronese combined a vigorous cross-hatching learned from Dürer's woodcuts with a free graphic stroke inspired by Parmigianino's drawings. This use of pen and ink alone recurs in other drawings of the period (5, 6, 7) but is soon supplemented by white heightening (4, 12, 16) and wash (3, 8, etc.). This became the standard mode for his drawings and the later sheets move towards the bold assurance found in Veronese's subsequent work.

From the outset of his career Veronese supplemented these preliminary sketches with chalk studies. That only (2) can be certainly dated to these years seems to be an unlucky accident of survival. A number of other chalk studies, which I believe to be autograph, also belong to this period (123, 124, 130, 133) and reveal the care with which Veronese worked out his compositions.

This approach is confirmed by (14) which may be a fragment of a cartoon for one of the frescoes in the crossing at Villa Maser (Fig 13). The drawing gives an important insight into Veronese's working procedure in his early period which can be aligned with that of contemporaries in Central Italy, including Taddeo Zuccaro.

1   Study for Christ preaching in the temple (actual size)

1   Study for Christ preaching in the temple

Pen and ink
7.8 × 17.4 cm

LOCATION New York, S. Schwarz
PROVENANCE Jonathan Richardson, Senior (Lugt 2183)
BIBLIOGRAPHY Tietze 1948 p 60; New York 1965 no 125;
   Rosand 1971 pp 203–204; Cocke 1971 pp 729–30

The drawing establishes the general composition of the painting of this subject now in the Prado (Fig 1), where Christ is raised up on steps to the left with two seated figures beneath him and the remaining scribes to the right. The group on the right does not yet include the man leaning in his chair to look up at Christ or the donor who stands behind the scribes identified by his cross of Jerusalem.[1] There is no indication of the architecture or of the Holy Family, who in the painting enter the Temple in the background in search of their son. The painting establishes this and (2) and (2v) as Veronese's earliest surviving drawings. It used to be dated to the 1560s before Michael Levey noted the date 1548 written in Roman numerals on the book of the scribe seated at the front of the canvas turning to look up at Christ.[2] This date has not won universal acceptance in the literature since many critics cling to the (mistaken) view that the Bevilacqua-Lazise altar from S. Fermo, now in the Museo di Castelvecchio, Verona (see under (165)) is datable to 1548.[3]

There seems to be no good reason for doubting the date of 1548 on the Prado canvas. David Rosand, who accepted the date, convincingly noted the comparative hesitancy of the present sheet and argued that the broad hatching was an indication of Veronese's earliest style. The same technique is handled with greater assurance and boldness, together with a reduction in the hatching, in the *Study for the Triumph of Mordechai* in Berlin of 1556 (6).

Rosand suggested that the interest in broad plastic forms as well as the handling revealed Veronese's training as a stone-cutter. The fact that the family name was 'spezapreda' does not mean that his father had been actively engaged as a stone-cutter.[4] Veronese himself abandoned the name, which he used when signing his letter to Cardinal Ercole Gonzaga in March 1553, by June 1555 in the contract for the *Transfiguration* in Montagnana.[5] Even if the family had been active as stone-cutters this would not explain the style of the present sheet which differs notably from the drawings attributed to earlier artists in Verona.[6]

In style it admirably illustrates Ridolfi's account of Veronese's early training:[7] 'nel principio della sua istitutione ritrasse le opere del Badile suo maestro e le carte del Dürero ... fatto adulto, si dilettò de' disegni del Parmigiano, ritraendo molti'.

The hatching on Christ, the scribe burrowing in a book and his neighbour follows the example of Dürer's woodcut's,[8] while the fluent graphic style with which the figures are established with its liberal use of *pentimenti* finds its precedent in Parmigianino's pen and ink sketches[9] (which continued to be sought after in the mid-sixteenth century).[10] The only element in Ridolfi's account which is open to question is the connection with Badile, for the figures in the present sheet, notably the pair seated at the left, are, as David Rosand observed, Michelangelesque in a way that is beyond Badile.[11]

Fig 1   *Christ preaching in the temple*, Prado, Madrid

NOTES

1   First noted by J. Allende-Salazar and F. J. Sánchez Cantón, *Retratos del Museo del Prado* (Madrid, 1919), pp 77–78

2   M. Levey, 'An early dated Veronese and Veronese's early work', *Burlington Magazine* 102 (1960), pp 107–111

3   Pignatti 50; the arguments against the date of 1548 for the Bevilacqua-Lazise altar were set out in my article of 1971

4   G. Biadego, 'Intorno a Paolo Veronese', *Atti del R. Istituto Veneto* Serie 7 Bd. 10 (1898), pp 99–111, and G. Trecca, *Paolo Veronese e Verona* (Verona, 1940), pp 15 and 17

5   Pignatti 251 docs 5 and 8; he is referred to as Paolo Caliari in the Montagnana contract which he signed 'Paullo Veronese'

6   See those assembled in the 1971 Verona catalogue, 1–25

7   P 345

8   See, for example, the curved hatching in the robes of Peter and the apostle behind Christ in the *Christ washing the apostles' feet* from the small Passion

9   See, for example, the *Studies for Venus disarming Cupid* in the Ecole des Beaux-Arts, Paris, A. E. Popham, *The Drawings of Parmigianino* (London, 1953), pl XLI

10   For the purchase of a volume of drawings in 1558 by Vittoria, see R. Predelli, 'Le memorie e le carte di Alessandro Vittoria', *Archivio Trentino* 23 (1908), pp 129–30

11   See also Cornwall, Colville collection (169)

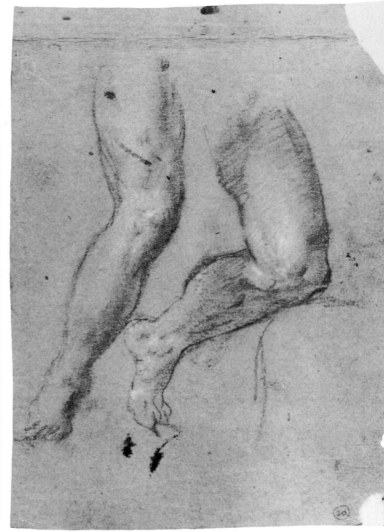

2   Study of a seated man

2v   Study of legs

2   Study of a seated man

2v   Study of legs

Black chalk on blue paper heightened with white
29 × 20 cm
LOCATION London, Sotheby 25 June 1970, 9
INSCRIBED in another hand: 'Palma'
BIBLIOGRAPHY Cocke 1971 pp 726–29

Sotheby's tentatively followed the old attribution to Palma inscribed on the recto. Their caution was understandable for the handling is calmer and more elegant than that of the comparable Witt collection chalk study by Palma for the *Passover* of 1575 in the sacristy of S. Giacomo dell'Orio. [1] The handling, although less accomplished and fluent, resembles that of the *St Lawrence* in the Museum Boymans-van Beuningen (73), which had long been recognised as an autograph chalk study by Veronese. The design on the recto is related to the seated man holding a book in the *Christ preaching in the temple* of 1548 (Fig 1), but differs in the pose of the head, in the book which he carries in his right hand and in the leggings and boots. His left leg, which in the Schwarz drawing had been shown tucked behind his other leg, is here extended by a *pentimento* in front of him. Although less certain than the related drawings, the care with which the loop of folds falling behind the right leg is drawn anticipates other, generally later, costume-studies including (67), (77) and (140).

The magnificent legs on the verso were by contrast drawn from life with the emphasis on outline of the later *Study of a seated nude* (55). The pose, although in reverse, echoes that of Titian's Uffizi study for the executioner in the Gesuiti *Martyrdom of St Lawrence*, a commission which was under way by November 1548. [2] As with the Schwarz pen and ink sketch, Veronese uses hatching, notably in the study of the drapery. The painterly approach to the chalk and white heightening on coloured paper, which matches the exciting use of scumbles in his paintings, derives from Titian's chalk studies. [3]

This is all the more notable since this aspect of Titian's work does not otherwise appear to have had an influence in Verona, and together with the working procedure of these two drawings reveal an artist looking beyond the bounds of his native city. The skill and accomplishment of the drawings is matched in the painting which breaks with the usual model, Dürer's woodcut of this subject. This had influenced the painting by Bonifazio de' Pitati, the most distinguished Veronese artist of the older generation, now in Palazzo Pitti, Florence. [4] This degree of innovation makes the question of Veronese's training academic but possibly Vasari was right when he referred to a period with Giovanni Caroto. [5] In April 1566, Veronese married Elena Badile, the daughter of one of the leading artists of a slightly older generation, who had died some six years before the marriage. [6] This may well have influenced Veronese's memory when he supplied the information on his training for Borghini in the early 1580s and substituted the name of Badile for that of Caroto. [7]

NOTES

1   Tietzes 1018, *see also* D. Rosand, 'Palma il Giovane as Draughtsman: The early career and related observations', *Master Drawings* 8 (1970), pp 148–62
2   Florence 1976 no 26
3   *See*, for example, Venice 1976 nos 26, the British Museum study for an apostle in the *Assumption*; 36, the Uffizi study of St Bernadino for the *Doge Francesco Donato presented to the Virgin* and 39, the Oxford study of a horseman
4   Bartsch 7, p 65, no 91 and D. Westphal, *Bonifazio Veronese (Bonifazio del Pitati)* (Munich, 1931), p 61 as a school picture, from the Sala del Consiglio del Dieci, the Palazzo Ducale, Venice
5   Vasari 3 p 370
6   Pignatti 254 doc 30 of 17 April
7   Borghini 1584 pp 561–63

3 Studies of Fame, Peace (?) and a cartouche

3   Studies of Fame, Peace (?) and a cartouche

Pen and ink and wash
25.6 × 31.1 cm

LOCATION Hamburg, Kunsthalle Inv. 1922/175 [1]
PROVENANCE August Grahl (Lugt 1199), his sale London,
     Sotheby 27 April 1885, 50
BIBLIOGRAPHY Cocke 1973 p 138

The drawing, which had been neglected in the earlier literature, prepares two of the frescoes that Veronese painted for Sanmichele's now destroyed Villa Soranza in 1551. [2] In the centre of the sheet, Fame, identified by the trumpets pressed to her lips, has been studied from one of the studio models, which were much used by Tintoretto; a *ricordo* on the upper right includes both wings in a study of the figure in flight. In the fresco of *Time and Fame*, now in the Duomo, Castelfranco (Fig 2), Fame [3] is larger in scale and has a greater *contrapposto* which brings it closer to Veronese's source, the angels which Giulio Romano had designed for Verona Cathedral. [4]

The remaining three sketches prepare a fresco lunette now lost showing a coat of arms supported by two females, which was removed by Filippo Balbi in 1816, and was included in lists of 1818 [5] and 1825, when it was one of the fragments on sale in London. [6] The cartouche, which must have surrounded the arms, is studied in detail at the top and is then shown as a summary oval supported by the raised right hand of one of the two ladies seated on a ledge, holding a palm in the other hand suggesting the identification as Peace. The pose is loosely echoed in reverse by her companion whose left hand is raised to support the other side of the cartouche. The purpose of these sketches suggests a possible reason for their inclusion on the same sheet. As with Peruzzi's frescoes on the ceiling of the Sala di Galatea in the Farnesina, Fame may have directed her clarion call to the family's coat of arms, presumably those of Benedetto Soranzo who had inherited from Alvise on the latter's death in 1548. [7] Although not mentioned by Ridolfi in his account of the villa, such a scheme might have been part of the entrance loggia, just as that at the Farnesina was in the Tiber loggia. [8]

Veronese designed the frame in two alternatives combining the curling strap-work with herms on the left and *ignudi* on the right. This is the first example of his interest in the decorative forms of the school of Fontainebleau, [9] an interest which continued in the sacristy and upper nave at S. Sebastiano but was reduced to minor details in the ceiling of the Sala dell'Olimpo at Maser. [10] His collaborator Vittoria shared this taste, but the present drawing anticipates his adoption of this system at Palazzo Thiene, Vicenza, by some two or three years. [11]

In style the drawing differs from the Schwarz sketch (1), partly because Veronese has here used pen and ink for studies from the model, a technique that is rare in his drawings. There is another factor at work, for just as the Fame reflects models by Giulio Romano, so the certainty with which the outlines are established reveals the influence of Giulio Romano's pen and ink drawings. [12]

Fig 2   *Time and Fame*, detached fresco, Duomo, Castelfranco

The style of the present drawing is reflected in a drawing of an allegorical lady in the British Museum with an old attribution to Zelotti (Fig 107) which has been linked tentatively with the Soranza frescoes.[13] This helps clarify the status of a group of drawings in Milan and one in Christ Church, Oxford which have been related to the Soranza frescoes.

The Milan drawings, all of which are in the same technique of wash on blue paper heightened with white, come from the Bolognini collection and have been discussed by both Mrs Tietze-Conrat[14] and Professor Arslan.[15] Mrs Tietze-Conrat, who noted that the drawings included motives from both Villa Soranza and Palazzo Trevisan, rightly contrasted them with Veronese's preparatory sketches but suggested that they were not copies but an example of the drawings made by his workshop. This seems to be wrong for they have the literal awkward quality of copies, which is different from the freedom of the drawings produced by Veronese's studio where artists aped his style with limited success. Her view is, however, infinitely preferable to that of Arslan who attributed the *Fame* and the *Neptune* to Veronese, and divided the rest between Zelotti and anonymous.

Professor Ballarin drew attention to the drawing of a priest, an altar and a woman with two children at Christ Church, Oxford (199), previously as Farinati or Zelotti, which he related to Ridolfi's description of the histories and sacrifices on the walls of Villa Soranza and attributed to Veronese.[16] This was greeted with caution by Byam Shaw in his catalogue where he linked the Oxford drawing with another in the British Museum (Fig 106) which added a man kneeling before the priest and a crowd with animals behind.[17] Byam Shaw compared this drawing to another with an old attribution to Zelotti in the Scholz collection arguing that they were both by Zelotti.[18] In spite of connections with Zelotti, notably in the heads, both sheets are weaker than the allegorical lady attributed to Zelotti in the British Museum (Fig 107) and belong rather with the group of drawings attributed to Alvise dal Friso (165).

The woman seen from behind supporting a child on her shoulder while another shelters under her robe, the round altar with classical decoration, the kneeling figure and the crowds ready for sacrifice are related to Veronese's slightly later *Anointing of David* in Vienna.[19] These drawings may be an independent variation on the Vienna canvas, but they may also reflect a lost stage in the design of the canvas by Veronese himself. In favour of this possibility, it can be argued that the changes from the drawing in the British Museum to the painting, the fluent relief-like grouping, the avoidance of Samuel's mannered pose and of the excessive emphasis upon the classical ornament of the altar resemble the revision of the Dresden *Presentation of Christ in the temple*[20] in the 1560 organ shutters in S. Sebastiano.[21] In either case, the drawings must be later than the Soranza frescoes and if the attribution to Alvise dal Friso is correct, reveal another aspect of his interest in Veronese's work of the 1550s.

NOTES

1 Its present location was kindly brought to my attention by Mr Philip Pouncey

2 Pignatti 104–106; the date is that of Veronese's *Glory* in the Pinacoteca del Seminario, Venice

3 Pignatti pl 9

4 F. Hartt, *Giulio Romano* (New Haven, 1958), pl 430

5 F. N. Vignola, 'Appunti sulla Pinacoteca Vicentina: Un affresco della Villa Soranza', *Bollettino del Museo Civico di Vicenza* 2 (1910), pp 17 and 18 republished the original from the *Giornale dell' Italiana letteratura* (1818), p 188. The lunette measured 6 ft 3 ins by 5 ft 6 ins

6 The list in the *Literary Gazette and Journal of Belles Lettres* (31 December 1825), pp 842 and 843 was republished by G. Schweikhart, 'Paolo Veronese in der Villa Soranza', *Mitteilungen des Kunsthistorischen Institutes in Florenz* 15 (1971), p 204. The lunette was no 1 (the arms were identified as those of the Morosini family, but no evidence was cited) with dimensions of 7 ft by 6 ft 2 in

7 B. Rupprecht, 'Sanmichele's Villa Soranza', *Festschrift für Ulrich Middeldorf* (Berlin, 1968), pp 324 ff. It is not clear whether the villa was completed by the time of Alvise's death in 1548

8 Ridolfi p 302 describes frescoes in the loggia, salone and two rooms which as Schweikhart noted, fitted with the plan of the villa by Albertolli of 1815, his fig 8 and p 199. For an alternative suggestion for the Time and Fame, *see* Dr L. Crosato-Larcher, 'Nuovi contributi per la decorazione della Soranza', *Arte Veneta* 31 (1977), pp 72–80; *see also* Cocke *M.K.I.F.* 1977 pp 211–18

9 Cocke 1972 pp 322–25

10 Pignatti pl 193, for the source of the frame, *see* Cocke *J.W.C.I.* 1972 p 242

11 W. Wolters, *Plastische Deckendekorationen des Cinquecento in Venedig und im Veneto* (Berlin, 1968), pl 55 and p 46 dating it to 1554

12 *See* from among the wide range of possible examples, the Chatsworth and British Museum drawings for the ceiling of the Sala of Atilio Regulus, E. Verheyen, *The Palazzo del Te in Mantua* (Baltimore, 1977), pls 35 and 36

13 Inv. 1950–10–115; Cocke *M.K.I.F.* 1977 pp 214–16 and fig 5

14 E. Tietze-Conrat pp 37–38 and figs 22 and 23, and Tietze and Tietze-Conrat 2171

15 E. Arslan, 'Note su Veronese e Zelotti', *Belle Arti* 5–6 (1948), esp. p 230; *see* (191) and (192)

16 Ballarin *Arte Veneta* 1971 pp 99–101; Inv. 1325

17 Byam Shaw 1976 cat 790; the drawing in the British Museum, Inv. 1950–2–11–8 (anon. school of Verona), is reproduced as his fig 52

18 Venice 1957 no 32

19 Pignatti 110 cat 48, with a date of *circa* 1555. The fluent composition appears to relate rather to paintings of the 1560s, the *Martyrdom of Sts Primus and Felician* in the Museo Civico Padua, for instance. The fact that the bridge in front of the fantastic view of Bethlehem on the right recurs in reverse in the Stanza di Bacco at Villa Maser (in both cases it is derived from the engraving of the Temple of Minerva by H. Cock) would seem to confirm a slightly later date

20 Pignatti 110 cat 49; I am not persuaded by the view, first argued by G. Fiocco, *Jahrbuch der Kunsthistorischen Sammlungen in Wien*, N.F. 1 (1926), pp 123–36, that they were pendants. Their external histories are different, their dimensions do not match and the compositions do not balance

21 Pignatti 116 cats 84 and 85. The later design presents the story with greater clarity, the altar is covered by a drape, the page with a bowl and the lady with the basket of doves both concentrate on Simeon. The blue of the Virgin's robe is the main accent so that even the gold mosaic ceiling does not distract from the main group

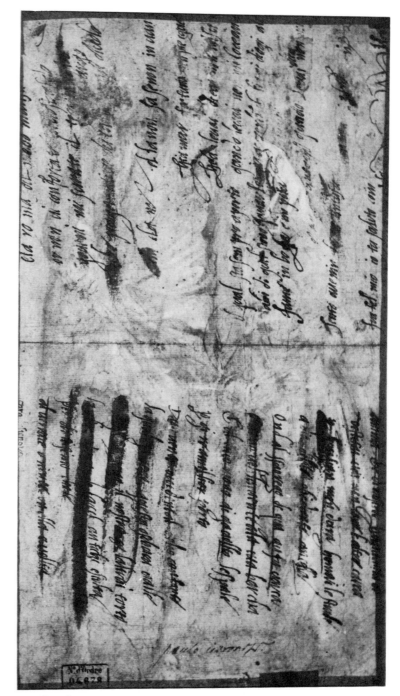

4v Set of notes

4 Study of Count Giuseppe da Porto with his son Adriano

Pen and ink and wash over grey chalk on buff coloured paper heightened with white

34.1 × 18.6 cm

LOCATION Paris, Musée du Louvre Inv. 4,678

INSCRIBED in chalk: 'P.S'; in another hand: 'Paul Veronese'

PROVENANCE Everard Jabach (Lugt 2961), no 362 in the Venetian section of his manuscript catalogue;[1] ceded to the French Royal collection in 1671

BIBLIOGRAPHY Tietze and Tietze-Conrat A2138 (perhaps Fasolo)

Veronese began this drawing on the back of a set of notes which have been partially crossed out (4v). Although earlier than any surviving autograph letters, they do not appear to be by Veronese.[2] Veronese made a detailed study in grey chalk including the notes 'P.S' to remind him of the fur lining of the cloaks (*peliccia* means fur). He reworked this preliminary sketch in the more precise medium of pen and wash, no doubt to help visualise the scaling up of the design. The pen and ink and wash, which corrects many details of the original chalk drawing, in the count's shoulder, the outlines of his cloak and left leg, etc., was heightened with white.

The drawing was made in preparation of the double-portrait from the Contini-Bonacossi bequest in Palazzo Pitti, Florence (Fig 3). On the basis of the age of the boy (he is about eight years old) the picture and the drawing can be dated to 1553 or 1554.[3] There are, as the Tietzes noted, considerable differences between the drawing and the painting. The view-point has been raised, the angle of the father's head is changed and his son turns to acknowledge his sister in the companion picture now in the Walters Art Gallery, Baltimore.[4]

The stiff, rather formal, character of the pen and ink resembles that in many of the independent *chiaroscuro* drawings (17–42), but the Tietzes bravely followed the logic of their argument that it was different from Veronese's and suggested that both portraits might be by Fasolo. A comparison between the Florence picture and Fasolo's *Portrait of Giuseppe Gualdo with his two sons* in Vicenza does not support this view.[5] Fasolo aims at grace but achieves stiffness both in the poses and the handling of the costumes, and the sitters are seen as though under a spotlight. The lighting of the Florence painting is softer, as is the very Venetian handling of the robes, and the figures are linked together with an easy naturalness that is beyond Fasolo but found in other certain portraits by Veronese.[6]

The Tietzes' view of the present drawing is consistent with their rejection of a number of the independent *chiaroscuro* drawings (25, 31, 38, 40). Its connection with the painting, the formal properties of the combination of chalk, pen and ink and wash with white heightening, and the links with the independent *chiaroscuro* drawings confirm its attribution to Veronese.

Fig 3   *Count Giuseppe da Porto with his son Adriano*, Palazzo Pitti, Florence

NOTES

1   Paris 1978 (unpaginated)

2   He engaged in a long correspondence with Marcantonio Gandini in Treviso about the purchase of land. The earliest letter is in the Wisbech and Fenland Museum dated 4 March 1578, Townsend bequest bt Puttick and Simpson 8 July 1847, 259 (brought to my attention by Dr John Gage). Lot 260 in the same sale is also at Wisbech (undated). Pignatti 257 doc 49 is the next of 20 March 1578, followed by the letter in the Fondation Custodia, Paris J. 5559 of 28 March 1578 (Fig 87). A further letter of the same year has no indication of the month, British Museum Egerton 2015. The others are: Pignatti doc 50, April 1578 and doc 51, of the same date; on 18 September 1582 Veronese received the letter from Gandini that he used for (93); on 1 June 1584 he wrote to Francesco Soranzo (Pignatti doc 63); the letter on the verso of (118) dates from 2 or 4 February 1588 (Pignatti doc 68). These documents show that the letters on the back of (115) and (116) are not by Veronese

3   Pignatti 20; D. F. von Hadeln, 'Two portraits by Paolo Veronese', *Burlington Magazine* 45 (1924), p 209 note 1 established that Giuseppe da Porto married Lucia Thiene in 1545. On the basis of the age of the son, whom he took to be about ten years old, he dated the pictures *circa* 1556. Pignatti rightly noted that he is younger, though not surely young enough to give a date of 1551 as he suggested. The portrait develops from that of Franceschini in Sarasota, dated 1551, Pignatti 19

4   Pignatti 21

5   Inv. A868, *see* F. Barbieri, *Museo Civico Vicenza. Dipinte e Sculture dal XVI al XVIII secolo* (Venice, 1962)

6   *The portrait of a man* in Malibu, Pignatti 103 and the *Portrait of a boy with dog* in New York, Pignatti 109

4   Study of Count Giuseppe da Porto with his son Adriano (*see also* colour plate)

5   Studies for the Triumph of Mordechai and the Coronation of Esther (actual size)

Fig 4   *The Coronation of Esther*, S. Sebastiano, Venice

Fig 5   *The triumph of Mordechai*, S. Sebastiano, Venice

5   Studies for the Triumph of Mordechai and the Coronation of Esther

Pen and ink

15 × 17.7 cm

LOCATION Paris, Musée du Louvre Inv. RF 38926

INSCRIBED by a later collector on the verso: 'S.P. n.o 25'

PROVENANCE Anon. (Lugt 2103a; sometimes described as the
Borghese collection);[1] private collection, France, acquired in
1982

BIBLIOGRAPHY Bacou 1

6   Study for the Triumph of Mordechai

6v   Studies of architecture

Pen and ink

12.6 × 11.3 cm

LOCATION Berlin-Dahlem, Staatliche Museen KdZ 26357

INSCRIBED 'amico' (?); in another hand on the verso: 'studi di
Paolo'; the provenance on the mount

PROVENANCE Marchese Jacopo Durazzo, Genoa; private
collection formerly on deposit in Berlin

BIBLIOGRAPHY Oehler p 34; Cocke *Burlington Magazine* 1972
pp 322–25; Bacou 1

These two studies were made in preparation of two of the great
canvases in the nave of S. Sebastiano, painted during the course
of 1556 (Figs 4 and 5).[2] They mark a development in Veronese's
graphic style by contrast with the *Studies of Fame, Peace (?) and
a cartouche* in Hamburg (3). Here Veronese draws with confident
foreshortening not characteristic of the 1551 study for a ceiling
decoration. Both sheets share a tightness in the handling of the
pen, lacking the freedom of his mature drawings, the Von Hirsch
Study for the Martyrdom of St George (52), for instance.

The main sketch in the Paris sheet (5) is already close to the
canvas of the *Coronation of Esther* (Fig 4) with the queen kneeling
to be crowned by Ahasuerus. The drawing reveals Veronese's

6   Study for the Triumph of Mordechai (actual size)

concern with decorum, since the king holds his sceptre in his left hand so that the right is free to crown Esther. The change in the painting must have been prompted by a concern to clarify the action. The group of onlookers to the right of the canvas also underwent considerable alterations. At first Mordechai was raised above Ahasuerus, he was then placed slightly lower but still above the soldier (Haman), an appropriate position from which to witness Esther's coronation. Attention was further focused on Ahasuerus in the final painting by the change in position of the foreshortened cornice which now coincides with the king's shoulders.

The sketches to the left of the Paris sheet reveal the care with which Veronese studied the soldiers leading Mordechai's horse in the canvas (Fig 5) who attract our eye to the central actor in the triumph, Mordechai. These sketches are variations on the theme initiated in the Berlin drawing (6). Here on the bottom right of the sheet, Mordechai, sceptre in hand, rides his horse as it is led by the two soldiers.

The grouping anticipates the painting where, in addition to changes in the costumes and poses of the soldiers, the discrepancy between the view-points has been removed. Mordechai's horse is seen from a higher angle than the soldiers and is not placed on

6v   Studies of architecture (actual size)

the same level, although this is masked by the cut at the bottom of the sheet, which is clearer on the verso.

The right-hand soldier is studied again on the upper left of the sheet in a pose that is close to that in the canvas as is the magnificent rearing horse underneath. From the 1450s onwards rearing horses had become popular in frescoes, organ shutters and decorative panels.[3] Jacopo Bellini took up the motif in his sketchbooks[4] and Pordenone used them both on the façade of Palazzo d'Ana[5] and also in his lost *Conversion of St Paul*.[6] Veronese transforms this tradition by the steepness of the fore-shortening and by the device of cutting off the horse's rear legs.

The combination of the rearing and striding horse in the Berlin drawing recalls the frescoes on the upper part of Niccolò Giolfino's house at 1 Corso Cavour, Verona, which have a traditional, but not necessarily reliable, attribution to Mantegna.[7] That Veronese was interested in these frescoes is further confirmed by his adaptation of the striding and leaping horses in the *Conversion of St Paul* in Leningrad[8] and of the leaping horses alone in the small grisaille of *Marcus Curtius*[9] in the upper loggia of the Trevisan Palace. Such an interest, although not the only element in the drawing, fits with his palette, echoing Mantegna's,[10] and with the relationship of the real and painted architecture in the organ shutters in S. Sebastiano, which transforms that of the S. Zeno altar.

The fact that the architecture in the drawing is shown on the right, the opposite side to that in the painting, suggests the possibility of a change in plan. Initially, all three canvases may have been on the same axis[11] with their architecture on the right. When Veronese realised that the canvas over the entrance was masked by the monks' choir he turned it and then switched the architecture in the *Triumph* to match the new arrangement. The steep angle of the cornice in the drawing echoes that in the octagons of the ceiling of the Sala di Psiche in the Palazzo del Te,[12] but in the painting the foreshortening focuses attention upon Mordechai.

At least three schemes, none intended for a ceiling, are worked out on the verso (6v). The top is dominated by a round two-storeyed temple, with a man indicated in front, which is flanked by a palace on the right with a view of a campanile between. This recurs on the left of the middle section where there are further buildings. These are divided from a triumphal arch with a balustrade over which small figures peer, and which is connected to another palace by a colonnade. In the bottom sketch the colonnade leads into a large hall where a figure is enthroned with drapes hanging to the right, a combination that, much simplified, forms the basis for the fresco of *St Sebastian before Diocletian* in the monks' choir.[13]

NOTES

1   Monte Carlo 1966 intro. The mark was, however, only added in the late eighteenth century, *see* London, Sotheby 9 July 1981, 132

2   The payments run from 16 January to 19 October 1556, Pignatti 252 doc 10

3   *See* Uccello's London, National Gallery *Rout of San Romano* and Piero della Francesca's *Battle of the Milvian Bridge* at Arezzo. Tura's organ shutters in Ferrara of 1468–69 may have been inspired by the Verona frescoes mentioned in note 7, E. Ruhmer, *Cosimo Tura, Paintings and Drawings* (London, 1958), pls 17 and 18

4   C. Ricci, *Jacopo Bellini e i suoi libri di disegni* (1908), pls 8 and 9

5   Known through the copy in the Victoria and Albert Museum, Tietze and Tietze-Conrat A 1332

6   The preparatory drawing, in the Pierpont Morgan Library was exhibited New York 1965 no 53

7   P. Nanin, *Disegni di Varie Dipinture a Fresco che sono in Verona* (Verona, 1864), pp 53–54 suggests the attribution which is disputed by G. Schweikhart, *Fassadenmalerei in Verona* (Munich, 1973), cat 73. The lower scenes, now perished, were attributed to Giolfino; the difference between the two parts and the popularity of the motif in the 1450s (*see* notes 3 and 4) support the attribution to Mantegna

8   Pignatti 323 as late; the horses at the bottom of the Von Hirsch *Studies for a Judith and Holofernes* (99) are reversed from those in the painting with which any connection appears arbitrary. The motif was inspired by the cartoon of Raphael's *Conversion of St Paul*, which had been in the Grimani collection since 1521, J. Shearman, *Raphael's Cartoons in the Collection of Her Majesty the Queen and the Tapestries for the Sistine Chapel* (London, 1972), p 139. Girolamo Grimani was Capo of the Consiglio dei Dieci in 1554, and may well have taken Veronese to Rome on his first embassy in 1555, *see* Cocke *J.W.C.I.* 1972 p 245

9   Pignatti pl 137

10   Cocke *Master Drawings* 1977 p 259

11   Perhaps reflecting the example of Titian's Santo Spirito ceiling in its original position, Cocke, 'Titian's Santo Spirito Ceiling: an alternative reconstruction', *Burlington Magazine* 113 (1971), p 734

12   F. Hartt, *Giulio Romano* (New Haven, 1958), pl 231

13   Pignatti pl 148

7 Studies of the Virgin and Child enthroned with saints (actual size)

7 Studies of the Virgin and Child enthroned with saints

Pen and ink
14 × 13 cm

LOCATION London, British Museum Inv. Ff–1–73

PROVENANCE Sir Peter Lely (Lugt 2092); P. H. Lankrink (Lugt 2092) with his number '6'; Lord John Somers (Lugt 2981)

BIBLIOGRAPHY Von Hadeln p 30 pl 28; Tietze and Tietze-Conrat 2095

In the centre of the sheet the Holy Family are enthroned with St John the Baptist, identified by his staff, and another saint sitting symmetrically at their feet. The Christ Child leans over in an effort to catch St John's staff and the vigour of his movement is repeated in the other sketches where he is in danger of falling off his mother's lap. She twists with her right leg forward, especially in the bottom left sketch, but is clearly intended for a central position.

The composition, which is shown as upright by the frame around the top sketch, cannot be linked with any surviving painting.[1] It is, as the Tietzes rightly emphasised, too energetic for the Bevilacqua-Lazise altar,[2] and although this new movement anticipates the altars of the 1560s[3] the handling finds its closest parallel in the Berlin *Study for the Triumph of Mordechai* of 1556 (6). This suggests a date in the late 1550s and fully justifies the attribution to Veronese which Von Hadeln argued at a time when it was classified with the doubtful drawings.

NOTES

1 The Tietzes suggested that it might prepare the destroyed picture in S. Maria dei Servi where the saints were St John the Baptist and Augustine; this is possible but the drawing does not suggest the 'pergolato' described by Ridolfi p 325; B. dal Pozzo, *Le Vite de' Pittori degli Scultori et Architetti Veronesi* (Verona, 1718), p 312 referred to a picture in the environs of Verona with the Virgin enthroned with two saints below

2 *See* under (165)

3 Notably that in S. Paolo, Verona of 1565 and the S. Zaccaria altar now in the Accademia (Pignatti 127 and 133)

8 Study of Eros and Anteros, Cybele and Venus with Cupid for Palazzo Trevisan (actual size)

8 Study of Eros and Anteros, Cybele and Venus with Cupid for Palazzo Trevisan

Pen and ink and wash

12 × 11 cm

LOCATION formerly London, P. M. Turner

INSCRIBED '25'

PROVENANCE Sir Joshua Reynolds (Lugt 2364); François Flaming (Lugt 991), his sale Paris, Petit 26 July 1919, 90; P. M. Turner; sold London, Christie 19 March 1975, 28

BIBLIOGRAPHY Borenius 1921 p 59; Von Hadeln p 27; Tietze and Tietze-Conrat 2110 (when in the Spanish Gallery, London); Cocke 1974 p 31

The drawing was first connected with the frescoes in Palazzo Trevisan by a previous owner, perhaps Sir Joshua Reynolds, in an inscription on the verso: 'The pictures for which this is a sketch painted on the outside of the Pala[zzo] Trevisano at Venice Cibele between two lions Two loves striving for a palm b[ranch] and two others extinguishing a torch by pouring water on it'. The identification is correct except that the badly faded frescoes were not on the façade but in the upper loggia (Figs 7 and 8). Eros and Anteros, who struggle for the palm and try to extinguish twin flames in their search for 'reciprocity in amorous relations,'[1] work out the roundels on the short walls (Fig 6). The drawing on the bottom right prepares the octagon of Cybele caressing her lion as one of the Spheres of Love (Fig 8). In the

Fig 6 *Eros and Anteros*, fresco, upper loggia, Palazzo Trevisan, Murano

Fig 7 *Jupiter, Janus, Saturn, Juno*, fresco, upper loggia, Palazzo Trevisan, Murano

Fig 8 *Neptune, Bacchus, Apollo, Cybele*, fresco, upper loggia, Palazzo Trevisan, Murano

remaining sketch, in which the sheet is turned on its side, Venus appears to punish Cupid who clings to her legs, perhaps by removing his bow, a motif that is developed on the ceiling from the lower room of the palace, now in the Louvre, where she is one of the seven Planetary Gods who submit to the power of Love (Fig 10).[2]

The site for the palace, which may have been designed by Daniele Barbaro,[3] had been in the family's possession at least since 1554 and Veronese's frescoes probably date from 1557, the year in which there are payments to one of Vittoria's assistants for his work on the decoration of the palace.[4] The drawings for the palace (9–11), including this one which I know only from a reproduction, look forward to the drawings of the 1560s with

their greater boldness of wash and with the fluent outlines conjured out of *pentimenti*.

NOTES

1 The phrase is that of E. Panofsky, 'Blind Cupid' in *Studies in Iconology* (New York, 1962), p 126 following the interpretation of V. Cartari, *Imagini dei Dei degli Antichi* (Venice, 1556). The ceiling illustrates the Sphere of Love as described by Empedocles, *see* Cocke 1974 pp 27–29

2 A. Caiana, 'Un Palazzo Veronese a Murano: Note e Aggiunte', *Arte Veneta* 22 (1968), pp 47 ff; for the literary source, an epigram by Philippus, *see* Cocke 1974 p 28

3 Ridolfi p 322

4 G.M. Urbani de Gheltoff, *Il Palazzo di Camillo Trevisan di Murano* (Venice, 1890) and R. Predelli, 'Le memorie e le carte di Alessandro Vittoria', *Archivio Trentino* 23 (1908), p 184

9   Studies of Jupiter (actual size)

9v   Studies of Juno (actual size)

9   Studies of Jupiter

9v   Studies of Juno

Pen and ink and wash
14.8 × 8.7 cm

LOCATION New York, Pierpont Morgan Library Inv. 90A
INSCRIBED in another hand on the verso: '34B no. 127'
PROVENANCE Charles Fairfax Murray; J. Pierpont Morgan
BIBLIOGRAPHY Tietze and Tietze-Conrat 2123; Cocke 1974 p31

The Tietzes, who wrongly identified the rapid sketches on the
recto as Cupid riding a dolphin, related the sheet to the ceiling of
the *Sphere of Love* from Palazzo Pisani (Fig 9), formerly in Berlin
and destroyed in the last war.[1] This is true of the upper drawing
on the recto where Jupiter astride his eagle anticipates the
painting, which probably dates from the 1570s, where he is
shown with his left arm outstretched to Venus in the centre of
the canvas. The two sketches directly beneath are variations on
this pose in which he is shown with both arms in front of his
naked torso. At the centre right there is another version, which is
difficult to make out, where he appears sitting in profile facing to
the right with his right arm down as in the fresco in the upper
loggia of Palazzo Trevisan of 1557 (Fig 7). The connection with
this arrangement is confirmed by the three schematic sketches
of the verso which are clearly related to Juno on the same wall
of Palazzo Trevisan (Fig 7), where, as in the drawings, she sits
caressing a peacock with her left hand. Veronese must have
retained this drawing in his studio and when commissioned to
repeat the theme of the Trevisan frescoes for Palazzo Pisani
decided that Jupiter's dramatic pose would fit with his new
interpretation of the elements: 'drawn together through love'.[2]

NOTES

1   Pignatti 140; nothing is known about the early history of the scheme since
the room in which it was first mentioned was only built in 1717, J. Schulz,
Venetian painted ceilings of the Renaissance (Berkeley, 1968), p122
2   Cocke 1974 p27, citing Empedocles; Jupiter stands for fire

Fig 9   *Jupiter, Juno, Saturn, Cybele and Venus*, formerly Staatliche Museen,
Berlin

10 Studies of Bacchus and Apollo with other figures

Pen and ink and wash

17.4 × 15.4 cm

LOCATION New York, Pierpont Morgan Library Inv. 1.90

INSCRIBED 'suitate' (?), '88'

PROVENANCE Sir Joshua Reynolds (Lugt 2364); Charles Fairfax Murray; J. Pierpont Morgan

BIBLIOGRAPHY Borenius 1921 p 59; Von Hadeln p 27; Tietze and Tietze-Conrat 2122; Cocke 1974 p 31

The seated figure at the top of the sheet is repeated below, where he is joined by a companion, in a sketch that obliterates an earlier version of the figure. To the left of this drawing is a lyre decorated on one side with a herm which recurs alone in the centre of the sheet. At the bottom of the drawing two seated figures are viewed from behind and next to them another similar figure turns backwards to look into a box (?) opened by a figure leaning forward. The bottom right of the sheet is dominated by a seated woman holding a large cup in her right hand, her right arm is shown again beside her, and the sketch of drapery at the top may well be hers.

The Tietzes rightly suggested a connection with the frescoes in Palazzo Trevisan, which can be substantiated by relating the two seated figures, under whose feet there is an indication of a floor, to the Bacchus and Apollo in the centre of one of the long walls of the upper loggia of Palazzo Trevisan between Neptune and Cybele (Fig 8). The inspiration of the *ignudi* on the Sistine ceiling, which must have been fresh in Veronese's memory after his visit to Rome with Girolamo Grimani,[1] is clearer in the drawing than in the admittedly battered fresco. Here Bacchus is intoxicated, to underline the connection between wine and women, and Apollo too reflects a further study of classical statues.[2] His lyre, an allusion to song and to the arts that is echoed in the set square introduced into the gods' attributes in the fresco from the lower room (Fig 10), is shown at his side and is sketched again on the left edge of the drawing.

NOTES

1 *See* under (6) note 8

2 *See* Cocke *J.W.C.I.* 1972 pp 243–45

10   Studies of Bacchus and Apollo with other figures (actual size)

11 Studies of Mercury, Venus and Cupid, Saturn, David (?) with other figures

11 Studies of Mercury, Venus and Cupid, Saturn, David (?) with other figures

Pen and ink

30.4 × 20 cm

LOCATION England, private collection

PROVENANCE Sir Joshua Reynolds (Lugt 2364); Paul Oppé

BIBLIOGRAPHY Von Hadeln pl 22; Venice 1939 p 213 no 1; Tietze and Tietze-Conrat 2104; London 1958 no 359; Cocke 1974 p 31

The seven sketches at the top left combine seated with foreshortened figures. The striding figure to the right is probably Mercury, an identification suggested by the three sketches underneath where he holds a caduceus. In the centre of the sheet Venus punishes Cupid in a sketch isolated from those below and to the right a naked figure, which recalls the Mercury, crosses his legs over a sickle, the attribute of Saturn, while in the next sketch on the right his legs are caressed by either an eagle or a swan. The remaining eight sketches prepare one design, which is most fully worked out in the draped figure to the right of centre on the bottom margin, where he stands in a *contrapposto* which brings his right knee forward to support an instrument which is probably drawn again on the bottom right.

The Tietzes, although hesitant about some of the handling, rightly noted the drawing's sculptural quality. The Venus and Cupid reflect the Venus Felix in the Belvedere, Rome, and Mercury combines the stride of the Apollo Belvedere with the attributes of Mercury.[1] These statues provided the inspiration for Venetian bronze statuettes which here formed Veronese's starting-point, just as in the *Studies of a Charity* (86) he made use of Vittoria's *St Sebastian*.

If the origin of the drawing is clear its intended function is less so, but the seated figure on the left of the sheet, holding what looks like a book, could represent a stage in the preparation of the Apollo in the upper loggia of Palazzo Trevisan (Fig 8), before the Morgan Library drawing for the same figure (10). Both the Mercury and the Venus and Cupid are related to one half of the ceiling from a lower room in Palazzo Trevisan, now in the Louvre (Fig 10), where they are foreshortened and Venus takes the punishment of Cupid further by holding him upside down.

The drawing at the bottom of the sheet may well be related to the David fresco next to the Angel of the *Annunciation* on the nave of S. Sebastiano (Fig 11).[2] Here the round headed niche in which he stands recalls that briefly shown on the left of the drawing and the harp is also similar to that on the right of the ex-Oppé drawing. Although usually dated slightly later than the frescoes in Palazzo Trevisan those on the upper walls of S. Sebastiano may, as this drawing suggests, be contemporaneous with them. Veronese received the final payment of five ducats for the frescoes on 8 September 1558 and a payment of 105 ducats on 31 March of the same year, which is always related to the start of the work.[3] When Veronese began work on the ceiling of S. Sebastiano in January 1556 he received only ten ducats, getting the major payment of sixty ducats in April when the

work was well under way.[4] This suggests that the 105 ducats were paid for work done either earlier that year or perhaps at the end of 1557, allowing for the winter break when the dampness of the plaster, and the danger from frost, would not usually allow work.

The present drawing differs from the others for Palazzo Trevisan in the absence of the wash, but it is developed from the Berlin *Study for the Triumph of Mordechai* of 1556 (6).

NOTES

1 H.H. Brummer, *The Statue Court in the Vatican Belvedere* (Stockholm, 1970), pp 44–71 and 123–29 and P.P. Bober, *Drawings after the Antique by Amico Aspertini, Sketchbooks in the British Museum* (London, 1957), p 52
2 Pignatti 69–75
3 Pignatti 252 docs 13 and 14
4 Pignatti 252 doc 10

Fig 10 *Venus and Cupid, Saturn and Mercury*, detached fresco, Musée du Louvre, Paris

Fig 11 View of the frescoes in the nave of S. Sebastiano, Venice

12   Studies of Neptune with tritons and sea horses (*see also* colour plate)

12v   Studies of flying putti

12   Studies of Neptune with tritons and sea horses
12v   Studies of flying putti

Pen and ink on red washed paper (on the recto it has faded to
pink) heightened with white
19.8 × 19.8 cm
LOCATION Paris, Musée du Louvre Inv. 11, 722
INSCRIBED '... per fa seguo per il mar si questi', 'tritoni',
'Bucina', 'tritoni'
PROVENANCE Everard Jabach (Lugt 2959); ceded to the French
Royal collection in 1671
BIBLIOGRAPHY Paris 1965 no 115; Paris 1977 no 77; Châtelet
pp 220–22

The drawing, which had been classified as anonymous by Jabach,
was recognised as a Veronese by Albert Châtelet, whose insight
was followed in the exhibition catalogues of 1965 and 1977. On
the recto there are twelve sketches for tritons, some of whom
blow shells while others, notably the figure at the top under the
first inscription 'tritoni' and the figure directly underneath, pull
shafts. The striding figure to the right of the sheet (he would
have been in the centre before it was cut) rides a shell indicated
at his feet and, in a variation on the pose shown just to the left,
cracks his whip. The putti on the verso, which has clearly been
cut on the left where a pair of feet can be made out, fly holding
arrows at the top of the sheet and a hurdy-gurdy (?) at the
bottom.

From this description it is clear that the drawing was made in preparation for the canal façade of the palace near San Canciano that Veronese decorated for Francisco Erizzo, which is known through its description by Ridolfi:[1]

'A contemplatione del Signor Francesco Erizzo indi dipinse pur à fresco nel porticale de suo palagio di San Cantiano, hor di casa Morosina (fabricato co' modelli di Andrea Palladio) strutture antiche, e paesi; e vi lasciò ancor a di sua mano di stucco la statua di Marte (l'altre furono dal Vittoria scolpite), nella quale osservasi la maniera del suo dipingere.

Nello aspetto verso il canale formò Nettuno trionfante sopra conchiglia tirata da Cavalli Marini con Tritoni intorno, che portano fanali, bandiere & arme diverse, e suonano bucine ritorte; e per lo cielo volano fanciullini can mazzi di freccie, carcassi, turbanti, zagaglie, e corone in mano, e la Fama suona tromba d'oro. Tra le fenestre fece a chiaro scuro Minerva e la Pace, & a piedi le Stagioni; per la Primavera Diana col cane; per l'Estate Cerere col cornucopia ripieno di frutti e di Biade; Bacco per l'Autunno, che preme un grappolo d'uva in bocca d'una tigre; & un vecchio involto in una schiavina per il Verno; e per ornamento delle fenestre fecevi torsi d'corpi, e sopra la porta due schiavi & altre bizzarie dipinte con tale tenerezza, che non si possono più soavemente colorire, à segno, che paiono della natura ivi prodotte'.

The sketches on the recto were made in preparation for the main fresco of Neptune on his seashell. The nearly square format with Neptune in the centre was conceived for the main field in the centre of the now destroyed palace, above the entrance from the canal, as it is shown in an engraving by Coronelli from the beginning of the eighteenth century, by which time the frescoes had disappeared (Fig 12).[2] The site was a more auspicious one than that on the façade of the Palazzo Dionysus Bellavite, now Terzi, in San Maurizio. Here the main axis is dominated by typically Venetian Serlian windows, reducing the space available for the frescoes,[3] which had already started to suffer by 1566 when Vasari, who mentions them in the second edition of the *Vite*,[4] was in Venice to collect material.[5]

Vasari also mentioned the frescoes on the façade of the Palazzo Cappello on the grand canal, on which Veronese collaborated with Zelotti,[6] but not those of Palazzo Erizzo. This, however, hardly seems an argument for dating them to after 1566,[7] for Neptune's gesture links with that of the gods on the ceiling formerly in Palazzo Trevisan of 1557 (Fig 10) and the handling of the recto with the drawings for the frescoes in the upper loggia of Palazzo Trevisan (8–11). The verso was doubted[8] before the connection with the Erizzo frescoes had been noted, but the handling of the wash has a dexterity and a lightness beyond the capability of the studio.

Fig 12   V. Coronelli, *Engraving of the Casa Morosina*, from the *Singolarità di Venezia* (Venice, *circa* 1709)

NOTES

1   Ridolfi p 324

2   V. Coronelli, *Singolarità di Venezia* (Venice, *circa* 1709), published and discussed by E. Bassi, *Palazzi di Venezia Admiranda Urbis Venetae* (Venice, 1976), p 275

3   Bassi p 251 reproduces the façade

4   Vasari 6 p 372 and Ridolfi p 303

5   J. Schulz, *Venetian painted ceilings of the Renaissance* (Berkeley, 1968), p 71 cat 14 quoting W. Kallab, *Vasaristudien* (Vienna, 1908)

6   *See* under (148). M. Boschini, *La Carta del navegar pitoresco* (Venice, 1660), *ed. cit.* A. Pallucchini (Venice, 1966), p 218 attributes the frescoes on Palazzo Nani on the Giudecca to Veronese. Ridolfi pp 359–60 gives a full description of them as deeds of Hercules and attributes them to Benedetto; Bassi p 515 reproduces the engraving of the now destroyed palace by Coronelli. *See* under note 2

7   This is implied by Bassi p 271; Francesco Erizzo had owned the palace from 1548

8   *See* Paris 1965 and 1977

13   Study for a ceiling with gods, goddesses and flying cupids

13 Study for a ceiling with gods, goddesses and flying cupids

Pen and ink and wash

31.4 × 21.2 cm

LOCATION formerly London, Arnal

INSCRIBED 'di Paolo V'

PROVENANCE Collection I.B.; Arnal, sold London, Sotheby 9 July 1924, 193

BIBLIOGRAPHY Von Hadeln p 27; Tietze and Tietze-Conrat 2111

The drawing, whose present whereabouts is untraced, has long been recognised as a study for a ceiling.[1] Various gods and goddesses are assembled on banks of cloud while in the centre of the sheet a female rides a chariot drawn by lions. Lions are the attribute of Cybele and she may well be the figure riding in triumph since the foreshortening of her head, as Philip Pouncey noted, does not allow us to see whether she is turreted.[2] Only two other figures are certainly identifiable. Apollo, holding his lyre on the left edge of the sheet, his head surrounded by an aureole, is repeated again to the right where he is seated. Almost in the centre of the sheet Diana is identified by the crescent moon as she rests her hand on a dog. The steep angle of the foreshortening, the suggestion of the curve in the clouds and of gods and goddesses seated around a central figure recur in the ceiling of the Sala dell' Olimpo at Maser where some of the individual motifs of this sheet are also developed.[3] In addition to Apollo and Diana, the lady underneath the lions pulling the chariot plays with a bird as does Juno at Maser, and just to the left the woman seen from behind with a child in front of her anticipates Venus with Cupid. It is possible that the drawing marks an early stage in the design of the fresco, before Daniele and Marcantonio Barbaro had decided upon the scheme of the harmony of the spheres with Thalia in the centre riding upon a great snake.[4] Here Veronese was still thinking of the Palazzo Trevisan frescoes (Fig 10),[5] especially for the flying putti, and had not yet imposed the great frame, a feature that is conspicuously absent from his surviving decorative drawings.

NOTES

1 The Tietzes related it to Ridolfi's description of the frescoes of the Palazzo Cappello, see under (148), apparently forgetting that those were façade frescoes, not a ceiling

2 C. Ripa, *Iconologia* (Rome, 1603), *ed. cit.* Hildesheim 1970 p58

3 Pignatti 193 cat 96

4 Cocke *J.W.C.I.* 1972 pp231–33

5 Of 1557. Since, as argued under (11), this may also be the date of the frescoes around the upper walls of S. Sebastiano, this would leave 1558 and 1559 for the work at Maser, probably done at the same time as Vittoria's, which was mentioned in a letter of 1559, see Cocke 1972 pp239–40

Fig 13   *A muse*, fresco, crossing, Villa Barbaro, Maser

14   Study of a woman's head

Black and white chalk on grey-blue paper, pricked
43.7 × 23.1 cm

LOCATION Florence, Galleria degli Uffizi Inv. S.7431
INSCRIBED 'P. Verones'
BIBLIOGRAPHY Von Hadeln 1911 p 397; Von Hadeln pl 49;
G. Fiocco, *Veronese* (Bologna, 1928), p 142 (Benedetto);
Tietze and Tietze-Conrat 2064; Joachim and McCullagh
under no 26

The drawing, which is pricked for transfer, was related by
Fiocco to the head of one of the servants in Benedetto's *Birth of
the Virgin* of 1577 from the Scuola dei Mercanti.[1] The Tietzes
rightly noted the differences and it is possible that it prepares the
musician with the violin on the crossing of Villa Barbaro, Maser
(Fig 13).[2] The lighting, the angle at which the head is viewed and
the complex hair are similar in both although in the fresco, her
eyes are open and she wears a string of pearls in her hair. These
changes could have been made in the course of painting the
fresco and the correspondence suggests that the present drawing
is a fragment of a cartoon. Although it is the only one to survive,
it seems likely that Veronese made others to help with his
decorative large-scale work and they may be reflected in a
number of drawings, which although clearly copies, differ from
the frescoes at Maser.[3]

NOTES

1   S. Moschini-Marconi, *Gallerie dell' Accademia, Opere d'arte del secolo XVI*
(Rome, 1962), p 77
2   Pignatti 97 pl 230; for the date of 1559, *see* Cocke 1972 pp 239–40 and (13)
note 5
3   A drawing for the *Venus as Abundance* is probably reflected in the copy
made by Van Dyck in his Italian sketchbook, ed. G. Adriani, *Anton van Dyck,
Italienisches Skizzenbuch* (Vienna, 1940/1965), p 37, *see also* Cocke *M.K.I.F.*
1977 p 217. A copy after the *Peace* in the Stanza del Tribunale dell' Amore,
London Old Master Galleries March 1968 (Zelotti), differs from the fresco in
the angle at which the head is set, in the omission of the shadow and of most of
the detail of the niche, all of which suggests that it is copied from a lost
drawing. The *Study of a decorative scheme* in the Albertina, Inv. 26666 is not
now given to Veronese, *see* Venice 1961 cat 45

14   Study of a woman's head (*see also* colour plate)

15   Study of a seated bishop

Oil (?) on paper

19.9 × 13.4 cm

LOCATION Chatsworth, Devonshire collection Inv. 282
PROVENANCE 2nd Duke of Devonshire (Lugt 718)
BIBLIOGRAPHY Cocke *Master Drawings* 1977 p 261

The painterly freedom of handling, which must have been inspired by the unusual technique,[1] has its closest parallel in the British Museum *Modello for Doge Sebastiano Venier's thanksgiving for the Battle of Lepanto* (87) from the end of the 1570s. The present drawing may well be earlier since the curved field in front of which the bishop sits to hold his book echoes the shape of the spandrels of the lower walls of the nave of S. Sebastiano decorated with twelve apostles. The scheme, although not documented, is generally dated to the early 1560s.[2] It could be an early stage in the preparation of the design, before Veronese had decided upon the togate costume. It was developed into the apostle, who reversed and more deeply into his book, is second from the left in the lower row of the *Study of twelve apostles* also at Chatsworth (16).

NOTES

1   I am grateful for the help of the late Mr Thomas Wragg in establishing the technique
2   Pignatti 77–83 noting that they must have been painted after the organ, finished by April 1560. In the course of the restoration, Tintori established that they were painted in tempera, a sense of experiment that recalls the present sheet, unlike the frescoes of the upper walls in true fresco, in T. Pignatti, *Le Pitture di Paolo Veronese nella chiesa di San Sebastiano in Venezia* (Milan, 1966), pp 103ff

15   Study of a seated bishop (actual size)

16   Study of twelve apostles

16 Study of twelve apostles

Pen and ink and wash on brown oiled ground heightened with
  white

25.2 × 40.2 cm

LOCATION Chatsworth, Devonshire collection Inv. 316
BIBLIOGRAPHY Florence 1976 p 161; Cocke *Master Drawings*
  1977 p 261

The drawing had been attributed to Palma Giovane before
Professor Rearick returned it to Veronese and connected it with
eight surviving apostles painted in tempera on the spandrels of
the nave of S. Sebastiano, probably soon after 1560.[1] Reading
from left to right in two lines the apostles are related to the
frescoes on the church, taken from the entrance, as follows: St
James with the staff on the top left appears as second from the
left in S. Sebastiano,[2] the next apostle, reading his book, is on the
end of the right wall,[3] the apostle leaning forward with a wall
indicated to the right is the first on the left[4] and the next apostle
sitting upright is the first on the right.[5]

The remaining three sketches on the top line are not related to
the surviving frescoes but the bottom left apostle is probably St
Thomas, second from right,[6] although his arms differ and he is
not holding the axe; the apostle deep in his book is the third on
the right;[7] St Andrew, identified by the cross he carries, is the
third on the left,[8] and the final figure is St Peter, at the end of the
left-hand side.[9] In the drawing he is reminiscent of Michelangelo's *Evening* in his pose and bare chest, which is covered in
the fresco where he wears both a robe and a tunic, a change that
is typical of the development which occurred in the course of the
execution of the frescoes. Although many of the figures were
conceived in relationship with the spandrels (this is especially
notable in the three sketches of end figures in the top line), the
drawing differs from the decoration in individual poses, the
apostles are not drawn in the sequence used at S. Sebastiano and
the egg and dart cornice is omitted together with the marquetry
windows and their elegant frames.[10]

The smudges of oil paint probably derive from the studio's
use of the drawing[11] both in the preparation of the frescoes and
subsequently when it was copied.[12] The rather precise handling
of the wash in the present drawing contrasts with that of later
sheets like the Chatsworth *Modello for the Martyrdom of St
Justina* (75) and resembles that of the early *Study of Count
Giuseppe da Porto with his son Adriano* in the Louvre (4), and
thus serves as a guide to the dating of Veronese's independent
chiaroscuro drawings (17–42).[13]

NOTES

1 Pignatti 77–83, *see also* (15) note 2; the remaining four figures prepare the
lost frescoes on the entrance to the nave
2 Pignatti pl 170
3 Pignatti pl 169
4 Pignatti pl 168
5 Pignatti pl 171
6 Pignatti pl 175
7 Pignatti pl 172
8 Pignatti pl 174
9 Pignatti pl 173
10 The apostles appear to be in front of the cornice, which is itself on a level
with the top of the arches, but they also appear to be slightly behind the arches
11 This was suggested by John Shearman's discussion of Sarto's drawings,
Andrea del Sarto (Oxford, 1965), p 158 note 2
12 Rearick in the Florence catalogue mentions Uffizi 7548S, attributed to
Schiavone (perhaps by Benedetto) and another sheet copying six apostles was
sold London, Sotheby 28 June 1979, 69 (studio drawing)
13 That Veronese would have made finished drawings to assist with the
decoration is suggested by the grey chalk *Copy after St Honofrius* which flanks
the main altar, Pignatti 132. The drawing, which measures 30.5 by 18.5 cm,
differs in detail from the fresco and may well have been copied from a now lost
drawing. It came from an anonymous private collection (Lugt 2103a) and is
now in a private collection in England

Chiaroscuro Drawings

The independent *chiaroscuro* drawings were among the most admired of Veronese's drawings, being the only ones mentioned by his first biographer Ridolfi in 1648 (19, 20, 41). Ridolfi's enthusiasm is understandable, for they were planned as independent works in preparatory drawings (21, 34) and executed with a brilliance and fluidity in the white heightening that was copied but never equalled (157, 162, 204). Veronese here turned to an older tradition of Venetian drawing with a sense of invention in conventional subjects, both religious and allegorical and in unusual variations on well-established themes.

There is no documentary evidence for the date of the series, which seems to me to have been produced if not in one burst at least in a concentrated, rather than a long drawn-out period. Internal evidence suggests a date in the late 1550s or early 1560s. Some of the allegorical figures (17, 23) were developed in paintings datable to the 1550s and 1560s with a sense of volume suggesting that the drawings are earlier. Their handling, too, resembles the controlled strokes of the *Study of twelve apostles* (16) from the beginning of the 1560s rather than the greater freedom of the 1575 *Modello for the Martyrdom of St Justina* (75). The inscriptions on the versos of a number of the series are in the first person, but were probably dictated by Veronese (perhaps at the end of his career) since they are not in his hand and are often inaccurate in minor details.

Drawings with inscriptions

17 Allegory of Fortune

Pen and ink and wash on green prepared paper heightened with
  white

27.6 × 20.2 cm

LOCATION Frankfurt, Städelschen Kunstinstitut Inv. 457

INSCRIBED on the verso (17v): 'Il Beneffitio una Donna vestita
  riccame[n]te et coronata da Re; et porga co[n] le mani
  corone; et scetri', 'P. Veronese n.o 1107', 'ex col Peter Lely'

PROVENANCE Sir Peter Lely (Lugt 2092, the 'L' cut); J. F.
  Städel by 1816

BIBLIOGRAPHY Tietze and Tietze-Conrat 2066; Paris 1967
  under no 144; Cocke *Master Drawings* 1977 pp 260 and 264;
  Malke no 12

The dismissive gesture with which the lady drops the bishop's
mitre to join the papal tiara, sceptres and crowns at her feet
identifies her as Fortune.[1] The identification as 'beneffitio' suggested by the unknown draughtsman responsible for the inscriptions[2] is a secondary one which derives from the proverbial
saying that someone is 'a beneffitio di fortuna' as an expression of
Fortune's capriciousness.[3] The attributes at Fortune's feet lie
on the ground to express the vanity of human ambition, as in the
Omnia Vanitas in the Frick collection (Fig 22) probably painted
for the Bavarian court by 1567.[4] Here the theme of the present
drawing was reworked with greater monumentality, especially
since Fortune may well once have taken up less of the sheet
which, by comparison with the *Triumph of Temperance over Vice*
in the Louvre (23), has probably been cut down.

NOTES

1 C. Ripa, *Iconologia* (Rome, 1603), *ed. cit.* Hildesheim 1970 p 169 'Fortuna
... e ne cadano varii istromenti appartenenti a varie professioni, come scettri,
libri, corone, gioie ...'; in the *Fortune* in the Sala del Collegio in the Palazzo
Ducale in the 1570s Veronese expressed the same idea by showing her with the
papal tiara etc in one hand and dice in the other, Pignatti pl 500

2 *See* under *Pittura Quarta* (19) note 5

3 Salvatore Battaglia, *Grande Dizionario della Lingua Italiana* 2 (Turin,
1962), p 172

4 Cocke *Pantheon* 1977 pp 120ff

17v Inscription

17   Allegory of Fortune

18   Allegory of Redemption

18 Allegory of Redemption

Pen and ink and grey wash on grey washed paper heightened
with white

61.3 × 42.1 cm

LOCATION New York, Metropolitan Museum Rogers Fund
Inv. 1961. 203

INSCRIBED by Jonathan Richardson, Junior in an English
translation of the original inscription, which is laid down:
'This Divine Poetry represents the Final Completion of the Great
and Sublime Mystery of the Redemption of the World: Foretold in
various Manners & Distant Times, by the Prophets & Sybils and in
its Due Time Fully Accomplished by the Virgin Mary's presenting
y First Author of Original Sin to the glorious Redeemer, her son'.
Richardson had added that:
'the Prophets are plac'd above and near their High Inspirers ...
while the Sibyl, whose Prophecies were by Compulsion, without
Their being let in to the Knowledge and Tendency of their own
high Illuminations, are only attentive to one another, Below'.

PROVENANCE Sir Peter Lely (Lugt 2093); Jonathan Richardson,
Junior (Lugt 2170); Sir Thomas Lawrence, thence Samuel
Woodburn, his sale London, Christie 4–12 June 1860, 1017;
Norblin Fils, his sale Paris 30 January 1863, 12; acquired
1961

BIBLIOGRAPHY New York 1965 no 129

Although this is the most ambitious and largest of all the
chiaroscuro drawings, it appears to have been trimmed at the
edges and may once have been slightly larger on all sides. It sums
up Veronese's interest in Titian and Michelangelo, which had
been so important in the 1550s.[1] The composition is a variation
on Titian's *Gloria*, which was despatched to the Emperor
Charles V by October 1554.[2] Adam is removed from the penitents
on the right of the canvas (including the shrouded figure of
the emperor) to be introduced to the Trinity by the Virgin on the
left of the sheet. The burst of heavenly light in the Titian
inspired Veronese's skilful combination of the coloured ground,
the wash and the white heightening. Each of the four sibyls
standing at the tomb carries a curling scroll derived from that of
Michelangelo's Delphic Sibyl, while their loose flowing robes
and prophetic appearance echo the Erythrean Sibyl.

The composition was developed in the 1574 Chatsworth
Modello for the Martyrdom of St Justina (75) with a greater
emphasis upon the circular movement in the heavenly figures set
in front of the light. Veronese learned this device from
Tintoretto[3] and used it to even more striking effect in the
Coronation of the Virgin in the Accademia (Fig 88), completed by
1586.

NOTES

1 Cocke *J.W.C.I.* 1972 p 245

2 This was noted by E. Panofsky, *Problems in Titian mostly Iconographic*
(London, 1969), p 65 note 20. Veronese was first documented as resident in
Venice in January 1555, but the commission for the redecoration of the rooms
of the Consiglio dei Dieci in the Palazzo Ducale may have meant that he was
there during 1554, Pignatti 251 doc 7 and 107 cats 25ff

3 The *Adoration of the golden calf* and the *Last Judgement* in the Madonna
dell'Orto, for instance, De Vecchi 156

19 Pittura Quarta: Virgin and Child surrounded by six angels (*see also* colour plate)

19 Pittura Quarta: Virgin and Child surrounded by six angels

Pen and wash on blue-grey paper heightened with white
37.7 × 28.9 cm

LOCATION Paris, Musée du Louvre Inv. 4,666

INSCRIBED in another hand on the verso (19v):[1]

'Pittura Quarta. Infiniti sono i modi e l'attitudine, c[he] sono state
dipinte di Maria Vergine, et sopra tutte da Alberto Durero, et
queste quasi tutte a un' modo sempre co[n] il figl[i]o in braccio, al
petto, et sempre nudo I greci, tutti lo facevano fasciato, forse
p[er] no[n] saper far nudi, et ancora p[er] piu divotione. Qua si
possano imaginare tutti colori i quali dipingono, et son valenti
huomini di disegno, c[he] ogni atto puerile, si può dipingere; cosi
vestito come nudo; Michiel Agnolo Buonarotti ultimame[n]te l'ha
fato adorme[n]tato mentre c[he] la Vergine legge. Resta adunq[ue]
c[ome] mai loveduto c[he] la Vergi[ne] sia in piedi a una culla; et lo
vadia vestendo; et farli attorno angeli, co[n] fiori et frutti in mano
co[n] istrume[n]ti musicali, et cosi mezzo vestito, et mezzo
spogliato o, in cuna, o fuori; senza altro Joseph, o Anna, ma angeli
solame[n]te.'

PROVENANCE Muselli collection, Verona by 1648; Pierre Crozat,
his sale Paris, Mariette 1741, part of 682;[2] acquired by
P. J. Mariette (Lugt 1852),[2] his sale Paris, Basan 1775, 242;
Prince de Conti, his sale Paris, Rémy 8 April 1777, 1133

BIBLIOGRAPHY Ridolfi p 321; Von Hadeln pl 57; Venice 1939
p 227 no 15; Tietze and Tietze-Conrat 2135; Paris 1967
no 144; Cocke *Master Drawings* 1977 p 263

This has long been one of the most admired of Veronese's
drawings, whose popularity in the nineteenth century led to
over-exposure in the Louvre with consequent fading.[3] It was
prized both for the marvellous fluency of the wash and the white
heightening and also for the inscription, which was quoted by
Ridolfi (with minor discrepancies)[4] when it may have formed a
part of its display in the Muselli cabinet.

The inscription, by an unidentified hand[5] emphasises the search
for *varietas* in a treatment of the Virgin and Child not found in
Dürer, whose engravings inspired Veronese's early work, or
Michelangelo. That Veronese was thinking of engravings is
confirmed by his description of Michelangelo's *Madonna del
Silenzio*, which was first engraved by Giulio Bonasone in 1561.[6]
This could well be the date for the composition, but minor
inaccuracies, the reference to the fruit and flowers held by the
angels and the failure to mention the strange implement (a pair
of tongs?) which the Virgin holds in her right hand, suggest that
the inscription may have been added when Veronese returned to
earlier drawings.[7]

Dürer's great Apocalypse series, with the text printed on the
back of the woodcuts, may well have provided the model for this
combination of word and image, whose very lack of precedents
reinforces the argument that the inscriptions were not a part of
the original plan.

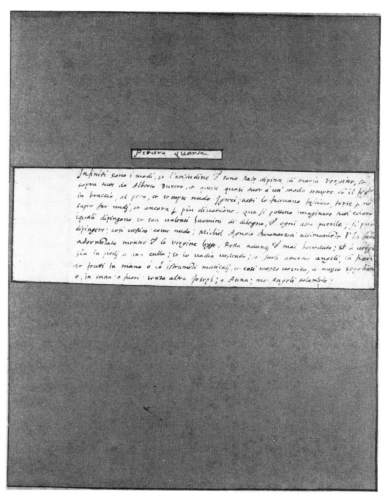

19v   Pittura Quarta

NOTES

1   This transcription was made by Von Hadeln p 321 note 1 of Ridolfi; the
drawing is now laid down except for the inscription

2   His mount with cartouches that reads: 'PAULI CALLIARI. Veronensis opus
eximium.'

3   This was noted by Roseline Bacou in the 1967 Paris catalogue

4   This was noted by Von Hadeln p 321 note 1 of Ridolfi

5   That it was not by Veronese was first argued by Rosand 1971 p 208; his
suggestion that it might be by Carletto does not bear comparison with the letter
on the verso of the Munich *Cupid and Psyche* (Fig 100), Cocke *Master Drawings*
1977 p 263 note 12

6   *Fortuna di Michelangelo nell'Incisione* (Benevento, Museo del Sannio,
1964), cat by M. Rotili, cat 25, based on a drawing in the collection of the Duke
of Portland; also engraved by G. B. de' Cavalieri in 1574

7   That it remained in the studio may be confirmed by the painting in the
collection of Antonio Zecchini in Pescara, which measured about the same size
as the drawing and was, to judge from the engraving by Dionigi Valesi, a school
derivation from the drawing, P. Ticozzi, *Paolo Veronese e i suoi incisori* (Venice,
Museo Correr, 1977), no 82; *see also* under *Pittura Sesta* (21) note 1

20   Pittura Quinta: Virgin and Child with St Anne and angels

Wash on grey paper heightened with white

33.5 × 39.1 cm

LOCATION New York, Mooney

INSCRIBED in another hand on the verso (20v):

'Pittura Quinta. Io ne ho fatto una p[er] la mia camera e da una parte del quadro e Maria Vergine; a sedere co[n] un' libro inan . . . et si sta co[n] gli occhi elevati, et co[n] le mani fermate una sul libro, l'altra al petto; et S. Anna a canto sede dorme riposatamente, et in questo mezzo p[er] tutto il quadro sono angeli intorno al Giesu [Crist]o inpiedi; co[n] va[rie] attitudini, et hanno in mano diverse cose, e le piu apporventi son queste. Una fenice; un pelicano; una co[rona] di stelle, una di gioe, una di spine; uno ha un sole un' altro una luna; et sparso p[er] terra Oliva, fiori, frutti; quasi un' mostrare; Noi angeli siami i suoi ministri, a governare il Cielo, et la terra; et sempre saremo come è scritto nella sacra scrittura la quale legge M[adonna] vergine et ammira; l'opera divina, et i se[di] celesti' together with a number of random sums

PROVENANCE Muselli collection, Verona by 1648; P. Crozat, his sale Paris, Mariette 1741, 680; Count Carl Gustav Tessin; Count Nils Barck (Lugt 1959); H. M. Calmann; Rudolf Heinemann

BIBLIOGRAPHY Ridolfi p 321; New York 1965 no 130; Birmingham, Alabama 1972 p 48

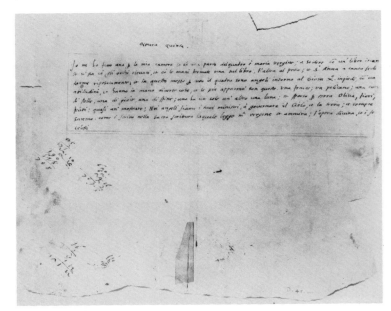

20v   Pittura Quinta

The composition is a variation of that of the *Pittura Quarta* in the Louvre (19) with the Virgin and Child in the centre emphasised by the column and by the nearly symmetrical grouping of the angels on either side. The inscription mentions the attributes held by the angels as well as the pelican in its piety on the left and the phoenix to the right, but refers to the Virgin as having one hand on her breast, a mistake confirming the view that it was added later. The back of the sheet includes a series of sums, similar to that on the verso of the sheet in Berlin, which may well be by Veronese and suggests that the backs of the drawings were not originally considered for inscriptions.

The retrospective tone of the reference to a picture of the same subject painted for the artist's *camera* also suggests that the inscriptions were added later, perhaps in the 1580s. None of the pictures mentioned in the Caliari collection by Ridolfi in 1648 fit.[1] The discrepancy is not surprising for the imagery of the *chiaroscuro* drawings with their extensive use of symbols, differs from the straightforward approach of the surviving devotional paintings.

As with the Uffizi study of *David and Moses* (26) the verso of the present sheet, with the inscription, appears to have suffered from more damage and trimming than the recto.

NOTE

1   Ridolfi pp 343–44

20　Pittura Quinta: Virgin and Child with St Anne and angels

Fig 14   *Copy after the Pittura Sesta*, Kunsthalle, Bremen

21v   Series of accounts

21   Study for the Pittura Sesta and for a Rest on the Flight into Egypt

Pen and ink and wash
19.5 × 20.2 cm

LOCATION Berlin-Dahlem, Staatliche Museen KdZ 26362
INSCRIBED on the verso (21v) with a series of accounts and in
    another hand: 'Studi di Paolo per una Cena'
PROVENANCE Marchese Jacopo Durazzo, Genoa
BIBLIOGRAPHY Von Hadeln pl 37; Tietze and Tietze-Conrat
    2044; Oehler p 33; Cocke *Master Drawings* 1977 p 264

Comparison with Veronese's autograph letters (Fig 87), for instance, supports the view, argued by the Tietzes, that the
accounts are autograph. This study is for the now lost *chiaroscuro*
drawing which Ridolfi described as Pittura Sesta in the Muselli
collection[1] and which is reflected in a copy in Bremen (Fig 14).[2]
According to Ridolfi the inscription on the verso of the Muselli
drawing read:

> 'Pittura Sesta. Se io haverò tempo giamai, voglio rappresentare
> sontuosa mensa sotto a nobil loggia, ove entri la Vergine, il Salvatore
> e Gioseppe, facendogli servire col più ricco corteggio d'Angeli, che
> si possà imaginare, che gli somministrino in piatti d'argento e d'oro
> regalate vivande e copia di pomposi frutti. Altri siano implicati in
> recar in tersi cristalli & in dorate coppe pretiose vivande, per
> dimostrare il ministero prestato da Beati spiriti loro Dio, come
> meglio nel fine del libro sarà dichiarato, per intelligenza de' Pittori e
> per diletto degli amatori della Virtù; della qual inventione io ne vidi
> un rarissimo disegno'.

The earliest design on the bottom right of the sheet shows
Christ offered a chalice with an angel on the right of the group
in the position used for Joseph in the main sketch. Where the
figures are set in front of a colonnade which, to judge from
the copy in Bremen, was not as skilfully developed as that of the
Feast in the house of Simon painted for the Servites by 1573, now
at Versailles. The remaining sketches at the top right of the sheet
were made in preparation for a *Rest*, and the seated Virgin on the
right edge with the sleeping Christ on her lap is connected with
the version in the Spector collection (30).

The combination of rapid pen and ink sketches, with many
pentimenti and rich wash defining some figures is one that
Veronese used throughout his career, but the loose, calligraphic
handling is close to that of the *Studies of Jupiter* in the Morgan
Library of 1557 (9).

21   Study for the Pittura Sesta and for a Rest on the Flight into Egypt

NOTES

1   Ridolfi p 321; the Tietzes noted that the composition is related to the painting that Ridolfi II p 113 described in the Curtoni collection. The disappearance of the painting makes judgement difficult, but none of the *chiaroscuro* drawings are squared, like the *modelli*, for transfer to canvas. The inscription together with the copy, which appears to reflect a drawing not a painting, makes it extremely unlikely that the drawings were made for painting, which like the school *Rest* in the High Museum of Art, Atlanta (Pignatti A5) may have been a derivation from the lost Muselli drawing, as was that, known through an engraving, which derived from the *Pittura Quarta* (19), esp. under note 7

2   The connection was first noted by W. Vitzthum, *Master Drawings* 4 (1966), p 185 pl 47. The Bremen drawing, which measures 39.6 by 53 cm, was acquired with an attribution to Alessandro Gherardini from Paul Brandt, Amsterdam, in 1957. The Muselli drawing was later in the collection of Pierre Crozat no 695 in the Paris, Mariette 1741 sale catalogue; acquired by Mariette in 1767 (Paris 1767 no 144) and was no 253 in the Paris, Basan 1775 sale of his collection

22v   Inscription

22   Triumph of Good Repute over Evil

Pen and wash on blue prepared paper heightened with white
27.3 × 19.8 cm

LOCATION Vienna, Albertina Inv. 1640
INSCRIBED in another hand on the verso (22v):
'Mentre c[he] il Sole girerà p[er] i segni celesti: la vita de i nobili da
ca . . . terra sotto i piedi il vitio; si come hanno i lor pass . . . fatto:
co[n] la destra hanno mostrato sempre chiarezza di vita, et co . . .
sinistra coperto attenuto sepolto ogni bruttezza c[he] potesse
scurare vita loro.   Una fama co[n] le ale et co[n] le trombe in
mano; c[he] la fama cat . . . tenga sotto i piedi, c[he] sara una brutta
femina co[n] alie di farf . . . et le trombe rotte. Da un canto un
putto co[n] trofei in bracc . . . di corone di scettri, et di dignità;
questo e p[er] il merito, d . . . altro canto un'altro putto p[er] il
giuditio co[n] libri, et olive c . . . et questi putti sien vestiti di
panneti a bene placito del pitt . . .   La fama c[he] ne portano i
mirabile, p[er] c[he] hanno atterato la . . . cattiva; et p[er] il mezzo
delle lettere e della Virtu si sono acquistati nobilta, dignita et
stato.'; in another hand: 'P. Veronese'
PROVENANCE Sir Peter Lely (Lugt 2092)
BIBLIOGRAPHY Stix and Fröhlich-Bum cat 159 (Farinati);
    Venice 1961 no 43 (Veronese)

The drawing clearly resembles the other allegorical drawings
including (17) and (23), as Oberhuber and Benesch noted in the
1961 Venice catalogue. The inscription (one of the longest to
have survived) has been trimmed on the right edge and the
reference to the sun and the zodiacal signs in the first line, which
is not echoed in the drawing in its present state, suggests that the
whole sheet has been cut down. It was probably once at least the
same size as the *Triumph of Temperance* (23) in the Louvre, and
may have included the sun with a selection of zodiacal figures.

22   Triumph of Good Repute over Evil

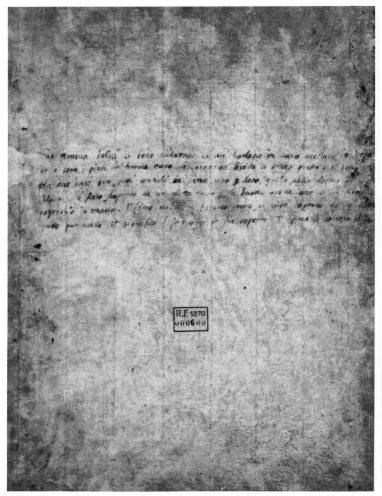

23v   Inscription

Fig 15   *Triumph of Patience over lack of self-restraint* (detail), Stanza dei tre Capi del Consiglio dei Dieci, Palazzo Ducale, Venice

23   Triumph of Temperance over Vice

Pen and wash on grey-blue prepared paper heightened with
   white
36.2 × 27.2 cm

LOCATION Paris, Musée du Louvre Inv. RF 600

INSCRIBED in another hand on the verso (23v):
   'Una femina belliss[im]a et bene adornata co[n] un horologio in
   mano questa e la Virtu et a sotto i piedi un'huomo nudo di
   carnagione livida e brun e questo e il vizio Item due vasi ben fatti
   antichi . . . uno p[er] lato quello della destra . . . e stato scoperto da
   uno putto nudo per la buon opinione ci se tiene . . . coperchio a
   mano. L'altro vaso alquanto[?] scuro, et vien aperto da uno altro
   putto pur nudo et significa . . . sia coperto che prima si conosce il . . .'

PROVENANCE W. A. Lestevenon; Marquis de Lagoy (Lugt
   1710); His de la Salle (Lugt 1333); presented to the Museum
   in 1878

BIBLIOGRAPHY Tietze and Tietze-Conrat 2131; Paris 1965
   no 114; Cocke *Master Drawing* 1977 p 264

The now sadly faded inscription has been cut at the right edge
(the left on the recto where the wall behind the putto appears to
have been trimmed), which suggests that the sheet was originally
wider, and that it was perhaps the same size as the *Pittura Quinta*
(20) in the Mooney collection. The inscription, which refers in
precise terms to the two smoking vases (that on the left is Good
Opinion), is more vague about the standing lady, whom it identifies simply as Virtue. The clock that she holds so prominently
suggests, however, that she embodies a specific virtue, that of
Temperance.[1]

   Together with Prudence, Courage and Justice, Temperance
joined the original three virtues, Faith, Hope and Charity at first
on an equal footing. By the mid-fourteenth century, under the
influence of Aristotle's Nicomachean Ethics with its emphasis
upon *mesure*, Temperance had become the supreme virtue. In
the eleventh century Temperance was shown holding a jug with
which she watered down her wine. By the fourteenth century
this changed and she was identified by a sandglass and then later
a clock. These attributes were sometimes accompanied by reins
and a bit, which could on occasions replace the clock.

23   Triumph of Temperance over Vice

Veronese painted a variation on the theme of this drawing on the ceiling of the Stanza dei tre Capi of the Consiglio dei Dieci in the Palazzo Ducale (Fig 15) in the mid-1550s,[2] with a vividness and power (allowing for the difference of view-point needed in a ceiling) that make it unlikely that the drawing could come after the ceiling. The *Temperance*, resembling a number of other allegorical drawings including the *Fortune* in Frankfurt (17) and the *Triumph of Good Repute* in the Albertina (22), looks forward to the bolder Truth in the *Omnia Vanitas* now in the Frick (Fig 22), probably commissioned for Albrecht V, Elector of Bavaria in 1567.[3]

NOTES

1   Lynn White, Junior, 'The Iconography of Temperantia and the Virtuousness of Technology' in *Action and Conviction in Early Modern Europe*, eds T. K. Rabb and J. E. Siegel (1969), pp 197–212

2   Pignatti 31; the frame of the ceiling was ready by 1554 when carpets and leather wall-hangings were installed; the ceiling was probably completed slightly later for it conforms in style with the canvases in the nave of S. Sebastiano of 1556. The picture's precise significance is as uncertain as its general message is clear; the stirrups may identify the woman as Patience (E. K. J. Reznicek, *Die Zeichnungen von Hendrik Goltzius* (Utrecht, 1961), p267), while the man's attitude and his failure to use the bridle suggest that he embodies lack of self restraint

3   Cocke *Pantheon* 1977 pp 120ff

Religious drawings

24 The angel appears to Zacharias

Pen and ink and wash on green tinted paper heightened with
white
27.5 × 18.4 cm
LOCATION London, British Museum Inv. 1971–10–30–2
INSCRIBED on the verso: 'Cat. M. de la Nous'

The drawing was included in an exhibition of recent purchases
soon after its acquisition where it was recognised as an autograph
early Veronese, perhaps intended as a *modello* for a lost altar.
This is, of course, possible although the early sources do not
record a picture of this subject.[1] It resembles the independent
chiaroscuro drawings, most notably *The supper at Emmaus* at
Chatsworth (35), in handling and in details like the foreshortened
head of the angel, comparable to that of Christ, in Zacharias's
gesture, similar to those of the apostles, and in the sketchy use of
the pen in the background.

The drawing preserves its original frame like the *Sts Mark,
Leonard and Francis* in the Morgan Library (32). It may be early,
for the drapery style does not achieve the bulk of *The supper at
Emmaus*, and the altar in the background is more conventional
than the frame of the organ of S. Sebastiano, which Veronese
designed in October 1558, where, for the first time in Venice, the
arch breaks into the pediment.[2]

NOTES
1 Pignatti pp 294ff, Index of Lost Works
2 Cocke *J.W.C.I.* 1972 p 246

24 The angel appears to Zacharias

25   Christ the Redeemer appears to Sts Peter and Anthony of Padua

Pen and ink on grey washed paper heightened with white
23.2 × 24 cm

LOCATION Paris, Musée du Louvre Inv. 4,667
PROVENANCE P. Crozat (Lugt 2951)[1]
BIBLIOGRAPHY Von Hadeln pl 61; Tietze and Tietze-Conrat
2196 (Benedetto); Cocke *Master Drawings* 1977 p 265

Von Hadeln's view that this is an autograph drawing seems preferable to that of the Tietzes who compared it with the Lille *Copy of Christ in Limbo* (178), which they believed to be by Benedetto. In spite of damage the treatment of the wash and the realisation of Christ's features are finer than in the Lille drawing. The skill with which the kneeling Sts Peter and Anthony of Padua are realised recalls the seated Virgin in the *Rest* (28).

The Christ is freely based on the statue that Michelangelo had delivered to S. Maria sopra Minerva, Rome, by 1524. The legs are seen from further to the left than in early copies (or modern photographs)[2] and this unusual aspect is combined with a reversal of the arms holding the cross. The skill with which the figure is reworked suggests that Veronese must have studied it carefully on his visit to Rome with Girolamo Grimani, which I believe to have taken place in 1555.[3]

NOTES

1   It cannot be identified in the 1741 sale catalogue but the cartouche inscribed with the number 715 together with the paraph is presumably his as is the inscription; 'Caliari Paolo Veronese École Vénitienne'
2   It was engraved, reversed, by Beatrizet, C. de Tolnay, *Michelangelo 3: The Medici Chapel* (Princeton, 1970), pp 177ff
3   Cocke *J.W.C.I.* 1972 pp 245–46

25   Christ the Redeemer appears to Sts Peter and Anthony of Padua

26   David and Moses

26   David and Moses

26v Studies of seated figures and a Virgin and Child

Pen and ink and wash on green prepared paper heightened with
   white (recto); pen and ink (verso)
19.8 × 25.6 cm

LOCATION Florence, Galleria degli Uffizi Inv. 12894F
INSCRIBED 'Paolo Veronese'; on the verso: 'de m Paulo
   Veronese'
PROVENANCE Lorenzo de'Medici (?)
BIBLIOGRAPHY Florence 1976 no 116; Cocke *Master Drawings*
   1977 p 265

26v   Studies of seated figures and a Virgin and Child

Rearick in his discussion of the drawing, whose old attribution to Veronese was first recognised as correct by Châtelet, linked both recto and verso with the decoration of S. Sebastiano (Fig 11). In neither case is this persuasive, although his dating of 1558 fits with that which I had argued for the *chiaroscuro* drawings. Neither the pose of the David and Moses nor their settings on rolling clouds are related to the figures in the frieze of 1558 in the upper part of S. Sebastiano. Rather they recall the prophets in the *Allegory of Redemption* in the Metropolitan Museum (18), and it was perhaps made as a trial for that great drawing.

The sketches on the verso show a seated figure on the left edge holding a scroll, a number of other figures which are cut off at the bottom and a seated man with a book on his lap near the centre of the bottom edge. On the right, a briefly indicated

Virgin holds a standing Christ Child whose legs are shown again at the top of the sheet, cut off at the edge, confirming that the sheet was once larger. Rearick related these elements to the main altar in S. Sebastiano, which was commissioned in 1559 but probably painted later.[1] In the altar, however, St John, like the other saints, looks up at the heavenly appearance of the Virgin and Christ Child and holds a staff, rather than a scroll. The two seated figures are perhaps closer (even though the connection is not beyond doubt) to the *David and a prophet* in the Morgan Library (27).

NOTES

1   Pignatti 132, convincingly dating the altarpiece to *circa* 1565

27   David and a prophet

27   David and a prophet

Pen and ink and wash heightened with white
26.6 × 19.6 cm

LOCATION New York, Pierpont Morgan Library Inv. 189
PROVENANCE Charles Fairfax Murray; J. Pierpont Morgan
BIBLIOGRAPHY Cocke *Master Drawings* 1977 p265

In style and handling the drawing is similar to the *Sts Mark, Leonard and Francis* (32) in the same collection. It may have been cut down, in which case the trees behind the prophet and the bush beside David would have taken up more of the sheet. The figures are related to the David and a prophet, usually identified as Isaiah,[1] on the chancel arch of S. Sebastiano painted in 1558 (Fig 11).[2] David's crown is similar in both, but in the drawing the figures are seated in a landscape and the colloquy is heightened in a way that suggests a connection with the prophets in the upper half of the *Allegory of Redemption* in the Metropolitan Museum (18). The drawing may also be related to the sketches on the verso of the *David and Moses* in the Uffizi (26), another drawing possibly connected with the *Allegory*.

NOTES

1   This, together with the nature of the action which does not suggest a rebuke, makes my earlier suggestion that the prophet is Nathan unlikely
2   *See* (11)

28   Rest on the Flight into Egypt (*see also* colour plate)

Fig 16   *Rest on the Flight into Egypt*, National Gallery of Canada, Ottawa

28   Rest on the Flight into Egypt

Pen and ink and wash on brown tinted paper heightened with
    white
31.6 × 23.7 cm

LOCATION London, British Museum Inv. 1854–6–28–4
PROVENANCE Gabriele Caliari, Venice (?); Sir Peter Lely
    (Lugt 2092); P. Crozat, his sale Paris, Mariette 1741, 682
    (one of three items); De Julienne sale Paris, Rémy 1767, 454;
    P. J. Mariette, his sale Paris, Basan 252
BIBLIOGRAPHY Von Hadeln pl 58; Tietze and Tietze-Conrat
    2090; Rosand 1971 pp 204ff; Cocke *Master Drawings* 1977
    p 266

This fine example of Veronese's mastery of wash and white
heightening, which is one of the three drawings prepared in the
sheet at Cleveland (34), remained in the studio where it was seen
by Van Dyck[1] and where it provided the starting-point for the
school copy now in the Samuel H. Kress collection, Atlanta,
Georgia.[2] Although I only know the picture from a photograph
it appears to be by the same hand as the *Christ and the Samaritan*
in St Louis,[3] which develops from a school drawing at Oxford.[4]

The artist of the St Louis *Christ and the Samaritan* has taken
considerable liberties with the Oxford drawing, adding a screen
of trees, changing the position of the bucket, the front of the well
and reversing the composition. All these alterations suggest that
the Oxford drawing may have been made with the painting in
mind.

Veronese himself developed the upright composition of the
present drawing into the oblong *Rest* now in Ottawa (Fig 16),[5]
which is undated, but whose treatment of the landscape resembles
that of the Sarasota *Rest*, probably completed by 1572 (212).

NOTES

1   His copy is on f. 2v of the Italian sketchbook, ed. G. Adriani, *Anton van
Dyck, Italienisches Skizzenbuch* (Vienna, 1940/1965); *see also* Cocke *M.K.I.F.*
1977 p 217, Ridolfi pp 343 and 361 describes the family collection which passed
to his son Gioseppe
2   Pignatti A5
3   Pignatti A281
4   Byam Shaw no 800
5   Pignatti 322; *see* under (74) note 1. Its dimensions, 166 by 264 cm, suggest
that it might be the *Rest* in La Favorita, Mantua in 1665 where it is called
a 'Quadro Lungo', whose dimensions as given in the 1709 inventory, 10 by
14 quarte, about 170 by 238 cm, match those of the Ottawa canvas, A. Luzio,
La Galleria dei Gonzaga venduta all'Inghilterra nel 1627–28 (Milan, 1913),
p 315

29   Rest on the Flight into Egypt

29   Rest on the Flight into Egypt

Pen and ink on blue-green paper heightened with white
24.8 × 19.8 cm

LOCATION Cambridge, Mass., Fogg Art Museum Inv. 1928.681

PROVENANCE Sir Thomas Lawrence, thence to Samuel
    Woodburn, his sale London, Christie 4–12 June 1860,
    bt Clement; Arozarena; J. P. Heseltine; Bellingham-Smith,
    their sale Amsterdam, Müller 5–6 July 1927, 8 (copy);
    Nebehay sold to Paul J. Sachs

BIBLIOGRAPHY Mongan and Sachs no 204; Tietze and Tietze-
    Conrat 2051; Rosand 1971 pp 204ff; Birmingham, Alabama
    1972 p 50; Washington 1974 no 24; Cocke *Master Drawings*
    1977 p 266

This is one of the three *chiaroscuro* drawings prepared in the
*Studies of the Virgin and Child with Sts John the Baptist and
Joseph* in Cleveland (34). It is slightly smaller than the *Rest* in the
British Museum (28), prepared on the same sheet, and a comparison suggests that it has been cut down and that there was
probably a strip of ground at the feet of the Holy Family and
another above the top of the tree. Restoring these losses would
reduce the emphasis upon the figures, making them similar to
those of the British Museum *Rest* and the larger *Rest* in the
Spector collection, New York (30).

30   Rest on the Flight into Egypt

30   Rest on the Flight into Egypt

Wash on grey prepared paper heightened with white
40.6 × 42.1 cm

LOCATION New York, Stephen Spector
PROVENANCE Mrs Llewellyn-Palmer; London 1962 no 10
BIBLIOGRAPHY Birmingham, Alabama 1972 no 49; Cocke *Master Drawings* 1977 p 266

Like the *Pittura Quinta* in the Mooney collection (20) this large[1] and ambitious drawing, which I know from a photograph, uses only wash underdrawing to achieve an almost impressionistic freedom of stroke especially in the wave-like movement of the leaves. This, together with its size, differentiates it from the other two versions of this subject (28 and 29), and the pose of the Virgin giving suck while holding onto a tree-stump with her right hand develops from the Berlin study for the *Study for the Pittura Sesta and for a Rest on the Flight into Egypt* (21). Here, however, her legs are stretched out in front of her as she sits on the grassy bank and turns to look at St Joseph collecting fruit into his basket.

NOTES

1   A copy from Lord Milford's collection, sold London, Christie 25 June 1974, is slightly larger, 42.5 by 44.5 cm. It shows that the present drawing has been cropped notably at the left and the bottom edges

31 Sts John the Baptist, Anthony Abbot and Andrew

31 Sts John the Baptist, Anthony Abbot and Andrew

Pen and ink and wash on grey paper heightened with white
28 × 23.5 cm

LOCATION Paris, Musée du Louvre Inv. 4,671
BIBLIOGRAPHY Tietze and Tietze-Conrat 2177 (workshop);
    Cocke *Master Drawings* 1977 p 266

The drawing has suffered considerable loss in the shoulder of the
Baptist and the hands of St Anthony, in spite of which it is
autograph and comparable with the *Pittura Quarta* in the same
collection (19). The Tietzes argued that the connection of the
kneeling page with the page in the *St Anthony Abbot enthroned*
from S. Antonio, Torcello, now in the Brera (Fig 17),[1] confirmed
their attribution of the drawing to the workshop. In the drawing
the page is reversed and differs both in the features of his face
and in his costume (the breeches are heavily slashed and the
bottom of his coat makes a simpler arabesque over them). The
differences suggest that both painting and drawing are autograph
and that when Veronese received the commission for S. Antonio
in 1570[2] he returned to the drawing which he revised to achieve
the greater monumentality of the altar.

NOTES

1   Pignatti A186
2   This was established by R. Gallo, 'Cinque Quadri Ignoti del Veronese alla
Mostra di Venezia', *Ateneo Veneto* 125 (1939), p 200 note 5, who published the
decision to gild the altars, including the main one, on 5 February 1570

Fig 17   *St Anthony Abbot enthroned*, Brera, Milan

32   Sts Mark, Leonard and Francis

32   Sts Mark, Leonard and Francis

Pen and ink and wash on grey prepared paper heightened with
white

29 × 21 cm

LOCATION New York, Pierpont Morgan Library Inv. I88
PROVENANCE Sir Peter Lely (Lugt 2092); P. H. Lankrink (Lugt
2090); William Mayor (Lugt 2799); Charles Fairfax Murray;
J. Pierpont Morgan
BIBLIOGRAPHY Tietze and Tietze-Conrat 2175 (workshop,
perhaps Benedetto); Birmingham, Alabama 1972 p 51
(ascribed to Veronese but citing the view of the Tietzes):
Cocke *Master Drawings* 1977 p 266

This fine drawing preserves its original frame,[1] like the *Angel
appears to Zacharias* in the British Museum (24), indicating that
in spite of its size it has not been cut down, unlike the related but
slightly later version in the Louvre (33). The Tietzes argued that
it was a studio drawing and compared it with the *Copy of Christ
in Limbo* in Lille (178). The comparison, however, underlines
the assurance with which the saints of the present sheet are
realised, matching that of the *Apostles*, for the spandrels of the
nave of S. Sebastiano (16), and the *Pittura Quinta* in the Mooney
collection, New York (20).

NOTES

1   It is shown in the old but feeble copy in the Real Accademia de San
Fernando, Madrid (Veronese), A. E. Perez Sanchez, *Catalogo de los Dibujos;
Real Accademia de San Fernando* (Madrid, 1967), pp 154–55

33   Sts Mark, Leonard and Francis

33   Sts Mark, Leonard and Francis

Pen and ink and wash on grey paper heightened with white
28.2 × 24.6 cm

LOCATION Paris, Musée du Louvre Inv. 4,672
INSCRIBED in another hand: 'Veronese'
BIBLIOGRAPHY Tietze and Tietze-Conrat 2178 (school drawing);
Cocke *Master Drawings* 1977 p 266

The doubts expressed by the Tietzes seem to be unjustified.
They may be due to the considerable damage and loss of the
white heightening that the drawing has suffered since the handling has close parallels to that of other autograph drawings,
notably the *Nymph pursued by a satyr* in the Ecole des Beaux-
Arts (41).

It is almost the same size as the related version in the Morgan
Library (32), but must originally have been larger for it has been
cut awkwardly at the top of the architecture eliminating some of
the rays of the stigmata to which St Francis responds. The
Morgan sheet is better preserved, with greater emphasis upon
the wash. The size of the present drawing suggests that it may be
a later reworking (although there is no significant difference in
date) with a greater complexity in the movement of the figures:
St Francis is seen from behind rather than from the front, and
there is a stronger diagonal linking the figures and a more
complex architectural setting.

34 Studies of the Virgin and Child with Sts John the Baptist and Joseph

34 Studies of the Virgin and Child with Sts John the Baptist and Joseph

34v Studies of architecture

Pen and ink and wash on grey-green paper, laid down
20.5 × 23.4 cm

LOCATION Cleveland Museum of Art, Gift of Robert
Hays Gries Inv. 39.670
PROVENANCE Dr Daniel A. Huebsch
BIBLIOGRAPHY Rosand 1971 pp 204ff; Birmingham, Alabama
1972 p 44; Cocke *Master Drawings* 1977 p 263 note 22

This drawing, which had previously been tentatively given to
Palma Giovane, was convincingly attributed to Veronese by
David Rosand. He related it to the drawings of the *Virgin and
Child with St John the Baptist* in Berlin (38), the *Rest* in the
British Museum (28) and that in the Fogg Art Museum (29).
These three drawings were worked out in general terms in the
three sketches of the upper tier, but without the details so skilfully realised in the *chiaroscuro* drawings. The sketch on the left,
which is related to the Berlin sheet (38), is the furthest from the
finished drawing where the *contrapposto* of the Baptist, deriving
in reverse from that of the Bruges Madonna, is changed for a
more intimate gesture as he turns to share his staff with the
Christ Child.

The group in the Berlin drawing was reworked in the *Mystic
marriage of St Catherine* in Montpellier (Fig 27)[2] and the lower
tier of the present sheet shows Veronese continuing to experiment with a range of poses for the Virgin and Child. The sketch
on the extreme left of the five clarifies the 'diving' pose used in
the British Museum drawing (28), the second could relate to the
Berlin drawing while the third is a rather more upright version of
that used in the Fogg drawing (29). The remaining two sketches
show the Virgin holding the standing Christ Child, a common
pose, which in the version on the right is not unlike that in the
*Virgin and Child with Sts George and Justina and a donor (Girolamo
Scrocchetto?)* in the Louvre, probably painted by 1554,[3] where
the Christ Child turns to acknowledge the kneeling donor.

The figure, of indeterminate sex, seated at the top right,
reverses the pose of the Virgin underneath in a way that looks
forward to the Joseph seated at the right of the *Rest* formerly in
the Borletti collection, Milan,[4] where he leans further forward to
look at the Christ Child. When the sheet is turned on its side the
architecture on the verso can just be made out, most notably a
cornice or base of a column (?) with a large roundel.

The connections with paintings, although loose, suggest a
date in the 1550s and the deeply bitten wash and the free
calligraphic handling have their closest parallels in the *Studies of
Jupiter* in the Morgan Library of 1557 (9).

NOTES

1 Although apparently not engraved (C. de Tolnay, *Michelangelo 1: Youth*
(Princeton, 1969), p 159), it was a common motif in Italy, from Raphael's *La
Belle Jardinière* to Parmigianino's *Vision of St Jerome*
2 Pignatti A210; it was in the collection of the Marchesi Carlo, Francesco,
Giovanni and Andrea Gerini by 1715, a collection which was formed by their
father Pierantonio, F. B. Salvadori, *Mitteilungen des Kunsthistorischen Institutes
in Florenz* 18 (1974), p 132. In style it compares, in my view, with other pictures
of the 1560s and the kneeling St Catherine appears to have been developed
from (55) of 1568.
3 Pignatti 130; the earliest reference, the De Brienne inventory of 1662,
mentioned a provenance from S. Giorgio Maggiore, ed. E. Bonnaffé, *Le
Catalogue de Brienne* (Paris, 1873), pp 34–35. The donor, although younger
and seen in profile, seems to be identifiable with the abbot of S. Giorgio,
Girolamo Scrocchetto, introduced in shadow on the right of the *Marriage feast*
from the refectory, of 1562–63, Pignatti 131. Scrocchetto was abbot of
S. Giorgio twice, from 1559 to 1564, when he commissioned the *Feast*, and
earlier from 1551 to 1554 when he may well have commissioned the small
picture in the Louvre, E. A. Cicogna, *Delle inscrizioni Veneziani raccolte ed
illustrate* 4 (Venice, 1824), p 264
4 Pignatti 321; the links with the Sarasota version noted by Pignatti suggest a
date from before 1572, *see* under (212). An engraving by A. W. Warren, issued
by G. Virtue, records the design when it was in the Cabinet Gallery, London.
It may have been the version sold by Dr Bragge, 1757, 48: 'A Riposo, an angel
bringing Flowers', without dimensions, London, Victoria and Albert Museum,
*The principal Collection of pictures sold by Auction in England in the years
1711–1759*, 2 vols, 1, p 467

35 The supper at Emmaus

Pen and ink and wash on green prepared paper heightened
   with white
42.1 × 57.5 cm

LOCATION Chatsworth, Devonshire collection Inv. 277
PROVENANCE Sir Peter Lely (Lugt 2092); 2nd Duke of
   Devonshire (Lugt 718)
BIBLIOGRAPHY Tietze and Tietze-Conrat 2055; Rosand 1966
   p 422 note 9; Royal Academy of Arts, *Old Master Drawings
   from Chatsworth* (1969), p 71; Cocke *Master Drawings* 1978
   pp 266–67

This marvellous large drawing was identified as a possible
modello by the Tietzes who attributed it to the studio. The
reaction against this view began with Rosand who, on the
suggestion of Roger Rearick, indicated that together with the
Temptation of St Anthony (36) it was an autograph early work.
The grass in the foreground of this masterpiece can be compared
with that of the tree on the left background of the *Nymph pursued
by a satyr* (41) and the white heightening resembles that of the
Pittura Quarta (19) where the foreshortening of the Virgin's
head is similar to that of Christ, although the bulk of the underdrawing is done with a brush instead of with a pen as in the
Supper.

Just as the Tietzes were wrong in assigning the sheet to the
studio, so too their view of it as a *modello* is open to question. It is
related to the later canvas of about 1560 now in the Louvre[1]
where the changes are greater than are usual between *modello*
(75) and painting (Fig 42).

There is a partial copy of the central group in Berlin (160).

NOTE

1 Pignatti 91; the early history and identity of the donors is unclear. It was
first mentioned in the 1635 inventory of Charles Emanuel II in Turin (Rome,
Le Gallerie Nazionali Italiani 3 (1897), p 60) with a note that it had been given
to the Duke of Créqui, who was then campaigning for Charles Emanuel in
Savoy, Michaud, *Biographie Universelle* 9 (Paris, 1854), p 466

35   The supper at Emmaus

36   Temptation of St Anthony (*see also* colour plate)

36 Temptation of St Anthony

Pen and ink and wash on grey prepared paper heightened with
white

41.4 × 35.6 cm

LOCATION Paris, Musée du Louvre Inv. 4,842
PROVENANCE Everard Jabach (Lugt 2961), no 65 in the Venetian
section of his manuscript catalogue (Veronese);[1] ceded to the
French Royal collection in 1671
BIBLIOGRAPHY Paris 1965 no 114; Rosand 1966 pp 421–22

Fig 18 *Temptation of St Anthony*, Musée des Beaux-Arts, Caen

The drawing, which had been attributed to Veronese by Jabach,
had in the intervening period been given to Farinati, and was
exhibited as such in 1965. In her catalogue entry, however,
Roseline Bacou noted that the quality of the execution supported
the traditional view that it was by Veronese. This was taken up
by David Rosand who, like Bacou, emphasised that the pliancy
with which the white heightening is handled matches Veronese's
technique in his certain *chiaroscuro* drawings.

The purpose for which the drawing was made and its relation
to the Caen canvas (Fig 18)[2] of the same subject are more open
questions. Rosand developed Bacou's idea that it might be a
modello into the hypothesis that it had been submitted to Cardinal
Ercole Gonzaga in the course of the preparation of the canvas,
which was ready for delivery to Mantua Cathedral by 1552. He
noted, however, that the changes from the *modello* to the painting
were more radical than in the other surviving *modelli*, suggesting
that it might be a later variation on the canvas. That this is so is,
in my opinion, borne out by the reversal of the saint's pose to
make him, rather than the tempter, the main focus of attention.
The change reveals the influence of the martyred saint in Titian's
Death of St Peter Martyr, formerly in SS. Giovanni e Paolo,
Venice.

The idea is further supported by the links with the *Study of
Count Giuseppe da Porto with his son Adriano* of *circa* 1554 (4)
rather than with the earlier *Study of a seated man* (2) and the
contrast with the sketchier *modelli* (75, 87, 88). This must stem
from a difference in function. The *modelli* were primarily intended
to help in the production of large-scale works and only secondarily
to be seen by the patrons, while the *chiaroscuro* drawings were
conceived as finished works of art.

NOTES

1   Paris 1978 (unpaginated)
2   Pignatti 22

37   Virgin and Child appear to Sts Thomas and Cecilia

Wash on blue paper heightened with white
36.7 × 26.1 cm

LOCATION Berlin-Dahlem, Staatliche Museen KdZ 5049
PROVENANCE Schiaminossi (?); Jonathan Richardson, Senior
  (Lugt 2184)
BIBLIOGRAPHY Von Hadeln 1911 p397; Von Hadeln pl60;
  Venice 1939 p226 no14; Tietze and Tietze-Conrat 2032;
  Cocke *Master Drawings* 1977 p267

The drawing has suffered serious damage from the mechanical and
crude use of a stylus, most probably at the hands of Schiaminossi,
who engraved the sheet (Fig 19) in the early years of the seventeenth century.[1] The use of the stylus strongly suggests that the
sheet was in Schiaminossi's own collection, at San Sepolcro.
This is the earliest indication of the appreciation of these drawings which continued in their display in the Muselli and Curtoni
collections (19, 20, 41).

Schiaminossi enlarged the design to show the low side of the
wall in front of which St Thomas kneels with the Virgin's girdle.
The frame lightly indicated around the drawing, like that of the
Sts Mark, Leonard and Francis in the Morgan Library (32) and
The angel appears to Zacharias in the British Museum (24),
shows that this is one of Schiaminossi's innovations, like the
deeper shadows, which transform Veronese's design into some-
thing more in keeping with Baroque taste.

NOTE

1   Bartsch 17, p234, no97; he was probably born in 1570 and the bulk of his
dated work is from the first two decades of the seventeenth century

Fig 19   Schiaminossi, *Engraving after the Virgin and Child appears to Sts Thomas and Cecilia*

37   Virgin and Child appear to Sts Thomas and Cecilia

38   Virgin and Child with St John the Baptist (actual size)

38 Virgin and Child with St John the Baptist

Pen and ink over traces of grey chalk on grey-green paper
   heightened with white
22 × 16.9 cm

LOCATION Berlin-Dahlem, Staatliche Museen KdZ 1549
BIBLIOGRAPHY Von Hadeln pl 56; Tietze and Tietze-Conrat
   2192 (Benedetto); Rosand 1971 p 204 (often ascribed to
   Benedetto); Cocke *Master Drawings* 1977 p 267

Together with the British Museum and Fogg Museum versions
of the *Rest* this was one of the three *chiaroscuro* drawings
prepared on the Cleveland sheet of *Studies* (34), although it
differs rather more from the initial sketch, most clearly in the
pose of St John the Baptist. This together with the handling
should belie the doubts expressed by the Tietzes. The use of the
wash in the Virgin's robe and the details of the drawing of her
mouth and nose seem to be inseparable from drawings that they
accepted as autograph, the Fortune in the Frankfurt *Allegory of
Fortune* (17), for instance, and it is notably superior in quality to
the copy in Turin.[1]

The format, which is small by comparison with the *Rest* in the
British Museum (28), suggests that it was cropped and that the
architecture, over which the Virgin is drawn, was the base for
buildings which rose to fill more of the page. The fallen capital
displayed beside the group recalls that in the Raphael school
picture, the *Madonna of the oak tree* now in Madrid. That
Veronese was interested in Raphael is shown by a copy he made
(now lost) of another Raphael school canvas the *Madonna della
Perla*, probably in the 1550s[2] while it was in the Canossa
collection in Verona.

NOTES
1   A. Bertini, *I Disegni Italiani della Biblioteca Reale di Torino* (Rome, 1958),
no 434. It is certainly early but hardly sixteenth century as Bertini suggests
2   This dating is suggested by Ridolfi p 299 who mentions it after the
Temptation of St Anthony of 1552 (Fig 18). Ridolfi's dating appears to be borne
out by its apparent influence on the Virgin in the *Coronation of the Virgin* on
the ceiling of the sacristy of S. Sebastiano, painted by 1555, Pignatti 39

Mythological and allegorical drawings

39 An allegorical female figure (Venice?)

Pen and ink and wash on grey prepared paper heightened with
   white
28 × 20.2 cm

LOCATION Norfolk, Holkham Hall, Leicester collection
PROVENANCE Sir Peter Lely (Lugt 2092); acquired by the
   1st Earl of Leicester
BIBLIOGRAPHY London 1948 no 29; London 1977 no 7; Cocke
   Master Drawings 1977 p 265

Popham's recognition of this as a typical finished drawing by
Veronese in the 1948 exhibition catalogue came too late for it to
be included in the Tietzes' corpus, although there can be no
doubt about the attribution of the faded figure which is clearly
related to those in the *chiaroscuro* drawings at Vienna, Frankfurt
and Paris (17, 22, 23). Its subject, however, is rather different,
for the orb, sceptre and castle are among the attributes with
which the Venice in the *Venice triumphant* in the Sala del
Maggior Consiglio in the Palazzo Ducale (Fig 57) rivalled Rome.[1]

The winged lion of St Mark's which is not included in the
preparatory sketch (88), was placed lower down the canvas just
above the conquered soldiers and it is possible that it was also
included in the Holkham sheet but was removed when the drawing was trimmed to its present size, which is notably smaller than
the best preserved of the series, the Vienna *Allegory of Victory*
(40). The drawing appears to have stayed in the studio to provide
the inspiration for the now lost *Cybele*, engraved when it was in
London in the early nineteenth century,[2] and for one of the
female allegorical figures in the room on the left of the salone in
Villa Giunti, Magnadola, which has not been photographed.[3]

NOTES

1   Wolters p 314: 'una venetia sedendo sopra citta et terre a imitatione della
Roma sedente sopra il mondo'

2   London, *Coesvelt Collection* (1836), no 75, together with a *Diana* (no 76);
they each measured 12 by 8 ins, and were probably the pair in the *Museo
Moscardo* (Verona, 1676), p 471

3   L. Crosato, *Gli Affreschi nelle ville Venete del Cinquecento* (Treviso, 1962),
pp 132 ff

39 An allegorical female figure (Venice?)

40   Allegory of Victory

40 Allegory of Victory

Pen and ink on blue prepared paper heightened with white
38.6 × 27.6 cm

LOCATION Vienna, Albertina Inv. 1636
PROVENANCE Sir Joshua Reynolds (Lugt 2364); Count Moriz
   von Fries (Lugt 2903); A. von Sachsen-Teschen (Lugt 174)
BIBLIOGRAPHY Stix and Fröhlich-Bum no 112 (workshop);
   Tietze and Tietze-Conrat A2187 (workshop); Venice 1961
   cat 44 (workshop); Paris 1975 cat 59 (autograph); Cocke
   Master Drawings 1977 p 265

The popular view of this drawing as a product of the workshop,
which began with Wickhoff in 1891, was challenged by Philip
Pouncey in his note on the mount suggesting that it is autograph.
In quality it compares favourably with the Rejected Attributions
(*see* 162, 165) and is close to *The supper at Emmaus* at Chatsworth
(35). The slightly awkward *contrapposto*, which suggests that the
sheet is early, was developed with greater assurance in the
Victory of the Peaceful Arts in the Louvre (42).

   The precise nature of the victory was once clarified by the
emblem on the flag, now almost impossible to make out. The
upward gesture of the right arm recalls the Christian Faith in the
Stanza della Lucerna at Maser,[1] and although the figure does not
hold a chalice the same meaning may be indicated by the contrast
with the ruins of paganism in which she stands.

NOTE
1   Pignatti pl 318; for the identification of the figure, *see* Cocke *J.W.C.I.* 1972
p 236

41 Nymph pursued by a satyr (Virtue pursued by Vice)

Pen and ink on blue prepared paper heightened with white
29.7 × 27.2 cm

LOCATION Paris, Ecole des Beaux-Arts Inv. 417

PROVENANCE Dr Curtoni, Verona; P. Crozat, his sale Paris,
Mariette 1741, part of 681; acquired by P. J. Mariette, his
frame, Mariette sale Paris, Basan 1775, 251; His de la Salle
(Lugt 1333); bequeathed in 1878

BIBLIOGRAPHY Ridolfi p 230; Tietze and Tietze-Conrat 2139;
Paris 1965 no 318; Paris 1967 no 145; Cocke *Master
Drawings* 1977 p 265

This drawing, which has been trimmed at the corners and may
have been about 10 centimetres larger (*see* 40), is one of the most
admired of Veronese's *chiaroscuro* drawings. Ridolfi describes
it as 'Un disegno a chiaroscuro della Virtù che fugge da un
brutto serpe, significato per il Vitio', while Roseline Bacou in the
1965 Paris catalogue groups it with drawings 'Conçues commes
des oeuvres en soi, véritables peintures en blanc sur support
coloré, ils composent l'un des aspects les plus significatifs de l'art
de Véronèse'.

Ridolfi's interpretation of the subject as Virtue pursued by
Vice, which was followed by Mariette in the 1741 sale catalogue
of the Crozat collection, is clearly right. The nymph is comparable
to the Virtue on the right of the *Benedetto Sanuto between Virtue
and Vice* now in Madrid,[1] which probably dates from the mid-
1550s, and the satyr, like the older Pan in the *Music* on the
ceiling of the Marciana,[2] embodies lust. The small but charming
dragons past whom the nymph dashes symbolise the moral
dangers from which she flees and may have been suggested by
the *Hypnerotomachia Poliphili*.

NOTES

1 Pignatti 261 and Cocke *Pantheon* 1977 p 123
2 Pignatti 63; E. Winternitz, *Musical Instruments and their Symbolism in
Western Art* (London, 1967), p 55 discusses the amorous character of Pan's
pipes

41   Nymph pursued by a satyr (Virtue pursued by Vice)

42   Victory of the Peaceful Arts (?)

42   Victory of the Peaceful Arts (?)

Pen and ink on green tinted paper heightened with white
28.4 × 21.4 cm

LOCATION Paris, Musée du Louvre Inv. 4,682
INSCRIBED 'Paolo Veronese' and an illegible note
PROVENANCE Everard Jabach (Lugt 2961), no 63 in the Venetian
    section of his manuscript catalogue;[1] ceded to the French
    Royal collection in 1671
BIBLIOGRAPHY Cocke *Master Drawings* 1977 p 265

Although ignored in most of the recent literature, I believe that
Jabach's attribution to Veronese is correct and that it is by the
same hand as the *Nymph pursued by a satyr* in the Ecole des
Beaux-Arts (41) and the *Allegory of Fortune* in Frankfurt (17).
    The identification of the figure is a more open question.
Jabach's suggestion that she is Pallas is unlikely, since she wears
neither helmet nor cuirass,[2] but implies the general significance.
The arts of peace, which are represented by the architecture on
the banner (trimmed at the top), triumph over the emblems of
war (cuirass, swords, helmet and palms of victory).

NOTES

1   Paris 1978 (unpaginated)
2   As she appears in the *Minerva and Mars* from the Fondaco dei Tedeschi,
formerly in Berlin, Pignatti 211

Middle Years

This section opens with a group of drawings which can probably be dated to the early 1560s although the function for which they were made is not known (43–50, Figs 20–23). It continues with an ever increasing number of preparatory sketches for paintings from the period down to *circa* 1578. The new maturity of Veronese's handling of pen and ink and wash is seen in comparing the *Study for the Martyrdom of St George* of 1566 (52) with similar but earlier drawings, (8) and (9) for instance. The breadth of handling and the sure decorative sense with which motifs are reworked is characteristic of the preparatory drawings in this middle period.

The *Study for the Martyrdom of St George* is also typical in establishing the main lines of the composition, many of whose details were changed in the final canvas. This is also true of the *Modello for the Martyrdom of St Justina* of 1575 (75) which, though squared for transfer, differs from the final painting. Analysis of these changes underlines the care and thought with which Veronese planned his canvases, a point that is confirmed by the *Studies for the Feast in the house of Levi* (69). The fluent mastery of these drawings is matched in the bold chalk costume-studies (67, 73, 77) and the pictorial studies of individual heads (54, 68, 76).

With the growth of his reputation, Veronese delegated the execution of more commissions to the workshop. The first drawings he prepared for others were unusually finished (64, 72), while later in the period, when Veronese was in even greater demand his assistants had to be well trained in transferring rapid sketches to canvas (79, 80).

43 Study of St John the Evangelist

Wash over grey chalk on blue prepared paper
26 × 16 cm

LOCATION Leningrad, Hermitage Inv. 7867
PROVENANCE Count Brühl; acquired in 1769
BIBLIOGRAPHY Dobroklonsky no 115; Dresden 1972 no 106

44 Study of St Mark

Wash over grey chalk on blue prepared paper
36.5 × 27 cm

LOCATION Leningrad, Hermitage Inv. 7868
PROVENANCE Count Brühl; acquired in 1769
BIBLIOGRAPHY Dobroklonsky no 113; Venice 1964 no 20;
   Dresden 1972 no 105

45 Study of St Luke

Wash over grey chalk on blue prepared paper
36 × 27 cm

LOCATION Leningrad, Hermitage Inv. 7863
PROVENANCE Count Brühl; acquired in 1769
BIBLIOGRAPHY Dobroklonsky no 114

There is a scratched out letter on the verso.

46 Study of St Matthew

Wash over grey chalk on blue prepared paper
35.5 × 27 cm

LOCATION Leningrad, Hermitage Inv. 7864
PROVENANCE Count Brühl; acquired in 1769
BIBLIOGRAPHY Dobroklonsky no 112

47 Study of a bishop

Wash over grey chalk on blue prepared paper
36 × 27 cm

LOCATION Leningrad, Hermitage Inv. 7866
PROVENANCE Count Brühl; acquired in 1769
BIBLIOGRAPHY Dobroklonsky no 118

48 Study of a saint (St James?)[5]

Wash over grey chalk on blue prepared paper
36 × 27 cm

LOCATION Leningrad, Hermitage Inv. 7861
PROVENANCE Count Brühl; acquired in 1769
BIBLIOGRAPHY Dobroklonsky no 117

49 Study of St George

Wash over grey chalk on blue prepared paper
36 × 27 cm

LOCATION Leningrad, Hermitage Inv. 7865
PROVENANCE Count Brühl; acquired in 1769
BIBLIOGRAPHY Dobroklonsky no 116; Venice 1964 no 21;
   Dresden 1972 no 104

50 Study of St Margaret

Wash over grey chalk on blue prepared paper
27.5 × 16 cm

LOCATION Leningrad, Hermitage Inv. 7741
PROVENANCE Count Brühl; acquired in 1769
BIBLIOGRAPHY Dobroklonsky no 119; Tietze and Tietze-Conrat
   2089; Venice 1964 no 24; Dresden 1972 no 103

This group of drawings, which clearly belong together, was first attributed to Veronese by E. K. Liphardt. He rightly drew attention to their connection with the *chiaroscuro* drawings, a point which is confirmed by a comparison of the robes in the *Study of St John the Evangelist* (43) with those of the prophet in the *David and a prophet* in the Morgan Library (27). Unfortunately, nothing is known about the purpose for which they were made. The framing of the male saints echoes that of the panels with the four evangelists around the *Coronation of the Virgin* in the sacristy of S. Sebastiano,[1] but they cannot have been intended for a ceiling. *St Margaret* (50) stands against a dark niche, which is not rounded at the bottom, with a *contrapposto* that is developed from that of the Fortune in the Frankfurt drawing (17) and anticipates the Truth in the *Omnia Vanitas* in the Frick collection (Fig 22).[2]

43   Study of St John the Evangelist

44 Study of St Mark

Fig 20   School of Veronese, *Study of the Virgin and Child with Sts Francis and George*, pen and ink and wash on grey-green paper heightened with white, Musée du Louvre, Paris

Fig 21   School of Veronese, *Study of St George*, pen and ink and wash heightened with white, Staatliche Museen, Berlin-Dahlem

Echoes of the drawings can be traced in Veronese's workshop. The St George was subsequently developed into the kneeling saint in the school *Study of the Virgin and Child with Sts Francis and George* in the Louvre (Fig 20)[3] and was more closely represented in another school drawing in Berlin (Fig 21).[4] The saint's pose is reversed with his left hand thrown wide in a gesture of appeal that echoes his dramatic stride; the absence of a setting in the Berlin drawing suggests that it may have been copied from a now lost drawing which developed the design of the Hermitage *St George*.[5]

NOTES

1   Pignatti 40–44

2   As noted in the 1964 catalogue; I believe that the Frick painting can be dated to before 1567, *see Pantheon* (1977), pp 120ff

3   As noted by Larissa Salmina-Haskell in the 1964 catalogue; the Louvre drawing, Inv. 4,681, measures 30 by 25cm, pen and ink and wash on grey-green paper heightened with white. There is a copy at Windsor, Popham and Wilde cat 1029 and another, from the Skippe collection, was sold London, Christie 20–21 November 1958, 230 (A)

4   Berlin-Dahlem, KdZ 22078, pen and ink and wash heightened with white

5   The *St Mark* was also copied by an unidentified member of the workshop in an elaborate washed sheet in the New Picture Room of Sir John Soane's Museum, *A New Description of Sir John Soane's Museum* (1977), p42. Its finished appearance further suggests that the designs of the Leningrad sheet were elaborated perhaps in lost drawings. The companion drawing (Fig 23), which shows a striding pilgrim holding the martyr's palm (possibly identifying him as St James), is based upon Dobroklonsky no 117. I am grateful to Larissa Haskell for confirming this since no photograph is available

49   Study of St George

No. 7741.

50   Study of St Margaret

Fig 22 *Omnia Vanitas*, Frick collection, New York

Fig 23 Follower of Veronese, *A saint (St James?)*, pen and wash, Sir John Soane's Museum, London

51   Studies of a suit of armour

51 Studies of a suit of armour

Wash on grey prepared paper heightened with white
38.1 × 25.3 cm

LOCATION Berlin-Dahlem, Staatliche Museen KdZ 5120
PROVENANCE Sir Thomas Lawrence (Lugt 2445); C. S. Bale; Sir
F. Seymour Haden; Von Beckerath[1]
BIBLIOGRAPHY C. Loeser, *Gazette des Beaux-Arts* (1902), p 482;
Von Hadeln p 55; G. Fiocco, *Paolo Veronese* (Rome, 1934),
p 85; London 1930 no 284; Venice 1939 no 52; Tietze and
Tietze-Conrat 2034; Verona 1971 no 68; Pignatti 76

The drawing studies with evident understanding and complete
technical mastery a typical late sixteenth-century suit of plain
armour, of a type that may well have originated in Brescia.[2] The
armour, as the Tietzes rightly noted, occurs throughout Veronese's
oeuvre beginning with the soldier standing under the throne in
the *St Sebastian before Diocletian* in the monks' choir of S.
Sebastiano.[3] This has led to a wide range of speculation as to the
precise purpose for which it was prepared including: a soldier in
the fragment of the canvas of *St Sebastian before Diocletian*
which covered the fresco in the monks' choir of S. Sebastiano;[4]
the armour in the portrait of Pase Guarienti in Verona[5] or that of
Agostino Barbarigo in Cleveland;[6] the saint in the centre of the
Sts Mark and Marcellian led to martyrdom, one of the lateral
canvases in the main chapel of S. Sebastiano.[7]

Although the drawing is close to the latter figure there are
minor but vital differences, as with the other examples which
suggest that it was not made with any specific commission in
mind but as an independent study. The finished quality of the
sheet is close to the *chiaroscuro* drawings of the late 1550s but the
certainty with which the wash realises the sheen of polished
metal is more advanced and accords with the Leningrad *St
George* (49) in the early 1560s.[8]

NOTES
1 Noted by Popham in the 1930 Royal Academy exhibition
2 I am grateful to Mr A. V. B. Norman of the Armouries for his help
3 Pignatti 73
4 Pignatti 76
5 Fiocco p 85; unlikely since Guarienti wears striped armour, Pignatti A375,
rightly rejects the attribution to Veronese
6 Venice 1939; Pignatti 172
7 Loeser 1902; Pignatti 134
8 An attractive red chalk study of a young man, perhaps intended as a St
George, wearing very similar armour was sold from the Skippe collection
London, Christie 20–21 November 1958, 226; Popham's doubts about the
attribution of the sheet, which I know only from a photograph, seem confirmed
by a comparison with the *Study of a kneeling magus* (67), formerly in the
Koenigs collection where the hatching of the black chalk is finer and more
evocative

52   Study for the Martyrdom of St George

Pen and ink and wash
28.9 × 21.9 cm

LOCATION formerly Bâle, Robert von Hirsch
INSCRIBED '... in V.te Et U^tas in tri.te/Trinitas in Unitate',
   'moro'
PROVENANCE Freiherr Max Heyl zu Herrnsheim (Lugt 2879);
   Emile Wauters (Lugt 911), his sale Amsterdam, Müller 15–16
   June 1926, 33; Robert von Hirsch, his sale London, Sotheby
   20 June 1978, 26
BIBLIOGRAPHY Borenius 1921 p 54; Von Hadeln pl 24; Tietze
   and Tietze-Conrat 2029; Cocke 1973 pp 138–39

The drawing, which has been laid down, includes the main
elements of the *Martyrdom of St George* (Fig 24) in S. Giorgio in
Braida, Verona, probably painted in 1566.[1] The saint is surrounded by soldiers, who include a moor, as the priest urges him
to sacrifice. The double line through the horse on the left
coincides with the buildings in the background. In the heavenly
sphere angels bear the martyr's palm and crown of laurel while
Faith, Hope and Charity, whose positions have not yet been
clarified, intercede with the Holy Family together with Sts Peter
and Paul and the angelic orchestra celebrates the saint's triumph.[2]

The drawing thus establishes a unique fusion of two moments
in the saint's legend: his refusal to sacrifice to idols and his
prayer before his martyrdom that all who called his name could
be helped.[3] That this may have been inspired by the Catholic
defence of the veneration of saints and of their images, embodied
in the decree of the Council of Trent of 3 December 1563,[4] is
suggested by the evolution of the saint's gesture of intercession
which in the painting includes the spectator. Veronese had not
evolved this pose in the drawing either in the sketch in the centre
of the sheet or in the alternative just to the right. His first idea in
the group under the back of the horse seen from the rear was
more conventional with the executioner stooping over the reclining saint whose pose, although it cannot be made out, must have
been similar to that of St Sebastian in the *Martyrdom of St
Sebastian* at S. Sebastiano.[5]

Fig 24   *Martyrdom of St George*, S. Giorgio in Braida, Verona

NOTES

1   Pignatti 161 and (53)
2   E. Winternitz, *Musical Instruments and their Symbolism in Western Art*
(London, 1967), pp 137–50 has established that in some cases angel concerts
reflect the practice of secular music of the period. Veronese here and more
especially in the *Mystic marriage of St Catherine*, Accademia, Venice, may
perhaps reflect the new prominence given to instrumental music in St Mark's
in this decade, E. Selfridge Field, *Venetian Instrumental Music from Gabriele to
Vivaldi* (Oxford, 1975), ch. 1
3   Cocke 1973 pp 138–39
4   The emphasis upon intercession, so notable in the upper section of the
altar, is not found in Altichiero's version of this subject in the Oratorio di S.
Giorgio, Padua. Both saints and their images had come under repeated attack
by Luther and the Calvinists. The council's decree on the veneration of saints
and of their images was the result of strong pressure from the French eager for
a reconciliation with the Calvinists. The council reaffirmed the traditional
view of images: 'in ipsa legunt qui letteras nesciunt' and earlier affirmed:
'Sanctos, una cum Christo regnantes, orationes suas pro hominibus Deo offere,
bonum, atque utile esse suppliciter eos invocare: et ob beneficia impetranda a
Deo per filium eius Iesum Christum Dominum nostrum, qui solus noster
Redemptor et Salvator est, ad eorum orationes opem auxiliumque confugere',
C-J. Hefele, *Histoire des Conciles: Tome 10, Les Décrets du Concile de Trente*,
ed. A. Michel (Paris, 1938), pp 592ff and H. Jedin, 'Entstehung und Tragweite
des Trienter Bildverehrung', *Theologische Quartalschaft* 116 (1935), pp 142–
82 and 404–28
5   Pignatti 135

52   Study for the Martyrdom of St George

53   Studies of the Virgin and Child, a horseman and a music-making angel (actual size)

53 Studies of the Virgin and Child, a horseman and a music-making angel

Pen and ink and wash

15.1 × 13.1 cm

LOCATION Rotterdam, Museum Boymans-Van Beuningen
Inv. I39

INSCRIBED on the verso, which has been cut at the left edge, with
a series of accounts (53v):

'Come apar p(er) R... dal 1560 fino a.../ pagia r.ta il 1564 a di 16
Zugno a conto/ a di 20 Zenier 1561 per.../ R.to Item mi Paulo
per il fito di questo e del mz.../ del trageto da Ms Giacomo
L(ire) 3 s(oldi) 14/ Come apar per... R.to Item L(ire) 27 s(oldi)
18/ a di 24 decembrio 1562/ a conto de fito R.to Item L(ire) 27
s(oldi) 18/ a di 22 Zener 1564/ a conto del fito schorso R.to Item
L(ire) 30/ a di 16 Zugno 1564/ R.to ho dal sopra deto L(ire) 37
s(oldi) 4 per una gramola vechia L(ire) 49/ E in tutto L(ire) 221/
e con ducati 4 che hano...'

PROVENANCE Sir Peter Lely (Lugt 2092); R. Houlditch (Lugt
1736); F. Koenigs (Lugt 1023a); acquired by D. G. van
Beuningen in 1940

BIBLIOGRAPHY Tietze and Tietze-Conrat 2072; Cocke 1973 p138

Veronese often seems to have been short of paper. He used
someone else's notes for the *Study of Count Giuseppe da Porto
and his son Adriano* (4), letters to him for the Rotterdam *Studies*
(56), the Von Hirsch *Studies* (99) and the Berlin *Adoration* (116),
a draft of a letter he never sent for the Fogg *Studies of a Baptism*
(125) and a page of his own accounts (as is shown by comparison
with the autograph letter of 1578 (Fig 87)) for the present drawing. The sketch among the accounts has been cut at the edges so
that it can no longer be made out (53v).

The purpose of the drawings on the recto must also have been
clearer before it was cut down: there is an Entombment at the
top, a figure kneeling at a prie-dieu underneath, beside whom
there is a rider on a horse with a music-making angel underneath
and a series of studies of the Virgin and Child. The horseman is a
reworking of the motif at the bottom of the drawing for the
Martyrdom of St George, formerly in the Von Hirsch collection
(52). The connection does not appear to be fortuitous for,
although reversed, the viol player just below echoes that on the
left of the Von Hirsch drawing. The sketches of the Virgin and
Child, which begin on the left-hand margin and continue in the
centre and right of the sheet, may relate to that at the top of the
Von Hirsch drawing, which is closer to the painting than any
other part of the drawing. These connections, together with the
series of accounts on the verso, tend to confirm the nineteenth-
century view[1] that Veronese painted the great *Martyrdom of St
George* (Fig 24) for S. Giorgio in Braida in 1566,[2] the year he
returned to Verona to marry Antonio Badile's daughter.[3] Stylistically this seems convincing since the *St George* anticipates the
St Jerome in S. Pietro Martire, which is documented as having
been executed in 1567.[4]

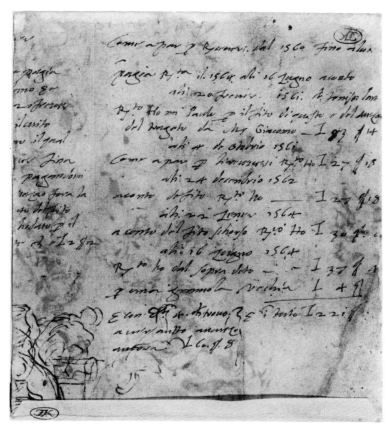

53v Series of accounts

NOTES

1 The tradition, accepted by the later literature, first appears in P. Caliari,
Paolo Veronese, sua vita, sue opere (Rome, 1888), p70

2 Pignatti 161

3 Pignatti 254 doc 30

4 Pignatti 159

54   Study of a Negro boy

54 Study of a Negro boy

Black and red chalk on buff paper
27.6 × 20.5 cm

LOCATION Paris, Musée du Louvre Inv. 4,679
INSCRIBED on the mount: 'Ex Collect. Abb. de Camps e Crozat,
nunc perié P. J. Mariette 1741'
PROVENANCE Abbé de Camps; P. Crozat, his sale Paris, Mariette
1741, part of 688; P. J. Mariette (Lugt 1852), his sale Paris,
Basan 1775, 247; Prince de Conti, his sale Paris, 8 April 1777,
1134
BIBLIOGRAPHY Von Hadeln 1911 p 397; Von Hadeln pl 51;˘
Venice 1939 p 216 no 4; Tietze and Tietze-Conrat A2133
(doubtful); Verona 1971 no 70 (Veronese)

The Tietzes' rejection of the present sheet together with the
related study in the Lehman collection (68), which has not found
acceptance,[1] rests upon two mistaken assumptions. They noted
that the reference in Mariette's sale to a connection with the
Martyrdom of St Justina in Padua (Fig 42) was wrong. Pallucchini,
however, had already justified Mariette's view by drawing attention to the appearance of this head on the left of the *Miracle of St
Barnabas* (Fig 25) painted for S. Giorgio in Braida, Verona, most
probably in 1566.[2] The connection serves to undermine the
Tietzes' second argument, the difference between the present
sheet and the *Portrait of a prelate* in Munich (193) which they,
wrongly in my opinion, saw as one of the few portrait drawings
by Veronese. Veronese rendered the texture of the young Negro's
head with an assured combination of red and black chalk on buff
coloured paper. The vividness of the handling anticipates the
drawings of Annibale Carracci, but the feeling for the surface of
the drawing is typically Venetian.

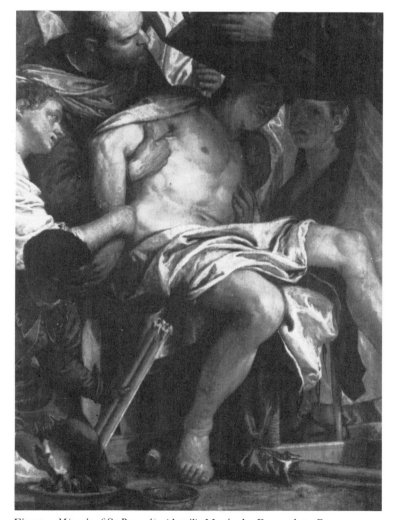

Fig 25 *Miracle of St Barnabas* (detail), Musée des Beaux-Arts, Rouen

NOTES
1 Bean and Stampfle in New York *Drawings* 1965 p 74
2 Now in Rouen, Paris 1965–66 p 254

55 Study of a seated nude

Black chalk on buff coloured paper heightened with white
40.2 × 29.6 cm

LOCATION London, Sotheby 15 June 1983, 26
INSCRIBED in another hand on the verso which is otherwise laid
   down: 'giovane coop', 'ope giov(?)'
PROVENANCE unidentified collector's mark

This striking life-study was rightly connected by Elizabeth
Llewellyn with the *Miracle of St Barnabas* painted for S. Giorgio
in Braida most probably in 1566 (Fig 25).[1] In the painting the
athletic nude looks up at the gospel with which the saint cures
him, and the awkward caesura where the left leg fails to join the
rest of the body is masked by drapery. The pose is reminiscent of
Michelangelo's *ignudi* on the Sistine ceiling, without quoting
any precisely.

The system of modelling is unlike that used by Central Italian
artists and is very different from that of the *Study of a Negro boy*
(54) for the same painting. *Pentimenti* in the back, right arm and
leg, produce a bold contour which is contrasted with the light
strokes of the black and white chalks which suggest the muscu-
lature. This is developed further in the painting where the legs at
the top of the sheet were used for the cripple beside the temple in
the background. They appear to have been added later for they
almost interfere with the head of the nude.

The almost abstract handling of the head is similar to that in
the *Study of the head and right arm of a man* (139). The modelling
of both sets of legs finds a close parallel in the *Study of legs* (2v),
which before the appearance of the present sheet was the only
surviving life-study from the nude or near nude by Veronese. It
was perhaps this rarity which tempted the unknown owner to
suggest in his notes on the verso that it was an early work.

NOTE
1 *See* above under (54)

55   Study of a seated nude

Fig 26   G. Barri, *Engraving after the Holy Family with Sts John the Baptist and Catherine*, British Museum, London

56   Studies for a Mystic marriage of St Catherine and the Holy Family with Sts Anne, John the Baptist and Catherine

Pen and ink and wash

30.4 × 19.9 cm

LOCATION Rotterdam, Museum Boymans–Van Beuningen Inv. I40

INSCRIBED 'sposi di laura', 'con S. Zuane', 'Con una Santa', 'Mad[onn]a'; on the verso a letter (56v), presumably to Veronese, from Castelfranco, dated 11 August 1568

PROVENANCE F. Koenigs (Lugt 1023a); acquired by D. G. van Beuningen in 1940

BIBLIOGRAPHY Von Hadeln pl 34; Koenigs no 13; Venice 1939 p 217 no 5; Tietze and Tietze-Conrat 2073

Veronese prepared a number of different compositions beginning with what may be a *Meeting at the golden gate* at the top, continuing with a number of variations on the theme of the *Mystic marriage of St Catherine*, which is indicated by the inscription 'sposi', and ending with a composition in which St Catherine stands to the right of the group while the infant St John plays with Christ's feet and St Anne sits by a wicker crib. The Tietzes rightly connected this latter sketch with the painting of this subject from the Norman Clark Neill collection, now in the Timken Art Gallery, San Diego.[1] While I know the San Diego picture only from photographs I doubt that it is autograph. An engraving made by Barri in the 1670s (Fig 26),[2] which differs notably in the landscape and the tree behind St Anne,[3] suggests that he may have known a now lost autograph version which was painted towards the end of 1568.[4] The composition and the motif of the Baptist playing with Christ's feet in the sketch at the bottom of the sheet were developed in the *Holy Family with Sts Barbara and John the Baptist* in the Uffizi.[5] The pose of the St Catherine in the centre of the sheet together with the active interplay with the Christ Child, as well as the wicker crib, are found again in the *Mystic marriage of the St Catherine* in the Musée Fabre, Montpellier (Fig 27).[6]

Fig 27   *Mystic marriage of St Catherine*, Musée Fabre, Montpellier

56   Studies for a Mystic marriage of St Catherine and the Holy Family
with Sts Anne, John the Baptist and Catherine

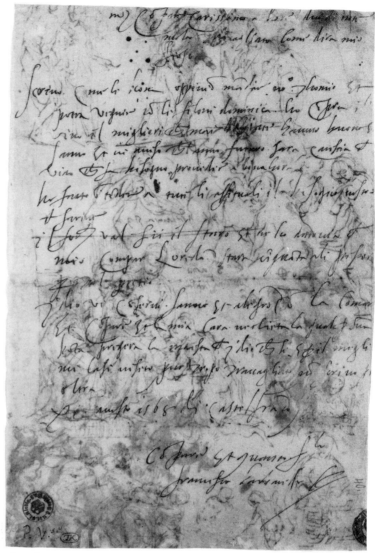

56v   Letter

NOTES

1   Pignatti 129

2   British Museum Inv. W.9.65; Barri appears to have been reliable in his engravings after the *Feast in the house of Levi* and the *Adoration of the shepherds* in SS. Giovanni e Paolo but frames the *Feast in the house of Simon* now in Turin, with two giant columns. These were not discussed by P. Ticozzi, 'Le incisioni da opere del Veronese nel Museo Correr', *Bollettino dei Musei Civici Veneziani* 20 (1975), no 22, but may be based upon the long lost frame described *in situ* by Ridolfi pp 307–308

3   The landscape in the San Diego painting does not appear to have been repainted as has that on the right of the Detroit *Mystic marriage of St Catherine*, to judge from Agostino Carracci's engraving of 1585, Rome, Calcografia Nazionale, *Le Incisioni dei Carracci*, cat by M. Calvesi and V. Casale (1965), no 118. Pignatti bases his ill-advised attribution to Benedetto on the handling of the landscape, A60

4   The Tietzes rightly connected the design with the picture which Ridolfi noted in the Caliari collection: 'Le Nozze di Santa Caterina Martire, e Sant. Anna che svolge una fascia' which was probably no 50 in the slightly later family inventory (Gattinoni), where Sts John and Anne are mentioned but not St Catherine, and the size, 7 by 9½ quarte or approx 119 by 161 cm, is similar to that of the San Diego painting, 104 by 155 cm

5   Pignatti 128; *see* under (160)

6   Where Veronese also re-used the pose of the Virgin and Child from the Berlin *Virgin and Child with St John the Baptist* (38); *see* under (34) note 2

57   Study for the Feast in the house of Simon

Fig 28   *Feast in the house of Simon*, Brera, Milan

57   Study for the Feast in the house of Simon

Pen and ink
13 × 26.5 cm

LOCATION Moscow, University
PROVENANCE Jonathan Richardson, Junior (Lugt 2170);
    Sir Joshua Reynolds (Lugt 2364)
BIBLIOGRAPHY engraved by S. Watts in C. Rodgers, *A collection
    of prints in Imitation of Drawings* (London, 1778); Borenius
    1921 p 59; Tietze and Tietze-Conrat 2117

The drawing marks an early stage in the preparation of the
canvas from the refectory of S. Sebastiano, now in the Brera
(Fig 28). Following Ridolfi, it is dated to 1570,[1] the year in which
Veronese received payment for unspecified work at S. Sebastiano.[2] The drawing establishes the twin curved tables, the
interplay of guests and servants, the play of the dogs in the
centre and the Magdalen anointing Christ on the left. That
the architecture is only indicated on the left reflects the sym-
metry which Veronese had introduced into the background of
the *Marriage feast at Cana* in the refectory of S. Giorgio. The
changes, most notably the addition of Martha standing behind
Simon's chair and of Judas in front of the table rising in protest
at the extravagance of the Magdalen's gesture,[3] help to concentrate attention upon the main action and to offset the more
diffuse reactions of the apostles and other guests.

NOTES

1   Ridolfi p 314; Pignatti 164
2   Pignatti 255 doc 37
3   Mark 14, 3–9 and Matthew 26, 6–13 identify the Feast as taking place in
Bethany in the house of Simon the Leper; John 12, 1–9 identifies Martha and
Mary as the hosts and Judas as the apostle who objected. Veronese had begun
the fusion of these two traditions in the *Feast* from SS. Nazaro e Celso, Pignatti
93, but it is made more explicit here

58   Studies for a Marriage feast at Cana (actual size)

Fig 29   *Marriage feast at Cana*, Gemäldegalerie, Dresden

58   Studies for a Marriage feast at Cana

Pen and ink
20.6 × 17.3 cm

LOCATION Berlin–Dahlem, Staatliche Museen KdZ 502
INSCRIBED 'D' 'D' 'O'
BIBLIOGRAPHY Van Hadeln pl 23; Tietze and Tietze-Conrat 2040;
    Oehler p 32

This is one of three drawings[1] for the series of four canvases
painted by Veronese for the Coccina family palace on the grand
canal most probably around 1571.[2] The earliest sketch at the top
of the sheet shows a group of guests sitting around a curving
table like that in the *Feast in the house of Simon* (57) with Christ
in the centre. This was elaborated in the sketch with servants
pouring out the newly made wine in the foreground and contem-
plating a glass. This figure stands besides the fat guest who is
based, as the Tietzes rightly noted, on a well-known Roman bust
which was wrongly identified during the Renaissance as Vitellius.[3]

The sketch at the bottom of the sheet repeats this seated figure
with the servants pouring wine but concentrates upon compres-
sing the heads of the guests on the left. In the canvas (Fig 29) two
are seen from behind to frame Mary and Christ. Christ is further
emphasised by the removal to the background of the servant
pouring wine. This allowed his head to be juxtaposed with the
miraculous glass of wine, illustrating John 2, 9: 'When the ruler
of the feast had tasted the water that was made wine, and knew
not whence it was (but the servants which drew the water
knew)'.

NOTES

1   *See also* (59) and (60)
2   R. Gallo 'Per la datazione delle opere di Paolo Veronese', *Emporium* (1939),
pp 145–52 established this date for the *Coccina family presented to the Holy
Family*, a date which must be extended to the whole group, Pignatti 167–70
3   *See also* (70)

Fig 30   *Christ carrying the cross* (detail), Gemäldegalerie, Dresden

59   Studies for Christ carrying the cross

Pen and ink and wash

20.1 × 29.6 cm

LOCATION London, Courtauld Institute, Princes Gate collection

PROVENANCE Sir Joshua Reynolds (Lugt 2364); Sir Thomas
   Lawrence (Lugt 2445), thence Samuel Woodburn, his sale
   London, Christie 4–12 June 1860, 1023; Sir Thomas Phillips,
   thence Fenwick, Cheltenham; Count Antoine Seilern,
   Princes Gate collection

BIBLIOGRAPHY Popham p 110; Tietze and Tietze-Conrat 2057;
   A. Seilern, *Italian Paintings and Drawings at 56 Princes Gate,
   S.W.7* (London, 1959), p 51 cat 102

This drawing is the second made in preparation for the series of
four canvases commissioned by the Coccina family about 1571.[1]
It reveals the extraordinary care with which Veronese adjusted
the details of the design to achieve the dramatic flow of the
composition (Fig 30).[2] In the main sketch he established the
rocky path to Golgotha with Christ whipped by an executioner
for stumbling under the cross. The cross is supported by Simon
the Cyrenian while its front is dragged by another executioner
as the cortège of horsemen disappears down a slope as in the
painting.

Veronese changed his mind and repeated Christ over part of
his initial sketch with the executioner dragging the cross now
seen from behind with alternative poses for Simon. St Veronica
bending forward to wipe Christ's face with her cloth is in a series
of sketches of two mourners on the right edge of the canvas.
Veronese devoted great care to this group but finally decided
that to show the fainting Mary supported by her companion
(whose drapery is tried out at the bottom of the sheet) would
have distracted from Christ's agony. He therefore substituted
for Mary a man whose vigorous gesture echoes that of the soldier
who in the picture pushes St Veronica away from Christ. Two
rather rapid sketches at the top left-hand corner appear to be
unrelated to this great design, for the framing and pose suggest a
half-length standing male portrait, which cannot, however, be
related to any surviving picture.

NOTES

1   Now at Dresden, *see also* (58) and Pignatti 169

2   R. Marini, 'Paolo, una strana fonte e una strana data', *Emporium* (1962),
pp 61–68 argued that the design derives from Schongauer's engraving of this
subject. But by 1571 this had been absorbed by Raphael in the *Spasimo di
Sicilia* and following him by Jacopo Bassano in a number of versions which
must have served as Veronese's starting-point

59 Studies for Christ carrying the cross

Fig 31   *Adoration of the Magi*, Gemäldegalerie, Dresden

60   Studies of a kneeling magus

60v   Study of a standing magus

Black chalk on blue paper heightened with white and reworked
    with pen and ink
28 × 40.2 cm

LOCATION France, private collection
INSCRIBED 'B'; on the verso: 'Turchi[n]a'; in another hand: 'Paolo
    Veronese'; on the verso: 'P. N. o 69', '411'
PROVENANCE Anon. (Lugt 2103a; sometimes described as the
    Borghese collection)[1]

The drawings on the recto were made in preparation for the
magus who kneels to kiss Christ's feet in the *Adoration of the
Magi* in Dresden (Fig 31), which is one of the series of four
canvases painted for the Coccina family, Venice, in about 1571.[2]
Veronese abandoned his first sketch, on the right of the sheet,
and drew the alternative sketch over the bottom of the drapery of
the earlier drawing. The magus's gesture in the left-hand sketch
includes the spectator and produces a more interesting play in
the folds of the drapery. These were used in the painting and
Veronese has indicated that he is happy with them by writing 'B'
besides the indication of the pattern of the brocade ('B' must
stand for either 'broccato' or 'brocchi', which mean the raised
pattern of the brocade).

The magnificent handling of the recto resembles that of the
now lost *Study of a kneeling magus* (67). In both these drawings
from the artist's imagination the broad hatching of the chalk
creates a rich pictorial effect on the blue prepared paper. In this
they differ from the more rapid study on the verso, which
appears to be a sketch from life, in which Veronese was struck by
the jewels worn by the sitter. The point is underlined by the
annotation 'turchina' which means a pale blue (turquoise)
precious stone. The drawing appears to have formed the starting-
point for the younger magus standing behind his kneeling companion. In the painting he wears a richly decorated collar rather
than a string of jewels, he looks attentively at the Holy Family
and his features are strongly idealised.

NOTES
1   Monte Carlo 1966 intro. The mark was, however, only added in the late
eighteenth century, *see* London, Sotheby 9 July 1981, 132
2   *See* under (59)

60   Studies of a kneeling magus

60v   Study of a standing magus

61   Study for the Allegory to celebrate the publication of the Holy League (?)

61   Study for the Allegory to celebrate the publication of the Holy League (?)

Pen and ink over red chalk and wash
21.6 × 31.1 cm

LOCATION Germany, private collection
INSCRIBED 'Sc. di Paolo'

This remarkable drawing which was brought to my attention by Julien Stock, underlines the care with which Veronese prepared the great finished version of this subject at Chatsworth (62). It offers a unique insight into Veronese's working procedure, for it reveals a type of chalk underdrawing which is generally worked over in pen and ink. Here the handling of the group of the Doge and Pope on the left conforms with that of other autograph drawings from the early 1570s to belie the old attribution to the school.

62   Allegory to celebrate the publication of the Holy League (?)

Pen and ink with wash on green tinted paper heightened with white
43.7 × 58.3 cm

LOCATION Chatsworth, Devonshire collection Inv. 278
BIBLIOGRAPHY Tietze and Tietze-Conrat 2165 (workshop); London 1973 no 73 (autograph); London, Hayward Gallery, *Andrea Palladio 1508–1580*, cat by H. Burns and B. Boucher (1975), no 283; Cocke *Master Drawings* 1977 p 265

The Tietzes' view that this important drawing was from the workshop was rightly challenged by Byam Shaw in the catalogue of the 1973 exhibition, where he also suggested it must refer to some important historical occasion, perhaps the Peace of Château Cambrensis of 1559. The presence of Sts James, Peter with his

62   Allegory to celebrate the publication of the Holy League (?)

keys and Mark in the sky throwing down palms recalls the *Allegory of the Battle of Lepanto*,[1] where they are joined by St Justina on whose feast day, 7 October 1571, the Holy League won their great victory over the Turks. The choice of saints is echoed in their representatives on earth, where the Pope and the Doge are joined by a mitred figure, perhaps Cardinal Granvelle, the representative of Philip II during the negotiations for the League.[2] This suggests that the sheet may have been inspired by the publication of the Holy League which on 6 July 1571 was celebrated by processions in the Piazzetta.[3] The general meaning is clear, although some details are hard to interpret. Faith holds a chalice to greet the representatives of the League, the power of whose arms is shown by the putti holding a spear crowned by the laurels of victory. The kneeling figure prepares the *fasces*, the symbol of the League's authority whose success is acted out on the right where a soldier holds an unbroken wheel, the emblem of good fortune which is further embodied in the cornucopia

carried by the female attendants. The idealised loggetta and library from which the scene is witnessed as the procession departs through the triumphal arch crowned by Justice were drawn in first using a ruler. Veronese had calculated the space for the major seated figures in the preparatory drawing (61) but many of the minor figures were drawn in over the architecture.

NOTES
1   Pignatti 166
2   L. Freiherr von Pastor, *History of the Popes* 18 (London, 1952), pp 367ff
3   E.H. Gombrich in *Studies in Renaissance and Baroque Art presented to Anthony Blunt* (London, 1967), p 62

63   Study of a pope between Sts Mark and James (?)

63   Study of a pope between Sts Mark and James (?)

Pen and ink and wash over traces of grey chalk heightened with
   white

25.9 × 24.3 cm

LOCATION Bayonne, Musée Bonnat Inv. 146

PROVENANCE Count Gelosi (Lugt 545); Thibaudeau; Marquis
   de Chennevières; L. Bonnat

BIBLIOGRAPHY Tietze and Tietze-Conrat 2191 (Benedetto);
   Bayonne 1960 no 181 (autograph); Venice 1979 no 37

The drawing was included with the autograph ones on the basis
of Jacob Bean's account of it in the catalogue of the drawings at
Bayonne. From a photograph it appeared to fit with the drawings
of the Middle Years, most notably the *Studies for a Rape of
Europa* (64). This appeared to be supported by the choice of
saints which was clarified in the weaker derivation in the British
Museum.[1] Here the lion included at the feet of the right-hand
saint identified him as St Mark, while the pilgrim's hat[2] suggested
that the remaining saint may be St James, in spite of the absence
of his usual emblem, the cockleshell. While the pope cannot be
identified the links with Spain, Rome and Venice suggested a
connection with the Holy League and the Battle of Lepanto of
October 1571.

Seeing the drawing, however, made me share the Tietzes'
doubts about the attribution. Neither the handling of the pen
and ink and wash over the grey chalk, nor that of the white
heightening resemble that of other, comparable drawings. The
graphic treatment of the figures is formless and inelegant. It is,
though, difficult to identify the member of the workshop responsible for this sheet, which must have prepared the more fully
worked-out designs in the Ambrosiana and the British Museum.
The Tietzes suggested that it was by Benedetto, but he is a
shadowy figure as a draughtsman and the handling of the
present sheet does not resemble that of the drawings which may
be by him (185, 189, 207).

NOTES

1   Inv. 1900–8–24–133; the sheet in the Ambrosiana was no 37 in the Venice
1979 exhibition
2   *Compare* the headgear worn by the pilgrims in the *Feast of St Gregory the
Great* in Vicenza, Pignatti 175

Fig 32   Workshop of Veronese, *Madonna of the Rosary*, Gallerie dell'Accademia, Venice

64 and **64**v   Studies for a Rape of Europa, the Madonna of the Rosary and a Pietà

Pen and ink and wash on blue-green paper heightened with
   white
29.6 × 27.4 cm

LOCATION Stuttgart, Koenig Fachsenfeld
INSCRIBED 'Di Paolo Caliari Veronese'
PROVENANCE Carl Faber; acquired in 1904[1]
BIBLIOGRAPHY Deusch pp 295–97; Pignatti 216; Bacou 7

Veronese prepared a detailed study of the *Madonna of the
Rosary*[2] for the workshop on the recto and included a small
sketch of Europa seated on the bull above it. This was elaborated
on the verso in sketches which are related to the *Rape of Europa*
painted for Giacomo Contarini, now in the Palazzo Ducale
(Fig 33)[3] together with sketches for the *Pietà* in Berlin.[4] *The
Madonna of the Rosary*, which was destined for S. Pietro Martire,
Murano, is dated 1573 (Fig 32) and this must be the date of the
Rape and the *Pietà*. This is an extraordinary achievement in the
year in which Veronese completed the *Feast in the house of Levi*
(Fig 35), the *Adoration of the Magi* for S. Silvestro (Fig 34), that
for S. Corona, Vicenza,[5] possibly the *Sts Lawrence, Jerome and
Prospero* for S. Giacomo (Fig 39) as well as the school *Trinity
appears to Sts Peter and Paul* also for Vicenza.[6]

64   Studies for a Rape of Europa, the Madonna of the Rosary and a Pietà

64v   Studies for a Rape of Europa, the Madonna of the Rosary and a Pietà

Fig 33   *Rape of Europa*, Sala dell'Anticollegio, Palazzo Ducale, Venice

The drawings for the *Madonna of the Rosary* and the *Pietà* were more fully worked out than those of the *Rape*, perhaps since they were intended for the studio. The paintings lost the exciting asymmetry of the drawing in the *Madonna of the Rosary* and the fluent interlocking of Christ and the supporting angels in the *Pietà*. This version lacks the assurance displayed by Veronese in the *Pietà* now in Leningrad.[7]

The sketches for the *Rape* show Europa riding on the bull but concentrate on her as she sits tentatively upon the seated bull and is decked out with garlands by her servants. The fluid sketch of this group in pen and ink and wash, which includes a variety of alternatives, is clarified by the masterful application of the white heightening. In the painting Europa and her attendants are realised with a fluency not found in the earlier version of this subject, in the Rasini collection, Milan.[8] There space had prevented the inclusion of the flying putti who Veronese studied with such care in (64).

NOTES

1   A.M. Zanetti, *Della Pittura Veneziana e delle opere pubbliche de' Veneziani Maestri* (Venice, 1792), p 263 claimed to own a drawing for the *Madonna of the Rosary*, which might be the present sketch

2   Pignatti A 214

3   Pignatti 216 – referring to the drawing but not the article by Deusch. Although relating it to the *Madonna of the Rosary* of 1573 he sees the drawing as confirming his dating for the *Rape of Europa* in the 1580s

4   Pignatti 329; the *Dead Christ appears to a monk*, Pignatti 330, is by the same member of the workshop

5   *See* (71)

6   Pignatti A 380

7   Pignatti 339. His dating in the 1580s does not fit with the colour, and the design was echoed in the *Study of a Lamentation and Supper at Emmaus* of 1574 (74)

8   Pignatti 151. Veronese rejected the moment used by Titian in his version of this subject painted for Philip II for an earlier moment in the narrative of Ovid's *Metamorphoses* Book II. This was chosen for the woodcut that accompanied this section of Dolce's translation of 1553, *Le Trasformationi* p 57

65   Study of a seated woman

65 Study of a seated woman

Black chalk on blue prepared paper heightened with white
30 × 19.3 cm

LOCATION Paris, Musée du Louvre Inv. RF 38935
INSCRIBED by a later collector on the verso: 'P.N.o 63'; on the
mount 'P.N.o 42'
PROVENANCE Anon. (Lugt 2103a; sometimes described as the
Borghese collection);[1] private collection, France; acquired in
1982
BIBLIOGRAPHY Bacou 7

This slight but energetic sketch was, as Roseline Bacou established, made in preparation for the servant in the middle distance
of the *Rape of Europa* of 1573 (Fig 32),[2] who leads the bull down
to the water. The *Studies for a Rape of Europa, the Madonna of
the Rosary and a Pietà* (64) concentrated upon Europa and her
attendants as she first sat on the bull and included a sketch of
her riding off but not the servant leading her.

That Veronese prepared such a relatively minor detail in a
chalk study is not without precedent, for this also appears to
have been the function of the earlier *Study of the head and right
arm of a man* (139). It suggests that by comparison with the
better known and preserved preparatory drawings many chalk
studies have been lost, or, hopefully, still await rediscovery.
Comparison with (139) underlines Veronese's development. The
pose of the servant in the present sheet is thrown off with a
vigorous handling of the chalk on the blue paper which anticipates
the *Study for Moderation* also in the Louvre (84). The extraordinarily rapid and inventive use of the white heightening is similar
to that with which Veronese clarified the main group in (64), and
with the brilliant handling of the painting itself.

NOTES

1   Monte Carlo 1966 intro. The mark was, however, only added in the late
eighteenth century, *see* London, Sotheby 9 July 1981, 132
2   *See* under (64)

66 Studies for an Adoration of the Magi

66   Studies for an Adoration of the Magi

Pen and ink on blue washed paper heightened with white
28.3 × 19.8 cm

LOCATION Haarlem, Teyler Museum Inv. B. 65
INSCRIBED 'Un rubō'
PROVENANCE Joachim von Sandrart; Christina Queen of Sweden;
   Cardinal Azzolino; Prince L. Odescalchi; purchased in 1790[1]
BIBLIOGRAPHY Von Hadeln pl 32; London 1930 no 287; Tietze
   and Tietze-Conrat 2070; Paris 1962 no 119; Stockholm 1966
   P 454

This outstanding drawing has long been recognised as one of the
preparatory sketches for the 1573 *Adoration of the Magi* from
S. Silvestro, now in the National Gallery, London (Fig 34). In
the sketches at the top right of the sheet, Veronese suggested the
ruined setting within which the Virgin presents the infant Christ
to the foremost kneeling magus, whose two companions are
presumably indicated in the standing figures to the left. The free
sketch contains many other ideas; a horse seen from behind, a
camel's head, Joseph in a variety of poses and the animals which
accompany the shepherds. In the centre of the sheet Veronese
worked out the pose of a kneeling page (reversed in the picture)
and a magus,[2] both seen from behind. Even the sketch at the
bottom of the sheet still differs considerably from the picture as
the figures are not yet composed into the flattened 'V' of the
canvas with the striding magus on the left as one arm. In the
drawing the composition is framed by the magus seen from
behind and the background of the composition is filled with the
rear-view of the horse which in the painting was abandoned,
presumably as being too intrusive.

NOTES

1   This was established in the Stockholm 1966 cat
2   Both occur in the *Adoration of the Magi* in S. Corona, Vicenza, probably of
   the same date, *see* (71)

67   Study of a kneeling magus (actual size)

Fig 34 *Adoration of the Magi* (detail), National Gallery, London

67 Study of a kneeling magus

Black and white chalk on blue paper
16.5 × 16.7 cm

LOCATION formerly Haarlem, Franz Koenigs Inv. I 119
PROVENANCE Emile Wauters (Lugt 911), his sale Amsterdam,
    Müller 15–16 June 1926, 34
BIBLIOGRAPHY F. Lee, *The Art of the Great Masters* (London,
    1913), p 55; Koenigs no 14; Tietze and Tietze-Conrat 2084

The Tietzes' doubts about this study for the *Adoration of the
Magi* of 1573 (Fig 34), which were based upon a comparison
with the *Study of St Lawrence* (73), seem unfounded. That part
of St Lawrence's dalmatic which appears in the painting (the rest
being behind the bible he reads) is established with the broad
parallel hatching used in this drawing. The energetic handling
echoes that of the slightly earlier *Studies of a kneeling magus* in a
private collection, France (60). Here Veronese combined the
pictorial combination of the chalk with the blue ground with a
vivid use of *pentimenti* in the shoulders, heads and hands. The
resulting pattern of folds and brocade is close to the painting,
where it was further elaborated.

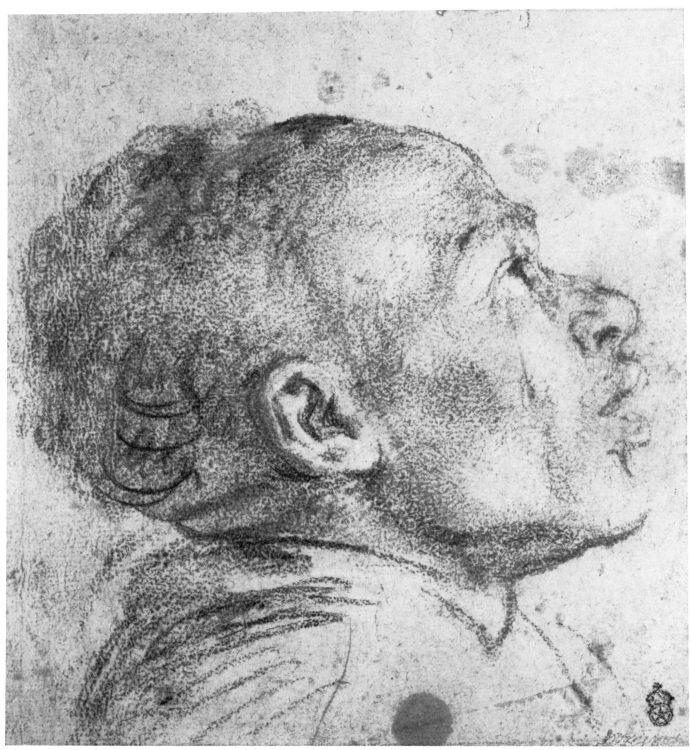

68   Study of a Negro (actual size)

68 Study of a Negro

Black chalk on brown paper
20 × 17.5 cm

LOCATION formerly New York, Lehman
PROVENANCE Richard Cosway; Charles Fairfax Murray;
A. G. B. Russell (Lugt 2770a), his sale London, Sotheby
9 June 1959, 12
BIBLIOGRAPHY Von Hadeln pl 52; London 1931 no 285; Venice
1939 p 217; Tietze and Tietze-Conrat A2108 (a later artist);
New York 1965 no 131 (autograph)

The Tietzes compared Veronese's three studies of Negro boys[1]
to the rather different drawings of women in Florence and
Chicago (14, 130). Against this, Bean and Stampfle rightly
argued that these drawings called to mind the many Negro boys
in Veronese's paintings. The handling, which the Tietzes found
to concentrate upon pictorial effects and to lack modelling, is,
given the very different function, comparable to that of the
Study for Liberality in the British Museum (70). This sketch of a
head looking upwards has parallels with the more generalised
Study of an apostle (76), recently on the London market.

Bean and Stampfle suggested that it might be related to a
Balthasar in an *Adoration of the Magi*. Their idea can be elaborated since I believe that the profile is similar to that of the Negro
page in the centre of the 1573 *Adoration* in the National Gallery
(Fig 34), although the connection has otherwise been overlooked
because of the difference in the hair.

NOTE

1   In addition to this drawing they are (54) and (135)

Fig 35 *Feast in the house of Levi* (detail), Gallerie dell'Accademia, Venice

69 Studies for the Feast in the house of Levi

Pen and ink and wash
30.9 × 20.9 cm

LOCATION Kassel, Staatliche Kunstsammlungen Inv. 1122
INSCRIBED 'ride', 'chines' and an illegible word
PROVENANCE acquired from a private collection in 1939
BIBLIOGRAPHY Oehler pp 27ff

The drawing includes a number of elements; five sketches of a winged lion of St Mark, turbaned servants, compositional sketches, details of architecture and servants pouring wine at the top. Here we can establish the connection with the *Feast in the house of Levi* (Fig 35)[1] painted for the refectory of SS. Giovanni e Paolo by 18 July 1573, the date of Veronese's appearance before the inquisition.[2] The servant on the left pouring wine into the cup, which is held by a young page seen from behind, is used on the left edge of the canvas (Fig 36) without the head marked 'ride'[3] and with the column moved to the other side. The profiles of the entablature are related to the small order in the painting. The figures beneath them were developed into the servant at the top of the right-hand flight of stairs carrying a large vase and his companion seen from behind who holds up a pitcher to fill the apostles' glasses.

These motifs are close to the picture. Those lower down the sheet are more remote but may, nonetheless, represent the initial plan, which I believe to have been for a *Feast in the house of Simon*.[4] The group of figures in the centre of the drawing seated in a half-circle around a central figure is repeated underneath where it is set within a roughly indicated architectural frame reminiscent of that which separates the servants in the upper sketch. Buildings are also suggested in the background on the left, where the ground appears to fall away and a figure kneels at the base of one of the columns. It is repeated towards the centre of the composition, which on the right is left incomplete because it runs into the sketches of the winged lion of St Mark. The kneeling figure is repeated again lower down between the standing men, whose pumpkin-like turbans recur in the servants in the background of the *Feast*. She holds a cup or jar which recalls the jar of ointment that the Magdalen used to anoint Christ's feet. The curved table lightly indicated in the sketch with the architectural frame recalls the *Feast* that Veronese had painted for the Servi.[5]

If, as I believe, this section of the drawing does represent the central moment of the Magdalen anointing Christ in the *Feast in the house of Simon*, we are still no closer to understanding the motives that led to the change of programme with Veronese's consequent appearance before the inquisition. His defence of the picture in terms of 'decorum'[6] has too often been underestimated by critics who believed him to be purely a decorative painter.[7] This analysis also adds considerable irony to his reply to the query if he knew why he had been called before the inquisition: 'I was told by the Reverend Father, who is the Prior of SS. Giovanni e Paolo, whose name I do not know, that the inquisition was here and that you illustrious gentlemen had ordered me to paint the Magdalen in place of a dog and I had replied that I would be glad to have done this and anything else for my honour and that of the painting, but that I did not think that a figure of the Magdalen could be added convincingly'.

NOTES

1 Pignatti 177
2 P. Fehl, 'Veronese and the Inquisition', *Gazette des Beaux-Arts* 58 (1961) pp 325ff whose transcription is followed by Pignatti 255 doc 40
3 This idea possibly suggested the servant behind St Peter in the centre of the canvas, Pignatti pl 458
4 Although the transcript of the appearance before the inquisition refers to it as an 'ultima cena', this cannot have been intended to refer to the *Last Supper* as opposed to other suppers mentioned in the gospels. When he was asked about other 'Cene del Signore' that he had painted, the inquisitor excluded the *Marriage feast at Cana* but allowed references to the paintings now in Turin, Milan and Versailles, all of which show the *Feast in the house of Simon*
5 Pignatti 176
6 He argues that the soldiers, about whom the inquisitor was especially unhappy, are suitable for a rich host, which further excludes the possibility that this is a *Last Supper*, and that, together with the servants: 'sono di fuori del luogo dove è il nostro Signore'
7 I have attempted to trace the development of this conception of Veronese's work in *Arte Veneta* 34 (1980), pp 96ff

69   Studies for the Feast in the house of Levi

70v   Study of a Roman bust (the so–called Vitellius)

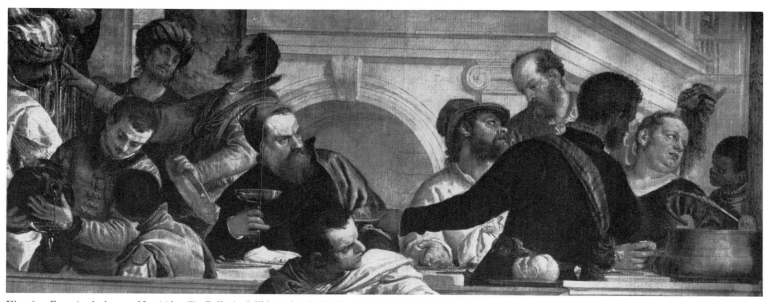

Fig 36 *Feast in the house of Levi* (detail), Gallerie dell'Accademia, Venice

70v Study of a Roman bust (the so-called Vitellius)

Grey chalk on grey-green paper heightened with white
21 × 22.5 cm

LOCATION London, British Museum Inv. 1969–4–12–4 verso
INSCRIBED '125', 'D 30990'
PROVENANCE sold London, Sotheby 27 March 1969, 8

This is a now faded study after the antique bust in the Grimani collection,[1] which was mis-identified in the Renaissance as Vitellius.[2] It is on the verso of the *Liberality* (70; *see* 84, 85) for the ceiling of the Sala del Collegio of about 1575–77. The verso may have been made slightly earlier for it is related to the fat man turning to the centre above the inscription 'FECIT' in the *Feast in the house of Levi* of 1573 (Fig 36). Veronese, who also used a different view of his head in the servant in a striped brocade seen in profile looking at Christ, had employed a comparable but more sculptural view of the head in the *Marriage feast at Cana* now in Dresden (Fig 29). The drawing, with its flattening of form and added emphasis upon the combination of the emperor's unsavoury lips and nose, is close to the head in the *Feast in the house of Levi* (Fig 36). Here, however, the model was transformed by a fresh observation of light and of flesh.

Vitellius's presence on the back of a drawing of *Liberality* and in these *Feasts* reminds us that Veronese was not so unlettered as is often supposed. Suetonius relates[3] that: 'But his [Vitellius's] besetting sins were luxury and cruelty. He divided his feasts into three, sometimes four a day, and was readily able to do justice to all of them through his habit of taking emetics. Moreover he had himself invited to each of these meals by different men on the same day, and the materials for any of them never cost less than four thousand sesterces'.

NOTES

1   M. Perry, 'Cardinal Domenico Grimani's legacy of ancient art to Venice', *Journal of the Warburg and Courtauld Institutes* 41 (1978), p234 no I establishes that it was in the Sala delle Feste on the second piano nobile of the Palazzo Ducale, behind the Sala dei Pregadi. O. Kurz, 'Early art forgeries from the Renaissance to the eighteenth century', reprinted in *Selected Studies* vol II (London, 1982), p185 suggests that it is a Renaissance forgery

2   A. N. Zadoks-Josephus Jitta, 'A creative misunderstanding', *Nederlands Kunsthistorisch Jaarboek* 23 (1972), pp3–12; the date of the identification is not clear

3   *Lives of the Caesars*, ed. & trans. J. C. Rolfe, Loeb ed. London Bk VII, XIII p267

Fig 37 *Adoration of the Magi*, S. Corona, Vicenza

71   Studies for an Adoration of the Magi

Pen and ink and wash

22.2 × 21.5 cm

LOCATION Paris, Musée du Louvre Inv. RF 38927

INSCRIBED with a series of figures partially crossed out:
'tro[m]beta', 'porta una cassa'; in another hand: 'Al Molto
Mag[co] S[r] Paolo Caliari Veronese Pictor Ecc[quo] Casa…'
Magior suo Hosana Venezia A[o] S. Samuele', the letter which
was re-used for the drawing is on the verso which is laid
down. Annotated by a later collector on the verso: 'd.Paolo
n.o 80'; on the mount: 'd.P.n.98'

PROVENANCE Anon. (Lugt 2103a; sometimes described as the
Borghese collection);[1] private collection, France; acquired in
1982

BIBLIOGRAPHY Bacou 9

In the upper of the two sketches the Virgin presents the Christ
Child to the kneeling magus, whose pose seen from behind with
arms outstretched in greeting establishes the connection with
the *Adoration of the Magi* in S. Corona, Vicenza (Fig 37). The
painting is undocumented but the inscription of 1573[2] in the
Cogolo family chapel may well refer to its completion, and hence
to the *Adoration of the Magi*.[3] Having established a pose for the
kneeling magus which clearly differentiates him[4] from those in
the other near contemporary versions (Figs 31 and 34), Veronese
developed the composition in the lower of the two sketches.

He retained the main group, set against the architecture, and
added the remaining magi with their followers. The composition
is reminiscent of the upper sketch in the *Studies for an Adoration
of the Magi* in Haarlem (37), most notably in the magus with
the pumpkin hat. In the painting, the composition was developed
and the magus on the left was moved to the centre and the chest,
indicated by the inscription, appears in the distance on the back
of one of the camels.

The bold combination of pen and ink and wash in both of the
sketches looks forward to the style of Veronese's late drawings,
the *Studies for a Last Supper and a Rape of Ganymede* (110) and
the *Studies for St Pantaleon heals a sick boy* (127).

NOTES

1 Monte Carlo 1966 intro. The mark was, however, only added in the late
eighteenth century, *see* London, Sotheby 9 July 1981, 132

2 J. T. Facciolius, *Museum lapidarium Vicentium* 1 (Vicenza, 1776), p239.
This was first noted by Von Hadeln in his note to Ridolfi p 318

3 Veronese had completed the *Feast* for Monte Berico by April 1572 (Pignatti
255 doc 39). The colour of the Vicenza painting, with its emphasis upon the
rich red suggests his awareness of Giovanni Bellini's *Baptism of Christ* which
stands nearly opposite it in the nave of the church. Like the *Feast*, the
Adoration was painted in Venice and the lighting is not taken from the
(presumably original) window to the spectator's right, and the architecture
does not match that of the frame

4 This throws doubt upon the identification of the magus as a portrait of the
donor, Marcantonio Cogolo, suggested by Pignatti in Palazzo Ducale, Venice,
Da Tiziano a El Greco. Per la storia del Manierismo a Venezia 1540–1590
(1981), p 10. Marcantonio Cogolo is clearly recognisable on the left edge of the
canvas, peering in at the scene behind the magi

71   Studies for an Adoration of the Magi

72   Study of a dead Christ and a skeleton

Pen and ink and wash on blue paper heightened with white
13.8 × 27.8 cm

LOCATION London, British Museum Inv. 1895–9–15–841
INSCRIBED 'QUI MORTEM NOSTRAM MORIENDO DESTRUXIT'
PROVENANCE Count Nils Barck; Thibaudeau; J. C. Robinson;
   Malcolm
BIBLIOGRAPHY Robinson no 396; Tietze and Tietze-Conrat
   2094; Cocke *Master Drawings* 1977 pp 260–61

The Tietzes rightly connected this drawing with Parrassio
Michele's 1573 altar in S. Giuseppe of *Parrassio Michele adores
the dead Christ* (Fig 38). They noted that this must be one of the
drawings which, according to Ridolfi, Veronese prepared for his
new friend.[1] The dead Christ of the painting, the inscription, the
instruments of the passion and the skeleton symbolising death
are so closely modelled on the drawing that it is unlikely, as the
Tietzes suggested, to have been used by Veronese in another
context, but must have been made for this altar.

Veronese's drawing is a moving document. The classically
inspired Christ[2] is realised with a strikingly free and loose
treatment of the white heightening, which contrasts with that of
the independent *chiaroscuro* drawings, the *Christ the Redeemer
appears to Sts Peter and Anthony of Padua* (25), for instance.

The altar is one of the first paintings to document the wide-
spread influence of Catholic evangelism.[3] This can be found in
late sixteenth-century Venetian testaments with their emphasis
upon the ineffectiveness of good works and passionate invocation
of Christ. Two testaments of 1556 and 1558, for instance, spoke
of the testator's firm and constant faith that:[4] 'not through any
merits of mine but of his pure goodness and Grace through Jesus
Christ who died for us on the Cross … God will gather my soul
to the merciful bosom of Christ'. Many of these testaments were
orthodox in their provision for mass, and the upper part of
Michele's altar (Fig 38) is dominated by the chalice borne aloft
by the angels. This must have been inspired by the Catholic
defence of the sacrament of the Eucharist, which had a considerable
influence on Tintoretto in the Scuola di San Rocco and also on
Veronese.[5]

Fig 38   Parrassio Michele, *Parrassio Michele adores the dead Christ*,
S. Giuseppe, Venice

72   Study of a dead Christ and a skeleton

NOTES

1   Ridolfi II pp 137–38 and D.F. von Hadeln, 'Parrassio Michele', *Jahrbuch der Königlich preussischen Kunstsammlungen* 33 (1912), pp 149–72

2   *See* the dead Actaeon in Roman sarcophagi, K. Weitzmann, 'The origin of the Threnos', *De Artibus Opuscula, Essays in Honour of Erwin Panofsky* (1961), fig 17

3   O.M.T. Logan, 'Grace and Justification: Some Italian Views of the sixteenth and early seventeenth centuries', *Journal of Ecclesiastical History* 20 (1969) pp 67–78

4   Logan p 76

5   *See also* (87). The reaction to Luther's doubts as to whether Christ was present in the sacrament of the Eucharist had begun with the 'non-liturgical worship of the host in the services of benediction in the forty hours' exposition which, much popularised by the Capuchins and Jesuits, was first performed in Milan in 1527', H.O. Evennett, *The Spirit of the Counter-Reformation* (Cambridge, 1968), p 38. The twenty-third session of the Council of Trent in 1551 had reaffirmed the Catholic belief in the presence of Christ, in transsubstantiation and in the duty to set aside feast days and to adore the sacrament of the Eucharist. This devotion influenced a number of Veronese's works from the end of the 1570s, the *Virgin and Child appear to St Luke* of 1581 in S. Luca, the *Sts Peter, Paul and John the Evangelist* in S. Pietro, completed by 1581, the *Christ with Zebedee's wife and sons* in the Burghley collection, Stamford, and the *Martyrdom and Last Communion of St Lucy*, Pignatti 263, A338, A289 and 279. C-J. Hefele, *Histoire des Conciles: Tome 10, Les Décrets du Concile de Trente*, ed. A. Michel (Paris, 1938), pp 240ff. For Tintoretto, *see* E. Hüttinger, *Die Bilderzyklen Tintoretto's in der Scuola di S. Rocco zu Venedig* (Zurich, 1962), esp. pp 34ff

Fig 39   *Sts Lawrence, Jerome and Prospero*, S. Giacomo dell'Orio, Venice

73   Study for St Lawrence

Grey chalk heightened with white
29.6 × 20.1 cm

LOCATION Rotterdam, Museum Boymans-Van Beuningen
   Inv.I93
INSCRIBED on the (renewed) verso: 'P:n.o 65'
PROVENANCE Anon. (Lugt 2103a; sometimes identified as the
   Borghese collection);[1] F. Koenigs (Lugt 1023a); acquired by
   D.G. van Beuningen in 1940
BIBLIOGRAPHY Tietze and Tietze-Conrat 2078

This drawing is a study for the central saint in *Sts Lawrence,
Jerome and Prospero* (Fig 39). The altar was painted for the
Malipiero chapel in S. Giacomo dell'Orio probably *circa* 1573
when the family appear to have undertaken the redecoration of
their chapel as a result of the death of Jerome Malipiero.[2] The
drawing must have been made after a pen and ink sketch, for
Veronese knew which parts of the dalmatic to omit. In the
painting he added a Virgin and Child and a single saint in the
two embroidered panels of the dalmatic and adjusted the angle
of St Lawrence's arms to coincide with the grid-iron resting
against the column to the side.

NOTES

1   Monte Carlo 1966 intro. The mark was, however, only added in the late
eighteenth century, *see* London, Sotheby 9 July 1981, 132

2   Pignatti 297; the picture is almost invisible in its present setting, but the
date was suggested by G. Costantini, *La Chiesa di San Giacomo dell'Orio*
(Venice, 1912), p 45 and Von Hadeln p 325 note 7 of Ridolfi

73 Study for St Lawrence

Fig 40   *Lamentation over the dead Christ*, SS. Annunziata, Ostuni

Fig 41   *Supper at Emmaus*, Museum Boymans-van Beuningen, Rotterdam

74   Study for a Lamentation over the dead Christ and a Supper at Emmaus

Pen and ink and wash

15.5 × 20.4 cm

LOCATION Berlin-Dahlem, Staatliche Museen KdZ 26358

INSCRIBED 'fraciones panis – Un riposo c[he] fa la Ma^a',[1] and
    with a series of accounts and numbers: '43, 44, 46, 48, 48',
    '14000, 12000, 1000200, 100'

PROVENANCE Marchese Jacopo Durazzo, Genoa

BIBLIOGRAPHY Van Hadeln pl 44; Tietze and Tietze-Conrat 2042;
    Oehler p 34; Cocke 1973 pp 139–40

The *Lamentation* on the left of the sheet was made in preparation
for the now sadly battered and abraded painting which the
Venetian Vice-Consul in Ostuni presented to the church of SS.
Annunziata, Ostuni in 1574 (Fig 40).[2] The drawing confirms
that in addition to the other damage that it has suffered[3] the painting has been cut at the top. It also reveals Veronese's interest in
the late *Pietà* by Titian to which Palma Giovane added his signature, but very little else, on Titian's death in 1576.[4] The grouping
of the drawing reflects the sweeping movement of the Titian
which in the painting is given a richer axial play by the added
emphasis upon St John the Baptist. Christ's pose in the Berlin
drawing, although in reverse, echoes that of Veronese's *Pietà* now
in the Hermitage which also played its part in the present design.[5]

Veronese's interest in Titian continues in the *Supper at Emmaus*
made in preparation for the large version in Dresden[6] and the
smaller but autograph canvas in Rotterdam (Fig 41).[7] Here the
extravagant gestures of the earlier versions at Chatsworth (35)
and the Louvre are abandoned as a result of Veronese's renewed
interest in Titian's treatment of the subject.[8]

74 Study for a Lamentation over the dead Christ and a Supper at Emmaus

NOTES

1 This could be a reference to the version in Ottawa, Pignatti 322 (*see also* under (28) note 5), where the landscape is more complex than that of the Borletti and Moscow versions, Pignatti 321 and A212, and closer to that of the version in Sarasota of *circa* 1572, *see* under (212)

2 Pignatti 187

3 The head of Christ, his right hand and the Magdalen's back have been slashed and restored; the overall damage suggests a false analogy with late pictures like the Budapest *Crucifixion*, but I believe that it must once have been closer in appearance to the *Crucifixion* in S. Lazaro dei Mendicanti, Pignatti 264, from the Ospedale degli incurabili, which would thus date from the period of the renewed building campaign which began in 1566, E. A. Cicogna, *Delle iscrizioni Veneziane. Raccolte ed illustrate* 5 (Venice, 1853), p 329

4 H. Tietze, *Titian Paintings and Drawings* (London, 1937), pl 288 and J. Wilde, *Venetian Art from Bellini to Titian* (Oxford, 1974), p 203

5 *See* under (64) note 7

6 Pignatti 92, it is not accessible. It is the version listed by Pignatti p 228 under the lost pictures in the 1626 inventory of Cardinal Alessandro d'Este; A. Venturi, *La R. Galleria Estense in Modena* (Modena, 1882), p 159

7 Pignatti 171

8 H. Wethey, *The Paintings of Titian I: the religious Paintings* (London, 1969), cats 142 and 143

75 Modello for the Martyrdom of St Justina

Pen and ink and wash on blue paper heightened with white
47 × 24 cm

LOCATION Chatsworth, Devonshire collection Inv. 279
PROVENANCE P. H. Lankrink (Lugt 2090); acquired by the 2nd
   Duke of Devonshire (Lugt 718), thence by descent
BIBLIOGRAPHY Tietze and Tietze-Conrat 2056; London 1969
   no 72; Verona 1971 no 65

The Tietzes, who rightly connected the drawing with the great
altar of 1575 in S. Giustina (Fig 42),[1] suggested that it might be
the *modello* which Ridolfi described in the rooms of the abbot of
the church in 1648.[2] This is possible but Lankrink (d. 1692) had
not bought directly from Italy but rather from the collections of
Charles I, Sir Peter Lely and the Earl of Arundel, who had
bought in Padua in 1615–17.[3] This suggests that the drawing
may have left Italy before it could have been known by Ridolfi.
It was clearly intended to be shown to the abbot, even though it
is squared, for the introduction of the view of the church of
S. Giustina in the background of the painting must have been
suggested by the patron.

   Ridolfi rightly noted of the picture: 'mà quella pittura poco si
gode essendo mal servita di lume e occupata da vastissimo
ornamento'.[4] The many changes from the drawing to the painting,

the expansion of the figure-style and the intensification of the
Tintorettesque back-lighting behind the Deesis, must have been
intended to remedy this problem. This is also true of the choice
of moment, which follows the tradition of the *Martyrdom of St
George* (Fig 24), rather than the legend of the saint's martyrdom.
This formed the basis for the version in the Uffizi[5] where in the
background the saint's coach, in which she is returning from
the country, is stopped on a bridge by Maximian's soldiers who
bring her before the emperor to be stabbed to death.[6]

NOTES

1   Pignatti 182; by 30 March 1575 Veronese is recorded in the Cividale
documents as working in Padua, presumably on this altar, and the *Ascension*
in S. Francesco (Fig 43) together with Benedetto; the payment that he received
from the abbot of S. Giustina on 27 October 1575 was explicitly for the altar for
their church at Conca, due to be finished by Easter 1576, which implies that the
Martyrdom was already complete, Pignatti 256 docs 43 and 44
2   Ridolfi p 317; he may, as the older literature assumed, have meant the
painting from the monastery now in the Museo Civico, *see* under (205) and
(Fig 108)
3   E. A. Safarik, 'Un capolavoro di Paolo Veronese alla Galleria Nazionale di
Praga', *Saggi e Memorie di Storia dell'Arte* (1968), pp 79–110
4   *Compare* this view with that of most modern critics, summed up by
Pignatti, Ridolfi p 317
5   Pignatti 181; the connection in style with the *modello* suggests a date of *circa*
1575, and it too may have been painted in or for Padua since it influenced the
canvas by a follower from the monastery (Fig 109)
6   S. Baring-Gould, *The Lives of the Saints* II (1914), pp 152ff

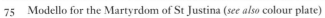

75   Modello for the Martyrdom of St Justina (*see also* colour plate)

Fig 42   *Martyrdom of St Justina*, S. Giustina, Padua

76   Study of an apostle (actual size)

76   Study of an apostle

Black and white chalk on blue paper
14.5 × 13.2 cm

LOCATION London, Sotheby 1 July 1971, 28 (1)
INSCRIBED 'Carletto C'; on the verso: 'C. C. no 45'; on the mount:
  'C. C. no 52'
PROVENANCE Anon. (Lugt 2103a; sometimes identified as the
  Borghese collection)[1]

The collector who annotated this sheet misunderstood the function of the drawing and made the head look down. That he is an
apostle gazing upwards is confirmed by the shoulders indicated
by the outline of his cloak. Although the head is a standard type
that recurs throughout Veronese's work, the drawing may have
been made to assist with the *Ascension* formerly in S. Francesco,
Padua of 1575 (Fig 43).[2] A number of the apostles' heads are
loosely based upon the drawing; probably the closest is the
apostle on the bottom framed by the outstretched arm of a
companion seen from behind, where the view-point was changed
to include his left eye, and the beard was also modified. The
connection with a painting dated 1575 excludes the attribution
to Carletto.[3] The fluent and pictorial handling of the chalk
masterfully complemented by the white heightening, is wholly
compatible with Veronese's certain chalk studies, including the
Study for the Portrait of a member of the Soranzo family (77).

NOTES

1   Monte Carlo 1966 intro. The mark was, however, only added in the late
eighteenth century, *see* London, Sotheby 9 July 1981, 132

2   Pignatti 282; overlooking the inscription which established that it was
commissioned by Laura Cumana in 1575, J. Salominis, *Inscriptiones Patavinae
sacrae et prophanae* I (1701), p 334 no 55; this was the year in which Veronese
and Benedetto are documented as working in Padua, *see* under (75)

3   Baptised 20 July 1570, Pignatti 255 doc 36; for a chalk study by Carletto, *see*
(217)

Fig 43   *Group of apostles* (detail), National Gallery, Prague

77   Study for the Portrait of a member of the Soranzo family

77 Study for the Portrait of a member of the Soranzo family

Black and white chalk on blue paper
30.1 × 20.7 cm

LOCATION London, Sotheby 25 June 1970, 2
INSCRIBED 'P' (to indicate the position of the fur on the cape); in another hand: 'di Paulo Veronese'

This magnificent drawing was rightly connected by Sotheby's with the *Portrait of a member of the Soranzo family* at Harewood House, Leeds (Fig 44).[1] The portrait is undocumented, but the conventional date of around 1575[2] is confirmed by the drawing whose handling contrasts with the earlier chalk studies (2v, 55, 139) and resembles that of the costume-studies from the 1570s (60, 67, 73). It serves to confirm the attribution of the *Study of a seated woman seen from behind* in the Uffizi (131) which was doubted by the Tietzes, and of the *Study of a lady with a fan* in the Scholz collection, New York (147).

The abstract handling of the cross-hatched chalk on the blue paper marks a move away from the study from life to drawing from the imagination. The resulting costume is close to the painting, where Veronese followed the indications of the highlights in the white heightening.

NOTES

1   Pignatti 270; its dimensions 184 by 113cm fit with those of the portrait which was no G.15 (together with its companion G.14) in the 1666 Renier sale, 11½ by 8 quarte, 196 by 136cm, as does the description of the man: 'a seder in Romana con dietro dell'architettura con cornice toccata d'oro', S. Savini Branca, *Il Collezionismo Veneziano nel' 600* (Padua, 1969), pp96ff; they came from the Reinst collection where Ridolfi p340 had identified them as members of the Soranzo family

2   It has the new sombreness of the 1570s and fits between the *Alessandro Contarini* in Dresden of *circa* 1571 and the *Grand-Duke Francesco I Medici* in Kassel, which must date from after 1574 when he was created Grand-Duke, Pignatti 141 and A132. Pignatti notes that the traditional identification of the Dresden portrait is thrown into doubt by the identity of the sitter with the *Portrait of a Contarini Admiral* in Philadelphia, Pignatti 108, identified as Tomaso Contarini in the Johnson collection. There appears to be no basis for this identification and the traditional view of the Dresden Contarini as Alessandro can be reconciled with the naval role that he assumes in the Philadelphia picture. Alessandro, son of Pandolfo, was sopraccomito of the galley S. Christopher in 1570, when he was wounded but not so badly as to be prevented from taking part in the naval victory at Lepanto in the following year, Capellari-Vivaro, Biblioteca Marciana, *Cod.Ital.Ser.VII 8304* p291

Fig 44   *Portrait of a member of the Soranzo family*, Harewood collection, Leeds

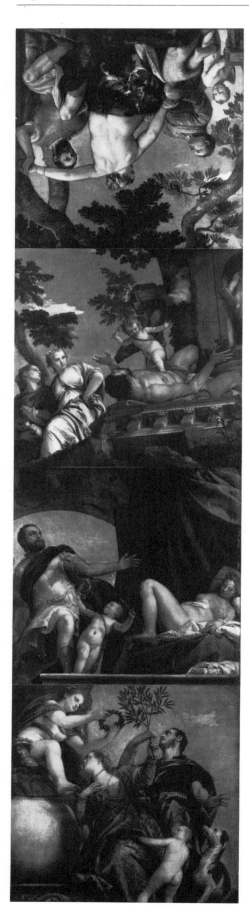

Figs 45–48 *The four
Allegories of Love
(Unfaithfulness, Scorn,
Respect, Happy Union)*,
National Gallery, London

78 Studies for the four Allegories of Love

Pen and ink and wash
32.4 × 22.3 cm

LOCATION New York, Metropolitan Museum Inv. 1975.150
INSCRIBED 'Carletto C'
PROVENANCE Anon. (Lugt 2103a; sometimes identified as the
 Borghese collection);[1] sold Los Angeles, Sotheby 21 May
 1975, 9
BIBLIOGRAPHY Jean-Luc Bordeaux, 'A sheet of studies for
 Veronese's Four Allegories of Love', *Burlington Magazine*
 117 (1975), pp 600–601

On this magnificent sheet, identified by Julien Stock and published by Jean-Luc Bordeaux, are studies for the four canvases
now in the National Gallery, London (Figs 45–48).[2] At the top
the reclining man in *Scorn* (Fig 46) is shown in five sketches
whose bold foreshortening suggests that Veronese may have
studied a wax model. The right edge is taken up with a sketch of
Happy Union (Fig 48), which although reversed contains the
major elements of the canvas and underneath, the clavichord
played by Cupid in *Unfaithfulness* (Fig 45). This is further
elaborated along the bottom of the sheet with the elements of the
final picture, *Respect* (Fig 47).

 The pictures, which were first mentioned in the 1648 list of
paintings removed from the Emperor Rudolph's collection in
Prague by the Swedes, are usually dated from the 1570s and the
drawing fits stylistically with the *Studies for a Venice enthroned*
of 1576 (83). Unfortunately, it brings us no closer to knowing for
whom the pictures were commissioned or their original lay-out.[3]
Since Allan Braham's perceptive account of the subject matter,
it has generally been assumed that they were intended as a ceiling (a point first suggested by Mariette in the *Recueil* of 1742)[4]
arranged in a diamond formation,[5] whose sequence was amended
convincingly by Royalton-Kisch.[6] This scheme is unlike any
known Venetian ceiling[7] and would require an enormous room,
the centre of whose ceiling would be left empty. Canvases of this
shape are more likely to be arranged in a line as in Titian's Santo
Spirito ceiling, where each canvas is viewed separately by the
spectator with his back to the door through which he enters the
room. Such an arrangement is entirely possible for the *Allegories
of Love*, although the first in the series, *Unfaithfulness*, was
probably reversed as in the great ceiling at S. Sebastiano.[8]

78   Studies for the four Allegories of Love

NOTES

1   Monte Carlo 1966 intro. The mark was, however, only added in the late eighteenth century, *see* London, Sotheby 9 July 1981, 132

2   Pignatti 234–36

3   That Van Dyck included partial copies after *Respect* and *Unfaithfulness* on pp 35 and 35v of his Italian sketchbook does not necessarily mean that he saw the canvases, but possibly the drawings, G. Adriani, *Anton Van Dyck Italienisches Skizzenbuch* (Vienna, 1940/1965) and Cocke *M.K.I.F.* 1977 p 217

4   *Recueil d'Estampes d'après les plus beaux Tableaux qui sont en France, dans le Cabinet du Roy, dans celuy de Monseigneur le Duc d'Orléans et dans d'autres cabinets* 2 (Paris, 1729–42), p 67 nos 25–28

5   'Veronese's Allegories of Love', *Burlington Magazine* 112 (1970), pp 205–210

6   'A new arrangement for Veronese's Allegories of Love in the National Gallery', *Burlington Magazine* 120 (1978), pp 158–62

7   J. Schulz, *Venetian painted ceilings of the Renaissance* (Berkeley, 1968)

8   This is suggested by the way in which the trees at the top of *Unfaithfulness* match those at the top of the second canvas, *Scorn*

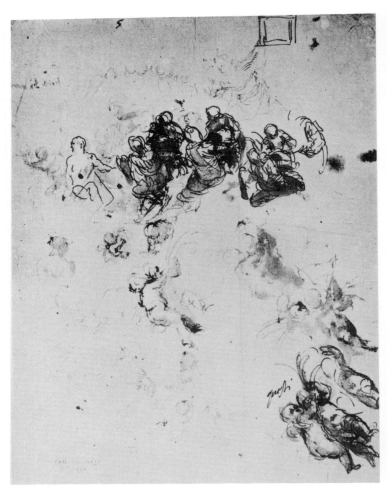

79 and 79v   Studies for a Virgin and Child in glory with saints and angels

**79 and 79v   Studies for a Virgin and Child in glory
with saints and angels**

Pen and ink and wash

26.7 × 20.2 cm

LOCATION formerly Haarlem, Franz Koenigs Inv. I 43
INSCRIBED 'testa bianca', 'questi'; in another hand: 'Paulo
    Veronese'; on the verso: 'Coll. Durazzo no. 3934.'
PROVENANCE Marchese Jacopo Durazzo, Genoa; Julius Licht;
    Otto Böhler
BIBLIOGRAPHY Von Hadeln pls 29 and 30; Koenigs no 12;
    Tietze and Tietze-Conrat 2076

The Tietzes rightly noted that the drawing differed from the
upper part of the *Martyrdom of St George* (Fig 24) which it
otherwise recalled. It is related to the similar section in the
school *Martyrdom of St Julian* (Fig 49) from S. Giuliano, Rimini,[1]
which was probably completed by 19 January 1578 when the
church was consecrated.[2] In both drawing and painting, the
heavenly apparition of the Virgin and Child is accompanied by
music-making angels (an angelic aureole, which appears to have
been cut in the painting), and by two saints the right-hand one of
whom is identified by his sword as St Paul.

In the painting only one angel bears down the martyr's palm
to the youthful St Julian, whose remains are preserved in S.
Giuliano, while his mother in the foreground urges him to
remain steadfast in the faith and to refuse to sacrifice.[3]

NOTES

1   Pignatti A263
2   It was first mentioned by Fr Scannelli, *Il Microcosmo della pittura* (Cesena,
1657), *ed. cit.* Milan 1966 pp 247–48, who mistakenly refers to it as being in
S. Vitale. The church had been ceded to the congregation of the Canons of
S. Giorgio in Alga in Venice in 1496, which would explain why the commission
was given to a Venetian artist; for this and the date of the consecration, *see
Ricordo delle Feste di S. Giuliano M. celebrato nella sua chiesa in Rimini*
(15–18 September 1910), p 9 (a photocopy of which was made available by
courtesy of the Biblioteca A Saffi, Forlì). The canons of S. Giorgio in Alga had
been in charge of Santa Maria dell'Orto from 1462, the church which adjoins
the Scuola dei Mercanti where Veronese was also working in 1578 (*see* 80),
E. A. Cicogna, *Delle iscrizioni Veneziane. Raccolte ed illustrate* 2 (Venice, 1827),
p 221
3   *Acta Sanctorum* (1867) Junii tomus Quintus pp 120ff

Fig 49   Workshop of Veronese, *Martyrdom of St Julian*, S. Giuliano, Rimini

80   Studies for a Visitation, St Nicholas in glory, Faith and Charity

Fig 50 *Visitation*, Barber Institute of Fine Arts, University of Birmingham

80 and 80v Studies for a Visitation, St Nicholas in glory, Faith and Charity

Pen and ink and wash
31 × 21 cm

LOCATION formerly Rotterdam, Museum Boymans–Van
  Beuningen Inv. I42
INSCRIBED 'Io Carlo', 'Joachi'; on the verso with accounts and:
  'Sefusse fato stride deletere [?] del dozo', 'Carita', 'Fede'
PROVENANCE F. Koenigs (Lugt 1023a); acquired by D. G. van
  Beuningen in 1940, thence to the Museum (not returned
  after 1945)
BIBLIOGRAPHY Von Hadeln pls 35 and 36; Venice 1939 p 225
  no 13; Tietze and Tietze-Conrat 2075; Cocke 1971 pp 726ff

Von Hadeln connected this sheet with the *Visitation* in Birmingham from S. Giacomo, Murano (Fig 50).[1] He rightly discounted
the reference to 'Carlo' in the inscription and attributed these
typically mature studies to Veronese. The sketches for the
Visitation begin at the top of the recto (80) with Elizabeth
walking down steps to grasp Mary's left hand. Further down the
sheet the meeting takes place on a level platform and Elizabeth's
pose comes close to that of the painting. In the sketch underneath
Zacharias (inscribed Joachim, but this appears to be a slip of the
pen, although according to the *Golden Legend* he was Elizabeth's
uncle)[2] is cut off by the frame indicated by a vertical line marked
by asterisks as he stands on a stone bridge with iron parapet.

The Murano painting is not dated, but the rapidly indicated *Charity* and *Faith* on the verso (80v) are studies for the monochrome school canvases that once flanked the *Annunciation* in the Scuola dei Mercanti. These are datable 1578 through the *Studies of a Charity, Sts Justina and Sebastian* (86), formerly in the Koenigs collection, a date also applicable to the *St Nicholas in glory* (Fig 51) from S. Nicolò dei Mendicoli, for which there are studies on the rest of the sheet.

The briefly sketched roundel at the top of the recto indicates the foreshortened balustrade which in the painting is broken only at the top and bottom. The group of the saint carried aloft by angels is worked out on both recto and verso where Charity and Faith appear to him and the poses of the angels holding the mitre and crozier and playing the viol are close to those of the canvas.

The drawing shows that when Sansovino wrote of the church in 1581 as:[3] 'restaurata in gran parte pochi anni sono' some of the paintings had been finished although the organ shutters probably date from 1582 (Figs 69, 70). The date is especially important since the ceiling has two alternative attributions, to Carletto Caliari,[4] baptised 20 July 1570,[5] and thus excluded from any role in a painting of 1578, and to Alvise dal Friso,[6] Veronese's nephew born *circa* 1554.[7] The attribution of the *St Nicholas in glory* to Alvise allows us to identify him as the member of the workshop responsible for a number of paintings, some of which are still attributed to Veronese,[8] as well as a small group of drawings including the Chatsworth variation on the Bevilacqua-Lazise altar which is related to the version in the Uffizi (149).

Fig 51 Alvise dal Friso, *St Nicholas in glory*, Gallerie dell'Accademia, Venice

NOTES

1 Pignatti A21, wrongly, in my view, as a school painting

2 G. Ryan and H. Ripperger, *The Golden Legend of Jacobus de Voragine* (London, 1941), p 519, Elizabeth's mother was Ismeria, the sister of Mary

3 F. Sansovino, *Venetia città nobilissima et singolare* (1581), *cit.* by J. Schulz, *Venetian painted ceilings of the Renaissance* (Berkeley, 1968), p 74

4 M. Boschini, *Le Ricche minere della pittura Veneziana* (Venice, 1674) Sestier Dorsoduro p 5

5 Pignatti 255 doc 36

6 Ridolfi II p 141

7 Von Hadeln p 144 note 4 of Ridolfi II mentions that he is listed as having died on 7 October 1609 aged about 65

8 *See* the list under (165) note 7

80v   Studies for a Visitation, St Nicholas in glory, Faith and Charity

81   Study of a standing lady

81   Study of a standing lady

Black and white chalk on blue prepared paper
29.9 × 17.5 cm

LOCATION Paris, Musée du Louvre Inv. RF 38929

INSCRIBED by a later collector: 'Dom. co Tintoretto'; on the
verso: 'I.T.N.o 26'; on the mount: 'I.T.N.o 33'; on the verso:
'Paolo'

PROVENANCE Anon. (Lugt 2103a; sometimes described as the
Borghese collection);[1] private collection, France; acquired in
1982

BIBLIOGRAPHY Bacou 6

The pictorial and expressive handling of the black and white
chalk on the blue paper resembles that of the *Study of a seated
woman*, also in the Louvre (65). It was made in preparation of the
Portrait of a lady with a dog[2] in the Thyssen collection (Fig 52)
where the sitter turns more to her right and a small dog sits on
the table beside her. The painting is not documented but most
authorities date it to the early 1570s, which is acceptable although
the present over-restored condition makes judgement difficult.

In spite of the *pentimento* in the left arm, the present sheet
does not appear to be a costume-study similar[3] to the *Study for
the Portrait of a member of the Soranzo family* (77). Its finished
character suggests that it was the pattern-sheet from which the
sitter chose her pose before the portrait session began.

NOTES

1   Monte Carlo 1966 intro. The mark was, however, only added in the late
eighteenth century, *see* London, Sotheby 9 July 1981, 132

2   Pignatti 174, wrongly in my view, as a school picture. He identifies it with
the painting in the Muselli collection in 1648, whose size as given in the 1662
inventory (3 by 2 braccia, 180 by 120 cm) is much larger than the 105 by 79 cm
of the Thyssen canvas. *The Baptism of Christ* from the Muselli collection,
Pignatti 220, measures 114 by 91 cm and was 2 by 1½ braccia in the 1662
inventory (120 by 90 cm) so that the discrepancy of the Lugano painting is
striking. It is tempting to suggest a more distinguished provenance. No 24 in
the 1640 inventory of Rubens's collection was a *Portrait of a lady with a little
dog* by Veronese, J. Denucé, *The Antwerp Art Galleries: Inventories of the Art-
Collections in Antwerp in the 16th and 17th Centuries* (Antwerp, 1932), p 57. In
1645 it was assessed as worth 220 gelders

3   There is no indication of the striped sleeves of the underdress, for instance

Fig 52   *Portrait of a lady with a dog*, Thyssen collection, Lugano

Designs connected with
the redecoration of the Palazzo Ducale
after the fires of 1574 and 1577

The disastrous fires in the Palazzo Ducale provoked a prompt reaction from the Venetian Senate. The destruction of the great decorative cycle in the Sala del Maggior Consiglio led to the appointment of a commission to draw up the historical and allegorical scheme to be carried out by the leading artists. Veronese's drawings underline the justice of Wolfgang Wolters's analysis of the programme in his publication of 1965/66. He argued that Tintoretto transformed certain aspects of the scheme for the central ceiling painting which he had been given by the commission. The 'tribunale altissimo' on which the doge and magistrates stand must have been intended to resemble the type of temporary structure often put up in the Piazza S. Marco, outside St Mark's. Such a setting had been included by Paris Bordone in his earlier *Fisherman gives the ring to the doge*, now in the Gallerie dell'Accademia.

Tintoretto, no doubt mindful of the *paragone* with Veronese, adopted the setting of Veronese's earlier *Assumption of the Virgin*, painted for S. Maria dell'Umiltà before 1568, with steps articulating the canvas. In the programme the doge is described as receiving the tribute of ambassadors from a number of countries. They are present at the bottom of the canvas but subsidiary to the doge who appears to be paying homage to Venice in the sky. The change must have been suggested by the tradition of the votive picture, with which Tintoretto was well versed.

The commission, while expecting artists to work within the norms prescribed by decorum, allowed this degree of liberty. This is confirmed by the changes that Veronese introduced into his *Venice triumphant* and in the drawings for the decoration of the Sala del Collegio and its Anticamera.

The programme for the *Venice triumphant* makes no mention of the great architectural setting, the main concern of the *modello* (88). The drawings for the *Venice enthroned* in the Anticamera of the Sala del Collegio show the gradual transformation from a passive seated Venice, to the active standing figure of the fresco, and a comparable transformation in the composition from a symmetrical centralised one to a more daring use of asymmetry (82, 83).

The leeway allowed the artists is further suggested by the *Modello for Doge Sebastiano Venier's thanksgiving for the Battle of Lepanto* (87). Although squared for scaling up it includes a dramatic change of plan. At the last minute Veronese added three heads behind the main group in the foreground partially for formal reasons, to heighten the contrast between the heavenly and earthly spheres, and also to introduce new protagonists, including Agostino Barbarigo and St Justina.

The documents about the redecoration of the Sala del Collegio suggest a sense of urgency. In October 1575 Veronese was still at work in Padua, by December of the same year he had received his first payment for work in the Sala del Collegio. This may explain his use of black chalk on blue prepared paper for the preparatory sketches for the allegorical figures on the ceiling of the Sala (70, 84, 85), since it eliminated one stage in the preparation of the design. These drawings also contrast with those for the rest of the redecoration of the Palazzo Ducale where the scale on which Veronese and his studio had to work led to a concentration upon the relationship of the figures to their settings (90, 91, 92 and 93). This had been true of earlier drawings, notably the *Studies for the Triumph of Mordechai and the Coronation of Esther* (5), but the style of these pen and ink and wash drawings marks the change to the greater range of the Late Drawings with their tendency to an increased abstraction of style.

82 and 82v   Studies for a Baptism of Christ and Venice enthroned

Fig 53   Carletto Caliari, *Copy after a design for the Venice enthroned*, pen and wash over grey chalk, H.M. the Queen, Windsor Castle (reproduced by gracious permission of H.M. the Queen)

82 and 82v Studies for a Baptism of Christ and Venice enthroned

Pen and ink and wash
20.3 × 28.8 cm

LOCATION New York, private collection
INSCRIBED 'Vene[z]ia che seli aprese[n]ta Tributi [dalle] provincie citta Castele p[er] il buo[n] governo ed [?] da grazie'; on the verso: '[Pr]imo nel fianco a la ba[n]da destra del Coligio', 'P. Verse 7.2'
PROVENANCE Sir Peter Lely (Lugt 2092); Sutton Palmer; C. R. Rudolf (Lugt 8811b)
BIBLIOGRAPHY J. Byam Shaw, *Old Master Drawings* 10 (1935), no 38, pp 22–24; Tietze and Tietze-Conrat 2106; New York 1965 no 127; Cocke 1973 pp 140–41

The function for which this fine drawing was made has been the subject of controversy since its publication by Byam Shaw. He tentatively connected it (on the basis of the inscription), with the *Venice enthroned between Justice and Peace* in the Sala del Collegio,[1] although cautiously noting the considerable differences and drawing attention to Palma Giovane's *Venice receiving the homage of Brescia, Udine, Padua and Verona* in the adjoining Sala del Senato. Two more drawings can be brought into the discussion to shed further light on the problem. The first (Fig 53) is in the Royal Library at Windsor with an old and convincing attribution to Carletto,[2] and the second is at Kassel (83). They offer confirmation of the view that this series of drawings was made in preparation of the *Venice enthroned* in the Anticamera of the Sala del Collegio (Fig 54).[3]

Veronese began by studying the *Venice enthroned* in the small sketch on the right of the recto of the drawing in New York (82), which he followed by that in the centre of the sheet. This was elaborated on the verso where Venice is shown seated in a niche flanked by columns, receiving tribute from a group of kneeling figures. A later stage in the same scheme is recorded in the drawing at Windsor (Fig 53) which Carletto appears to have copied from a now lost *modello* by his father.

Fig 54   *Venice enthroned*, fresco, Anticamera of the Sala del Collegio, Palazzo Ducale, Venice

The circular design shown in the Windsor drawing must have been abandoned after February 1576, when Marco Angelo del Moro stuccoed the octagonal frame of the fresco.[4] This is included as an afterthought around the upper of the two sketches on the sheet in Kassel (83). Here the niche flanked by columns resembles that shown in the drawings in New York and Windsor, but the central female figure, Venice, no longer seated, stands on the edge of a platform. As in the fresco she holds out a crown and parchment as a reward to the figures indicated at her feet. The cornucopia included in the fresco is also indicated in the lower sketch on (83) as are the bishop's mitre and staff which are also held out by her youthful companions.

The asymmetry and daring foreshortening of the much re-painted fresco resemble the *Justice and Peace* in the Collegio, while the early designs prepared in these drawings (82, 83, Fig 53) look back to the tondi which Veronese had painted for Sansovino's Library in 1556.[5] Byam Shaw related the Baptism on the left edge of the drawing to the *Baptism of Christ* from S. Giovanni in Malta, now in the Palazzo Pitti (Fig 95), but that painting appears to have been evolved at the end of Veronese's life from the *Studies for a Baptism* in the Fogg (125) and the National Gallery of Scotland (126). No version of the Baptism corresponds with the present design, but the pose of the Baptist is similar to that in the version in a private collection in London,[6] which could have been produced by the member of the studio who painted the Courtauld Institute version early in the 1580s (Fig 74).

NOTES

1 Pignatti 194

2 Pen and ink and wash over grey chalk, 22 by 22.2 cm; Popham and Wilde no 1923; for a discussion of Carletto's drawings, *see* under (188). The *Study of St John the Baptist*, Inv. 1952-1-21-62 in the British Museum (it is pricked for transfer) is clearly by the same hand as the Windsor drawing

3 Pignatti A353; suggesting the intervention of Montemezzano; the fresco can hardly be judged in its present condition and was attributed to Veronese by Ridolfi p 333

4 Von Hadeln p 333 note 2 of Ridolfi

5 Pignatti 61–63

6 Pignatti 220; it is the *Baptism* described in the Muselli collection by Ridolfi p 320 subsequently in the 1662 inventory where the three angels are noted, and the size, 2 by 1½ braccia, approx 120 by 90 cm, corresponds with those of this version, 114 by 91 cm, G. Gampori, *Raccolta di cataloghi e d'inventarii inediti* (Modena, 1874), p 186

83   Studies for a Venice enthroned

Pen and ink and wash
24.8 × 20.6 cm

LOCATION Kassel, Staatliche Kunstsammlungen Inv. 1124
INSCRIBED in four roundels: 'IN TUTO IUSTUS', RELLIGIO EX OPERIBUS', 'VERA DIGNO SCITUR', 'NUMEN FORTI ROBUR', 'QHK'
PROVENANCE acquired from a private collection in 1939
BIBLIOGRAPHY Oehler pp 27 ff; Cocke 1973 pp 140–41

This fine sheet is, as was argued under the previous entry (82), in spite of the considerable differences, an early stage in the preparation of the *Venice enthroned* (Fig 54) in the Anticamera of the Sala del Collegio. It must have been made in February 1576, soon after Marco Angelo del Moro began work on his octagonal stucco frame, here shown as an afterthought round the upper sketch. The lettering in the four roundels, which could be Veronese's first scheme for the inscriptions in the adjoining Sala del Collegio, emphasises the Collegio's role in the preservation of liberty and religion through strength.[1]

NOTE

1 Pignatti 193; the inscriptions are arranged as follows: '*Custodes Libertatis*' beneath the *Venice enthroned with Justice and Peace*, above which is '*Reipub Fundamentum*' which also stands in relation to the *Faith and Sacrifice* in the centre as does the '*Nunquam derelicta*' with the '*Robur Imperii*' next to the *Mars and Neptune*. Sinding-Larsen (1974) pp 256 ff argues that the central oval is the climax of the programme of the room which he interprets as an Eucharistic allegory. Such a view ignores the small ovals with classical scenes as well as the generalised allegories in the 'T' and 'L' shaped canvases. It is also difficult to reconcile with the ceiling which reads as a sequence of related but equal parts, an arrangement inspired by the Collegio's duties as the supreme legislative body, as the ministry of war and as the department responsible for religion (A. da Mosto, *Archivio di Stato di Venezia* (Rome, 1937–40), pp 22 ff and p 213)

83   Studies for a Venice enthroned

70   Study for Liberality (*see also* colour plate)

70   Study for Liberality

Black and white chalk on blue paper
20.4 × 22.5 cm

LOCATION London, British Museum Inv. 1969–4–12–4
INSCRIBED 'moderacia', 'di Paolo Veronese'
PROVENANCE sold London, Sotheby 27 March 1969, 8
BIBLIOGRAPHY Bacou 4

84   Study for Moderation

Black and white chalk on blue prepared paper
22.5 × 18.3 cm

LOCATION Paris, Musée du Louvre Inv. RF38 931
INSCRIBED 'Canto . .'; by a later collector on the verso: 'P.n.o
   61'; on the mount 'P.n.o 56'
PROVENANCE Anon. (Lugt 2103a; sometimes described as the
   Borghese collection)[1]
BIBLIOGRAPHY Bacou 4

85   Study for Industry

Black and white chalk on blue prepared paper
22.5 × 19 cm

LOCATION France, private collection
INSCRIBED 'P.n.º66'; in another hand and on the verso:
   '[Qu]alunque volta considero suovanissimo di quanto o...../
   ..solamente su alla humana natura la dignissima ang... di
   per prima(?)/scriveva con la quale le cose che per bino del
   tempo si corrompe.../... delle buon ricevute(?)'. The
   inscription is repeated in another hand at the top of the sheet
   where it is cut off: 'Qualunque la volta considero ... di
   quanto con una mente'; by an old collector on the mount:
   'Paolo'
PROVENANCE Anon. (Lugt 2103a; sometimes described as the
   Borghese collection)[1]
BIBLIOGRAPHY Bacou 4

Redecoration of the Sala del Collegio had begun immediately after the fire of 1574 and the ceiling was far enough advanced for Veronese to receive his first payment on 23 December 1575, and what is possibly the final one by April 1578.[2] These three drawings were made in preparation for three of the irregularly shaped canvases which flank the central allegories in their square and oval ones (Figs 55a–c). The broad and vigorous handling of the black and white chalk on the blue prepared paper shows the haste with which Veronese invented the designs.

In (70) he concentrated upon the complex drapery and the eagle's wing, which like the angle of the figure's head differs notably from the painting. The other sheets are further from the final paintings. That in the Louvre (84) has no indication of the costume which spills out to fill the 'T' shaped canvas, or of the rich detail of the underdress and ermine-lined cape. Both here and in (85) the handling of details, notably the hands, is rather clumsy and abstract. Of the three sketches (85) is furthest from the final painting. Veronese has established the raised arms with which the figure holds the lightly indicated spider's web at which she glances, together with the folds across her lap. In the painting the pose is reversed, and the costume was worked out in great detail, as were the basket and architecture which fill the rest of the awkwardly shaped canvas.

The scheme of the redecoration of the Sala del Collegio showed *Justice and Peace before Venice* over the tribunal, *Faith* in the centre of the ceiling and *Mars and Neptune* towards the doors. The allegories have both a general significance and a specific one in terms of the Collegio's responsibility for managing the meetings of the Senate. This must be alluded to in the *Justice and Peace*, while the *Faith* alludes to its control of religious affairs and *Mars and Neptune* to its role as ministry of war both at sea and on the *terrafirma*.[3]

These central canvases were accompanied by eight allegorical ladies, three of whom were prepared in the present set of drawings. In spite of the old identification of (70) as Moderation it is more likely to represent Liberality. This virtue had long been associated with the eagle, although the gesture of giving up a feather (the ultimate triumph of the Collegio's pen-pushing bureaucrats) is an invention of Veronese or of his adviser.[4] *Liberality*, which is at the end of the ceiling above *Mars and Neptune*, is coupled with *Fortune*[5] since those on whom fortune smiles should in turn be generous. Next come the pair of canvases prepared in (84) and (85). The identification of the spider's web held by (85) as an attribute of Industry goes back to Isidore of Seville and was long popular in the middle ages.[6] The ermine of her companion can be an attribute of Purity, but this seems out of place in the present scheme and less appropriate than the alternative identification as Moderation.[7] Here too the pair are linked as are the remaining four canvases which couple *Vigilance* with *Mildness*,[8] and the Good of the State (*Felicitas Publica*) with *Faith*.[9]

NOTES

1   Monte Carlo 1966 intro. The mark was, however, only added in the late eighteenth century, *see* London, Sotheby 9 July 1981, 132

2   G. Zorzi, 'Nuove rivelazioni sulla ricostruzione del Palazzo Ducale', *Arte Veneta* 7 (1953), pp 123 ff and S. Mason Rinaldi, *Arte Veneta* 34 (1980), pp 214–19

3   Cocke, *Veronese* (London, 1980), p 84 and A. da Mosto, *Archivio di Stato di Venezia* (Rome, 1937–40), pp 1, 22 and 213

4   According to the *Fior di Virtù* (Florence, 1491), *ed. cit.* (trans. N. Fersin, Library of Congress, 1953), pp 35 ff the eagle is a type of Liberality in that he leaves half his dead prey for lesser birds, an image used by Pisanello on the reverse of one of his medals for Alfonso I of Aragon, G. F. Hill, *Pisanello* (London, 1905), pl 59 and p 197

5   This identification, rather than Recompense favoured by Pignatti, is suggested by the dice which she holds in one hand to offset the rewards in the other

6   F. McCulloch, *Medieval Latin and French Bestiaries*, University of North Carolina Studies in the Romance Languages and Literature 33 (1960), p 171

7   This was popularised in the *Fior di Virtù*, *see* note 4

8   The crane is the attribute of Vigilance, the lamb that of Mildness, C. Ripa, *Della più che novissima Iconologia* (Rome, 1630), pp 74 and 172

9   The caduceus and the cornucopia are the attributes of *Felicitas Publica*, the loyal dog that of Faith, Ripa, p 245

Fig 55a   *Liberality*, Sala del Collegio, Palazzo Ducale, Venice

84 Study for Moderation

Fig 55b *Moderation*, Sala del Collegio, Palazzo Ducale, Venice

85 Study for Industry

Fig 55c *Industry*, Sala del Collegio, Palazzo Ducale, Venice

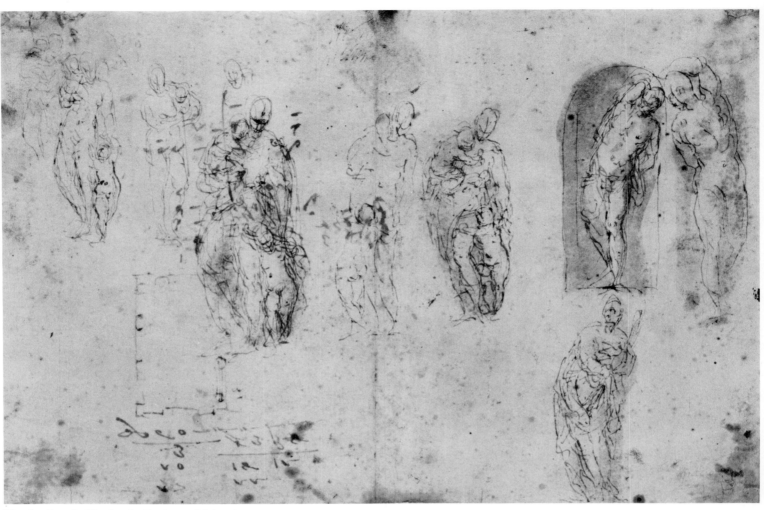

86   Studies of a Charity, Sts Justina and Sebastian

Fig 56   *Doge Sebastiano Venier's thanksgiving for the Battle of Lepanto*, Sala del Collegio, Palazzo Ducale, Venice

86   Studies of a Charity, Sts Justina and Sebastian

Pen and ink and wash

21.2 × 31.3 cm

LOCATION formerly Haarlem, Koenigs

INSCRIBED with a partial series of accounts

PROVENANCE Count Jacopo Durazzo, Genoa; Pribram; De Burlet, Bâle; F. Koenigs, thence by descent to Mrs A. K. M. Boerlags-Koenigs; sold London, Sotheby 26 June 1969, 69

BIBLIOGRAPHY L. Planiscig, *Venezianische Bildhauer der Renaissance* (Vienna, 1921), p 560 fig 614 (Aspetti); G. Fiocco, 'Austellung Venezianischer Kunst in München', *Zeitschrift für bildende Kunst* (1931/32), p 160 (as for the Sala del Collegio); Tietze and Tietze-Conrat 2030 (in the De Burlet collection)

The drawing, as Fiocco rightly realised, was made in preparation for the grisaille saints flanking *Doge Sebastiano Venier's thanksgiving for the Battle of Lepanto* above the Tribune of the Sala del Collegio (Fig 56).[1] St Sebastian's pose on the right edge of the sheet, before he is shown in a niche, recalls the *modello* by Alessandro Vittoria in the portrait by Veronese in the Metropolitan Museum, probably painted in 1575.[2]

The remaining five sketches of Charity surrounded by children are related to the monochrome figure, painted by the workshop to flank the *Annunciation* (now in the Accademia),[3] which was to go over the doorway of the (destroyed) Albergo of the Scuola dei Mercanti.[4] There is no way of reconstructing the plan of the room in which the canvases originally stood but it is possible that it is recorded in the ground-plan to the left of the sheet, which is linked with some random accounts.

NOTES

1   *See* the discussion under (87)

2   Pignatti 277 is unclear about the identification of the sitter for which *see* Cocke *Veronese* 1980 p 82

3   Pignatti 310; the background appears to have provided the model for the façade of S. Maria Nova in Vicenza on which work began in 1585 and which was completed by 1594. Lodovico Trento made his executors provide for the construction of the church in 1578; 'nel modo che e obligato con le monache per instrumenti', but although Palladio must have made plans for the church by 1578 they are unlikely, as Puppi has claimed, to have included the façade since the broken pediment does not correspond to his church designs. The motif had been introduced by Veronese in the organ and main altar at S. Sebastiano by the end of the 1550s and his work must have influenced the otherwise unknown designer of the façade of S. Maria Nova, L. Puppi, *Andrea Palladio* 2 (Milan, 1973), pp 425–26

4   The Scuola had moved to their new site next to the Madonna dell'Orto in 1570, when they took over the one-storey building of the Scuola di S. Cristoforo. Palladio played a small part in the design of the new building for he complained in 1572 about the failure to pay him and later he received fifteen ducats in place of the twenty-five he claimed. A description of the Scuola in November 1846 makes no mention of the Albergo, although the *Annunciation*'s position above the doorway must have led to the emphasis upon the architectural setting, R. Gallo, 'Andrea Palladio e Venezia', *Rivista di Venezia* n.s. 1 (1955), pp 37 and 40

87   Modello for Doge Sebastiano Venier's thanksgiving for the Battle of Lepanto

87 Modello for Doge Sebastiano Venier's thanksgiving for the Battle of Lepanto

Oil over grey chalk on paper coloured red, squared in grey chalk

30 × 40.7 cm

LOCATION London, British Museum Inv. 1861–8–10–4

BIBLIOGRAPHY Sir Karl Parker, *Old Master Drawings* (March, 1930), pp 66–67; Tietze and Tietze-Conrat 2092; S. Sinding-Larsen, 'The changes in iconography and composition in Veronese's *Allegory of the Battle of Lepanto* in the Doge's Palace', *Journal of the Warburg and Courtauld Institutes* 19 (1956), pp 298–301; Sinding-Larsen 1974 pp 96–98

Although squared for transfer the *modello* differs notably from the painting (Fig 56) above the Tribune of the Sala del Collegio, which had presumably been painted between 1577 (the year of Venier's election as Doge) and March 1578, when Venier died.[1] Sinding-Larsen argued that the drawing corresponds to Sansovino's 1581 description of the decoration and that it had a coherent iconography lacking in the painting which had been altered probably after 1582, perhaps as a result of the planned addition of Tintoretto's *Votive painting of Alvise Mocenigo*.[2]

This thesis is to be rejected on grounds of style (the painting appears to me to be autograph and of one piece), of iconography, as is argued below, and because it misreads the drawing. Here Veronese had already begun the process of revision (as Parker mentions), most notably in the section above the chalice where Venier's fellow victor at Lepanto, Agostino Barbarigo, is introduced over the flag together with St Justina. These heads were added behind Venice at a late stage to heighten the contrast between the kneeling figures in the foreground and the angelic host in the heavens. The handling of the white heightening over the grey of the figures achieves the painterly freedom and expressiveness found in the *Modello for the Paradise in the Sala del Maggior Consiglio* in Lille (Fig 62). In the painting the kneeling Faith with the chalice and Venier remain but the standing figure between them has been changed from Venice to St Justina. They kneel not before St Mark,[3] who supports Venier's cloak, but before Christ the Salvator Mundi with Barbarigo standing just behind Venier. Sinding-Larsen objects that these changes, especially those made to St Mark, Venice and St Justina, render the picture: 'quite meaningless in parts' and feels that the concentration of gestures upon Faith: 'make sense but is hardly an elegant solution'.[4]

The gestures are not, however, intended to emphasise Faith but rather the chalice which is given added significance by being placed under Christ's foot. The changes therefore function both at a public level, as Sinding-Larsen has noted, Christ being a more suitable figure to receive thanks than St Mark as the Victory was won in the name of Christendom rather than by Venice alone, and at a private level since Venier's devotion to Christ the Saviour parallels that of Parrassio Michele's painting earlier in the decade (Fig 38) and echoes the passionate invocations of Christ that were such a feature of Venetian testaments.[5]

NOTES

1 Pignatti 283; the suggestion that the picture was posthumous rests on a misreading of Ridolfi, Sinding-Larsen 1974 p 98 note 1. When Ridolfi p 332 says that Veronese painted the portrait of the Doge 'con la sola imaginatione' he did not mean that the Doge was dead but referred to the imagination with which Veronese worked. This is clarified by Ridolfi's use of the phrase in his general summing up of Veronese's work, p 346, where he comments that he used only few wax models and owned hardly any rich materials: 'Poichè solo aiutato da una felice retentiva, formava le cose vedute con la sola imaginatione; alle quali aggiungeva con l'ingegno sempre gratia e nobiltà'

2 This is his later position, earlier he suggested that the change took place in the seventeenth century; his interpretation, 1974 pp 98 ff and 254 ff, of Tintoretto's *Votive painting* as a celebration of the peace concluded with the Turks in 1573 is open to the objection that contemporaries defended it as a failure dictated by prudence, not as a victory, see the *Discorso sopra la pace de' Veneziani co' Turchi* by Paolo Paruta printed on p 427 of his *Opere Politiche* 2 vols, ed. C. Monzani (Florence, 1852)

3 The military saint who accompanies him could, by analogy with the *St Sebastian exhorts Sts Mark and Marcellian* in S. Sebastiano, be St Sebastian

4 Sinding-Larsen 1974 p 97

5 *See* under (72)

88 Modello for the Venice triumphant

Pen and ink and wash on red prepared ground heightened with
   white, squared

52.5 × 35 cm

LOCATION Leeds, Harewood House, Earl of Harewood

INSCRIBED 'P. Veronese cat. 35'

PROVENANCE Sir Peter Lely (Lugt 2092); P. H. Lankrink (Lugt
   2090); perhaps Palmer sold London 1755, 21;[1] Earl of
   Pembroke by 1772,[2] thence by descent; sold London,
   Sotheby 5 July 1917, 438

BIBLIOGRAPHY S. A. Strong, *Facsimiles of drawings by the Old
   Masters in the Collection of the Earl of Pembroke and
   Montgomery at Wilton House* (London, 1900), no 3; Von
   Hadeln pl 62; T. Borenius, *Catalogue of the Pictures and
   Drawings at Harewood House* (Oxford, 1936), no 74; Venice
   1939 no 18; Tietze and Tietze-Conrat 2101; Wolters p 298
   fig 12; Verona 1971 no 67

This magnificent drawing for Veronese's major contribution to
the Sala del Maggior Consiglio (Fig 57) dates from 1578–82.[3] It
influenced Rubens in the handling of the warm ground of his oil
sketches, where he achieved a comparable richness. Veronese
began by establishing orthogonals for the Salomonic columns,
for the flanking niches and for the smaller order. He then
projected the magnificent architecture on to this framework,
changing his mind about the depth of the underside of the
triumphal arch which is cut down to the more limited view of
the painting by a second line, which he then washed in. The figures (as Borenius noted) were drawn over the setting. Veronese

follows the programme drawn up for him in showing Venice like
Rome accompanied by virtues with the contented people looking
up,[4] but departs from it notably in the architectural setting and
in the victorious Venetian soldiers with their defeated enemy.[5]
Veronese drew upon earlier detailed studies like that in Berlin
(89) only to find, as so often with his *modelli*, that the figures
were too small and that there was room at the bottom which he
filled with the armour and the drum from the Berlin sheet.

NOTES

1   London, Victoria and Albert Museum, English Manuscripts, Reserve
S. 12, Sale Catalogues, *The principal collections of pictures sold by auction in
England in the years 1711–1759* I, p 349 bt Lord Verney

2   This was noted in the Sotheby sale catalogue

3   *See* (89)

4   *See* Wolters, and Sinding-Larsen pp 230–31; it is possible that the seated
lady on the right holding a doge's cap and sword-hilt is Security, since the
spear is the attribute of Security (C. Ripa, *Iconologia* (Rome, 1603), *ed. cit.*
Hildesheim 1970 p 453), while the naked lady at Venice's feet seems more likely
to embody Liberality, her pose recalling that of fertility etc.

5   Sinding-Larsen's, p 230, interpretation of the four men clinging to the base
of the columns as: 'li quattro fanciulli che significano li quattro stagioni
dell'anno correspondenti alla felicità, et contento universale di Populi' of the
programme seems far-fetched

88 Modello for the Venice triumphant

89   Studies of horsemen, a captive, a dog and a drum (actual size)

89 Studies of horsemen, a captive, a dog and a drum

Pen and ink and wash
16.2 × 10.2 cm

LOCATION Berlin-Dahlem, Staatliche Museen KdZ 22070
BIBLIOGRAPHY K. Badt, *Paolo Veronese* (Cologne, 1981), p 47

This drawing was discussed by Professor Wolters in a paper given at Cambridge in 1971. It is one of what must have been many made in preparation for the Harewood *modello* (88) for the *Venice triumphant* in the Sala del Maggior Consiglio (Fig 57). The pike of the horseman seen from behind, which was abandoned in the painting, can be made out in a *pentimento* in the *modello* (88) under the trumpet of the right-hand rider. Originally, the horse was shown in steeper foreshortening which was corrected in the light of the present drawing. Although the Berlin drawing thus preceeded the *modello*, Veronese returned to it when he found the *modello* too small and re-used the drum just behind the seated dog, but without the soldier sitting on it. The drawing must date from after February 1578, when the programme was drawn up by Giacomo Marcello and Giacomo Contarini with the collaboration of Jacopo Soranzo and Francesco Bernardo,[1] and from before 1582 by which date the decoration was known to Borghini.[2]

NOTES

1 Wolters pp 271 ff. Veronese had painted the *Rape of Europa* (Fig 33) for Giacomo Contarini. Recently S. Mason Rinaldi has suggested that the scheme may have been drawn up by the end of February 1578 and work, by Francesco Bassano, began almost immediately, *Arte Veneta* 34 (1980), pp 214–19

2 Borghini pp 561–63. He had, however, been collecting his information in 1582, *see* (99) and J. Schulz, *Venetian painted ceilings of the Renaissance* (1968), pp 107–111

Fig 57 *Venice triumphant*, Sala del Maggior Consiglio, Palazzo Ducale, Venice

Fig 58   Workshop of Veronese, *Defence of Scutari by Antonio Loredano* (detail), Sala del Maggior Consiglio, Palazzo Ducale, Venice

90 and 90v Studies for the Defence of Scutari by Antonio Loredano

Pen and ink and wash

12.3 × 21.5 cm

LOCATION Oxford, Ashmolean Museum Inv. P2 742

INSCRIBED 'questa e la Nincio'; on the verso with various accounts including: 'onzi 2 piu del le nuvole'; in another hand: 'P. Ver. so f. 1', 'Caliari'

PROVENANCE Sir Joshua Reynolds (Lugt 2364): R. Langton Douglas, by whom presented in 1936

BIBLIOGRAPHY Parker no 742

Parker rightly connected these studies with the *Defence of Scutari* (Fig 58) flanking the *Venice triumphant* in the Sala del Maggior Consiglio which were finished by 1582.[1] The sketch of the oval on the verso of the present sheet shows, as Parker noted, the care with which Veronese flanked the richness of the great central canvas with the more sombre octagonal battle scenes. The combination of the foreground horsemen seen from behind the leaping horses in the distance recalls Titian's *Battle of Cadore*, destroyed in the fire of 1577.[2] Veronese's concentration upon the kneeling woman who pleads with the departing Turkish horsemen for protection established the narrative in its own right.

NOTES

1   Borghini pp 561–63 but based on material collected in 1582, *see* under (89) note 2

2   C. Hope, *Titian* (London, 1980), pp 95–97 as the *Battle of Spoleto*. This identification although often suggested, is made extremely unlikely by the prominence given to the cannon which had not been introduced into European warfare by the twelfth century

90 and 90v   Studies for the Defence of Scutari by Antonio Loredano

91   Studies of figures and architecture

Fig 59   Workshop of Veronese, *Conquest of Smyrna* (detail), Sala del Maggior Consiglio, Palazzo Ducale, Venice

91   Studies of figures and architecture

Pen and ink and wash
32.5 × 22.5 cm

LOCATION Kassel, Staatliche Kunstsammlungen Inv. 1121
INSCRIBED 'aristide [?]' 'capitanō'
PROVENANCE acquired from a private collection in 1939
BIBLIOGRAPHY Oehler p 34; Cocke 1973 p 143

In spite of its complexity, this is one of the most striking of Veronese's studies of architecture. There is, however, no coherent pattern because different ideas are jotted on top of each other. The architectural frame, drawn in perspective at the top of the sheet, has another domed (?) building sketched over it in ink and a complex campanile next to it. Another campanile near the right edge appears to have been drawn over the study of the left-hand side of an achitectural frame, which has a distant relationship with the upper part of that shown on the Fitzwilliam *Study for a Finding of Moses* (102). These fantastic buildings recall the backgrounds of many of Veronese's paintings without, so far as I can see, being closely linked with any.

Other figures and motifs dotted around the sheet seem to have been made in preparation for the *Defence of Scutari* (Fig 58) and the *Conquest of Smyrna* (Fig 59). These include the leaping horse next to the inscription as well as the cannon further up the sheet, motifs which also resemble those in the *Studies for the Defence of Scutari by Antonio Loredano* (90) and the *Studies for a Judith and Holofernes, David and Goliath and other compositions* of 1582 (99).

The drawing is significant since it shows that Veronese prepared the wall-paintings for the Sala del Maggior Consiglio at the same time as those for the ceiling.[1] This is confirmed by the group of figures at the bottom, two of whom are picked out by asterisks, which is related to that part of the Munich study drawn in preparation for the *Recognition of Pope Alexander III by Doge Sebastiano Ziani* (93).[2] The wall-paintings were manifestly executed by the studio, possibly after Veronese's death, but had been assigned to Veronese in the programme drawn up in 1578. This drawing shows that Veronese prepared them in 1582, when other artists, most notably Federico Zuccaro,[3] were at work on the wall-paintings. Veronese developed the design for the walls in *modelli* formerly in the collection of his heirs in Venice,[4] which were last mentioned in France in the eighteenth century.[5]

NOTES

1   It was referred to Paolo by Bardi p 31, but Bardi does not discriminate between the plan and its execution; Ridolfi p 355 attributed it to the heirs and p 345 noted the *modelli* in the Caliari collection

2   Wolters p 308, where it is assigned to Veronese together with the companion picture *Pope Alexander III and Doge Sebastiano Ziani send ambassadors to Frederick Barbarossa* (Fig 61)

3   *Allgemeines Lexikon der Bildenden Künstler, Thieme-Becker* 36 (Leipzig, 1947) p 573

4   Ridolfi p 345 refers to two *chiaroscuro modelli*; by the time of the 1682 inventory there was only one, no 857, Gattinoni p 40 with dimensions of 2 by 2½ quarte, about 34 by 42 cm

5   The *Recognition of Alexander III* was part of no 684 in the Pierre Crozat sale, Paris, Mariette 1741 p 73, subsequently no 248 in the Mariette sale, Paris, Basan 1775 p 43. The oil grisaille of the *Sending of the ambassadors* was sold Paris, Boileau 4–9 March 1782, C. Blanc, *Le Trésor de la curiosité* 2 (Paris, 1857), p 55

92   Studies for Pope Alexander III recognised by Doge Sebastiano Ziani
and Pope Alexander III and Doge Ziani send messengers to Frederick
Barbarossa

92v   Study of barges

Fig 60   Workshop of Veronese, *Pope Alexander III recognised by Doge Sebastiano Ziani*, Sala del Maggior Consiglio, Palazzo Ducale, Venice

Fig 61   Workshop of Veronese, *Pope Alexander III and Doge Sebastiano Ziani send messengers to Frederick Barbarossa*, Sala del Maggior Consiglio, Palazzo Ducale, Venice

92   Studies for Pope Alexander III recognised by Doge Sebastiano Ziani and Pope Alexander III and Doge Ziani send messengers to Frederick Barbarossa

92v   Study of barges

Pen and ink and wash
29.8 × 21.7 cm

LOCATION Vienna, Albertina Inv. 44718

INSCRIBED 'Pap[?]ia ed g.sedenn or per il P.ta di Nimisia [?] se il P.t . . .', 'Capitano', 'F' on various figures

PROVENANCE Luigi Grassi (Lugt 171b); acquired in 1923

BIBLIOGRAPHY Stix and Fröhlich-Bum no 108; Von Hadeln p 27; Tietze and Tietze-Conrat 2152; Degenhart pp 207ff; Venice 1961 no 42

The older literature rightly connected the main flow of sketches on the right of the sheet with the *Pope Alexander III recognised by Doge Sebastiano Ziani* (Fig 60) on the walls of the Sala del Maggior Consiglio. The Tietzes convincingly suggested that the three sketches with architecture on the left also marked an early stage in the *Messengers* canvas (Fig 61). The architectural setting is closer to Paris Bordone's *Presentation of the ring to the Doge* than that of the final canvas,[1] which, however, is indicated in the related sheet in Munich (93).

NOTE

1   S. Moschini-Marconi, *Gallerie dell' Accademia, Opere d'arte del secolo XVI* (Rome, 1962), no 117

93 Studies for Pope Alexander III recognised by Doge Sebastiano Ziani, and Pope Alexander III and Doge Ziani send messengers to Frederick Barbarossa

Pen and ink and traces of wash
30.2 × 20.8 cm

LOCATION Munich, Staatliche Graphische Sammlung
Inv. 1951:63
INSCRIBED 'questo', 'sozo 6', 'tetrolo 5', 'pontili', 'Schiavi', 'Capitano' (twice), 'Comito'
BIBLIOGRAPHY Degenhart pp 207ff

The drawing, as Degenhart argued, develops the three left-hand sketches of the Vienna drawing (92) of enthroned figures with others kneeling before them to a form which, although reversed, is clearly connected with the *Pope Alexander III and Doge Sebastiano Ziani send ambassadors to Frederick Barbarossa* in the Sala del Maggior Consiglio (Fig 61). Veronese introduced figures clinging to a column further down the sheet where he was also concerned with the *Recognition* (Fig 60), to which the sketches of gondolas and barges relate.

Degenhart suggested that the drawings may have originated with the commission for the *Frederick Barbarossa recognises the Anti-Pope Octavian* painted by Veronese for the walls of the Sala del Maggior Consiglio between 1562 and 1564 and destroyed in the fire of 1577.[1] According to this hypothesis the drawings would then have been re-used by Veronese's heirs for the outstanding commissions in the later campaign. Against this, it can be argued that the drawings are related too closely to the subsequent commissions for them to be earlier sheets re-used by the workshop, that Ridolfi saw *modelli* for the paintings in the Caliari collection,[2] and that the drawings with which Degenhart compared these sheets dated from the 1570s and early 1580s, not the 1560s.[3]

NOTES

1　Vasari 6 p 371 and Ridolfi p 304; the payments are Pignatti 253 and 254, docs 20 and 25
2　Ridolfi p 345, *see* under (91) notes 4 and 5
3　They are: *Studies for a Marriage feast at Cana* (58) in Berlin of *circa* 1571, which Von Hadeln believed to date from the 1560s; the *Studies for the Feast in the house of Levi* (69) of 1573 at Kassel, but not previously connected with the painting; the *Studies of figures and architecture* at Kassel (91)

93   Studies for Pope Alexander III recognised by Doge Sebastiano Ziani, and Pope Alexander III and Doge Ziani send messengers to Frederick Barbarossa

94   Studies for a Coronation of the Virgin and apostles

Fig 62   *Modello for the Paradise in the Sala del Maggior Consiglio, Palazzo Ducale*, Musée Wicar, Lille

94   Studies for a Coronation of the Virgin and apostles

Pen and ink and wash

15.3 × 20.7 cm

LOCATION Berlin-Dahlem, Staatliche Museen KdZ 26356
INSCRIBED 'Fio', 'issepo', 'apostoli', 'S.P.', 'Monica'
PROVENANCE Marchese Jacopo Durazzo, Genoa
BIBLIOGRAPHY Von Hadeln pl 40; Tietze and Tietze-Conrat 2038; Oehler p 33; Byam Shaw p 214

95   Studies for groups of saints and a Coronation of the Virgin

Pen and ink, laid down

30.2 × 21 cm

LOCATION Berlin-Dahlem, Staatliche Museen KdZ 26360
INSCRIBED 'Monica', 'andrea', 'Borto'
PROVENANCE Marchese Jacopo Durazzo, Genoa
BIBLIOGRAPHY Von Hadeln pl 42; Tietze and Tietze-Conrat 2041; Oehler pp 33–34

96   Studies of apostles

Pen and ink and wash

30.1 × 21.1 cm

LOCATION formerly London, Henry Oppenheimer
INSCRIBED 'Mouese', 'Zuane', 'Mate'
PROVENANCE Sir Peter Lely (Lugt 2092); W. Esdaile (Lugt 2617), his sale London, Christie 18–25 June 1840, 437; J. Thane; Henry Oppenheimer, his sale London, Christie 13 July 1936, 206; Rasini, Milan
BIBLIOGRAPHY Borenius 1921 p 54; Von Hadeln pl 41; Tietze and Tietze-Conrat 2116

The first mention of Veronese's involvement with the *Paradise* to replace the destroyed fresco at the end of the Sala del Maggior Consiglio is in 1587, when Bardi refers to the plan to collaborate with Francesco Bassano.[1] This was abandoned both because of the diversity of their styles and Veronese's death in the following year.[2] The commission had evidently been awarded on the basis of a competition for which the *modelli* by Veronese, in Lille (Fig 62),[3] Francesco Bassano in the Hermitage, Palma Giovane in the Ambrosiana and Tintoretto in the Louvre survive.[4] The date of the competition is uncertain but Voss's attribution of a drawing for the *Paradise* to Federico rather than Taddeo Zuccaro may provide a guide,[5] Vasari refers to Federico's plans to repaint the fresco during his earlier stay in Venice, 1563–64,[6] but the drawing may well have been made on the second visit in 1582.[7] At this time he was working on the walls of the Sala del Maggior Consiglio,[8] which would suggest 1582 as the date of the surviving *modelli* including Veronese's.

The Lille *modello* (Fig 62) established the broad massing of the composition but none of the figures are identifiable by the attributes which are so prominent in the present drawings, a

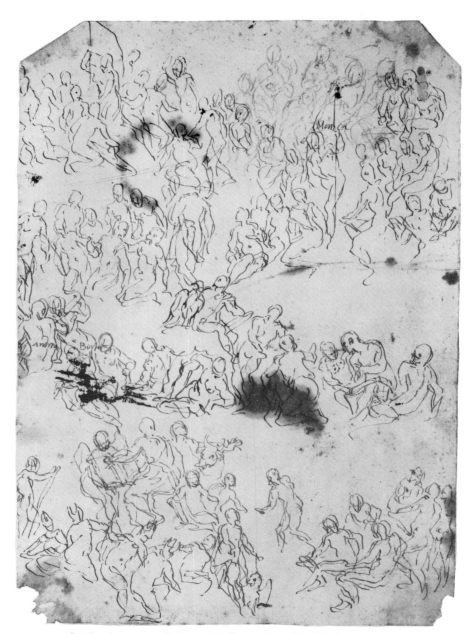

95   Studies for groups of saints and a Coronation of the Virgin

point that is further underlined by the inscriptions. The drawings therefore were not made in preparation for the *modello* but mark the next stage, that of detailed planning for the painting undertaken after the competition. A date of around 1585–86 is further confirmed by the connections between the *Coronation* (94) and the drawing in Christ Church (117) for the painting from Ognissanti completed by 1586, although as both the Tietzes and Byam Shaw have noted, the differences make it unlikely that the Berlin drawing is related to the *Coronation* from Ognissanti (Fig 88).

The three drawings are closely linked. The *Coronation* on one of the Berlin sheets is repeated on the verso of the other (94, 95).

St Monica is indicated by an inscription just to the right of the Trinity in the *Coronation* sketch (95) and recurs as the centre of a group of the figures in the upper part of the recto of the other Berlin sheets (94), which includes three of the Evangelists clearly identified by their attributes, eagle, ox and angel. They are repeated in the sheet from the Oppenheimer collection (96) together with St Mark, although the lion is not absolutely clear and the inscription, as Borenius noted, reads 'Mouses'. These interests confirm Ridolfi's account of the division of labour between Francesco Bassano and Veronese:[9] 'essendo à lui [Veronese] destinato la parte della Trinità e degli Angeli, come più proportionata al di lui operare'.

96 Studies of apostles

NOTES

1 Bardi p 46

2 Ridolfi p 345

3 Pignatti 232; Ridolfi p 345 refers to two sketches for the *Paradise* in the Caliari collection; by the time of the 1682 inventory one had been sold and that which remained, Gattinoni p 42 no 897, measured 7 by 5 quarte, about 109 by 85 cm (the inventory is clear about the proportions which are very different from those of the Lille sketch, 87 by 234 cm). On 15 April 1825, G. Rasini wrote from Pisa to Count Teodoro Lechi in Brescia of the discovery of an original sketch for the 'sfondo' in the Sala del Maggior Consiglio, but it is unclear whether this is a reference to the Lille *modello*, F. Lechi, *I Quadri delle Collezioni Lechi in Brescia* (Florence, 1968), p 100

4 *See* Paris 1965 p 259 and C. de Tolnay, 'Il *Paradiso* del Tintoretto; note sull' interpretazione della tela in Palazzo Ducale', *Arte Veneta* 24 (1970), pp 103–111

5 H. Voss, 'A project of Federico Zuccaro for the *Paradiso* in the Doge's Palace', *Burlington Magazine* 96 (1954), pp 172–75, mentioning the passage in Vasari but confusing it with the later visit. He was corrected by W. Vitzthum,

Burlington Magazine 96 (1954), p 291. A further drawing in the Louvre is no 49, Musée du Louvre, *Dessins de Taddeo et Federico Zuccaro*, cat by J. Gere (Paris, 1969)

6 Vasari 7 (1962) p 62; *see also* W. R. Rearick, 'Battista Franco and the Grimani chapel', *Saggi e Memorie di Storia dell' Arte* 2 (1958–59), pp 107–139

7 *See* under (91) note 3. *See also* J. Schulz, 'Tintoretto and the first competition for the Ducal Palace Paradise', *Arte Veneta* 34 (1980), pp 112–26. I am still not persuaded by his account of a first competition in 1562–64. The two drawings by Zuccaro fit, if not in style, then certainly in iconography with the others. The differences between the *modelli* by Tintoretto could be explained by the need to revise his scheme when the commission passed to him after Veronese's death in 1588

8 The Tietzes, 2041, overlook these interconnections and suggest that the Berlin sheet was made in preparation for a now lost *Paradise* described by Ridolfi p 328 as having been painted for 'alcune monache'

9 Ridolfi p 345

97 and 97v   Studies for Peter of Amiens exhorts Doge Vitale Michele

Fig 63   *Peter of Amiens exhorts Doge Vitale Michele*, Pinacoteca Nazionale, Lucca

97 and 97v   Studies for Peter of Amiens exhorts Doge Vitale Michele

Pen and ink and wash
14 × 27.3 cm

LOCATION Budapest, Museum of Fine Arts Inv. 2408
INSCRIBED 'capitano'; on the verso: 'Id [?] todero', 'P.o. ala VS destra del P.v. Primo i[n]facia ma roverso'
PROVENANCE Poggi (Lugt 617); Esterházy (Lugt 1965); O. Képtár (Lugt 2000)
BIBLIOGRAPHY Venice 1939 p 223 no 11; Tietze and Tietze-Conrat 2049; Venice 1965 no 32

The drawing, as has long been realised, was made in preparation for the painting of this subject (Fig 63) which Ridolfi saw in the Caliari collection. He noted that together with the companion *Doge Antonio Venier condemns his son to prison* they: 'dovevano servir per tesser arrazzi per lo Collegio'.[1] The commission, which was given by the Senate, is unfortunately undated but the inscription on the verso shows that Veronese had a specific site in mind and was aware of the reversal caused by weaving.

Surprisingly the canvas (Fig 63), which is still covered by a discoloured layer of varnish, is not pricked for transfer and there is, apparently, no record of the tapestries in any of the accounts or descriptions of the Palazzo Ducale. It is possible that, in spite of the care which Veronese lavished on this great autograph painting, it was never used for a tapestry.

The failure to proceed with the weaving may be explained by the subject matter. There was a fictitious tradition,[2] reported by Sansovino in the *Cronico Veneto* for 1097,[3] that Peter of Amiens persuaded Doge Vitale Michele to join his popular crusade.

Peter of Amiens, however, never visited Venice and is therefore omitted by Sansovino in his biography of Vitale Michele, which reflects the official view of Sabellico's Venetian history.[4]

Veronese would have been familiar with Sabellico who is frequently cited in the scheme for the redecoration of the Sala del Maggior Consiglio,[5] notably for the history scenes on the walls on which Veronese worked in 1582 (91). At the top of the late drawing in Berlin for the Prague *Christ washing the apostles' feet* (119), Veronese wrote: 'Il Sabellico di la instoria'. This can hardly refer to the *Washing* but might be a reminder to check on Sabellico's account of the career of Doge Vitale Michele.

The recto of the Budapest sheet shows a brilliant use of multiple *pentimenti*. There are two versions of Peter, two of the boy leaning forward, four of the column in the background and two of Contarini who was to accompany Peter. The verso reveals the decisiveness with which Veronese brought that fluent sketch nearer to its final form.

NOTES

1   Ridolfi p 344; they were nos 15 and 16 in the 1682 inventory ed. Gattinoni p 2 with dimensions of 12 by 19 quarte (the Lucca *Peter* measures 210 by 312 cm). It was acquired for the Tuscan collections by 1713, M. Chiarini, 'I quadri della collezione del Principe Ferdinando di Toscana', *Paragone* 301 (1975), p 71 no 72

2   H. Hagenmeyer, *Petrus Eremita* (Leipzig, 1879), pp 373–80

3   F. Sansovino, *Venetia città nobilissima et singolare* (Venice, 1581), *Cronico Veneto* p 14 and p 228v for the life of Vitale Michele who played an important role in the crusade

4   M. A. Coccius Sabellicus, *Le Historie Vinitiane*, ed. & trans L. Dolce (Venice, 1544), pp 50ff

5   Wolters p 311, for instance

Late Drawings

During the last eight years of his life, Veronese completed a large number of commissions both in Venice and outside. For the city, in addition to his involvement with the redecoration of the Palazzo Ducale, he was responsible for work in S. Maria Maggiore (98, 109), in S. Nicolò dei Mendicoli (6), for the Bonaldi family (101), for San Giuliano (110) and for Ognissanti (117). Outside commissions for which drawings survive include that for Charles Emanuel I, Duke of Savoy (99), the Gonzagas of Mantua (102), the Emperor Rudolf II (106), the Accademia Olimpica, Vicenza (113), S. Maria Maddalena, Treviso (115), Giovanni Setti, parish priest of Toscolano (118) and S. Giovanni in Malta, Padua (125, 126). This is not a complete list since it is confined to drawings and makes no mention of the many important commissions whose patronage is not known, the series subsequently in the collection of the Duke of Buckingham, for instance (119).

Not even so prolific an artist as Veronese could execute this amount of work unassisted, and the drawings reveal the care with which he prepared designs for the workshop. There is a contrast between those works designed by Veronese and executed under his supervision (99 and 102, for instance) and those like the *Study for a Christ healing at the pool of Bethesda* (122), where the lack of understanding of the initial design suggests that it was elaborated by the workshop after Veronese's death. The care with which Veronese guided his assistants is underlined by the *Study of the head of an old man looking down* (112) for the old man in the centre of the *Entombment* now in Geneva.

While this fluent chalk study is similar to earlier drawings, notably the *Study of an apostle* (76), the pen and ink drawings develop a new sense of abstraction in their handling of the graphic means, whether form emerges from a welter of strokes or from a single, rather awkward line.

98   Studies for an Assumption of the Virgin and an Adoration of the Magi

Fig 64   *Assumption of the Virgin*, Gallerie dell'Accademia, Venice

98   Studies for an Assumption of the Virgin and an Adoration of the Magi

Pen and ink and wash over traces of red chalk
21.7 × 21 cm

LOCATION New York, private collection
INSCRIBED 'Paolo'
PROVENANCE Luigi Grassi (Lugt 1171b), his sale London,
   Sotheby 13 May 1924, 16; Robert Lehman[1]
BIBLIOGRAPHY Von Hadeln p 27; Tietze and Tietze-Conrat
   2124; New York 1965 no 128

The sketches in the upper part of the sheet were made in
preparation for the *Assumption of the Virgin* over the main altar
of Santa Maria Maggiore, now in the Accademia (Fig 64);[2] this is
especially clear in the half-kneeling Virgin, her hands folded in
prayer. The sarcophagus raised above a flight of steps and
balustrade is shown in the central sketch where the apostles[3]
recall Titian's *Assuntà*. Their expressive gestures were abandoned in the painting for poses which develop from the 1575
Apostles now in Prague (Fig 43).

The Tietzes argued that the sketches for an Adoration were
made in preparation for the *Adoration of the shepherds* in
SS. Giovanni e Paolo.[4] In view of the almost complete difference
between drawing and canvas this idea was doubted by Stampfle
and Bean in the New York catalogue. They drew attention to the
relationship of the Holy Family and two animals on the right of
the drawing with the comparable section of the *Adoration of the
Magi* of 1573 in the National Gallery, London (Fig 34). The
Virgin in the Lehman drawing is shown from the side rather
than the front and the kneeling Magi do not repeat the distinctive

Fig 65   Workshop of Veronese, *Adoration of the Magi*, Musée des Beaux-Arts, Lyons

poses of either the preparatory sketch (66) or the painting (Fig 34). The present drawing therefore was probably made for one of the later *Adorations* which continued the fusion of the *Adoration of the Magi* with the *Adoration of the shepherds* that Veronese had begun in the great canvas in the National Gallery,[5] and the Holy Family with animals by their side is related to the workshop *Adoration of the Magi* now in Lyons, which came from the Palazzo dei Camerlenghi (Fig 65).[6]

Neither the *Adoration* nor the *Assumption* is documented but they can be dated to *circa* 1580. The apostles in the *Assumption* are developed from those of the 1575 painting formerly in Padua and the treatment of the heavens is not yet so richly contrasted as in the *Coronation of the Virgin* of 1585–86 (Fig 88). The free abstracted style of the Lehman drawing is similar to that of other drawings from around 1580, notably the *Studies of Venice enthroned* of 1578 (82) and the *Studies* formerly in the Von Hirsch collection of 1582 (99).

NOTES

1   I am grateful to Dr George Szabo of the Metropolitan Museum who kindly informed me that the drawing did not pass to the Museum

2   Pignatti A244; there may be some studio intervention in the angels in the background but for the most part it seems to me to be autograph. For another painting from the same church, *see* under (109)

3   The Tietzes suggested that they are related to those on the *Assumption* now in SS. Giovanni e Paolo from S. Maria dell' Umiltà (Pignatti A334); the composition is very different and the autograph but damaged ceiling of S. Maria dell' Umiltà was completed by 1567 (it was mentioned by Vasari in 1568)

4   Pignatti 158. The traditional date of 1560 for this badly rubbed and repainted canvas is confirmed by the way in which it appears to have formed the starting-point for Zelotti's fresco in the drum of the dome of S. Maria, Praglia, of the early 1560s and for Veronese's own ceiling of S. Maria dell' Umiltà, completed by 1567 (*see* note 3); the picture was first mentioned by F. Sansovino, *Venetia città nobilissima et singolare* (Venice, 1581), p61

5   Pignatti 287, the ceiling from S. Nicolò ai Frari, now in SS. Giovanni e Paolo, and 300, the school picture in the *Ateneo Veneto* of 1576

6   Pignatti A149

99 Studies for a Judith and Holofernes, David and Goliath and other compositions

99v Studies for a Raising of Lazarus (?)

Pen and ink and wash
29.8 × 19.4 cm

LOCATION formerly Bâle, Robert Von Hirsch
INSCRIBED 'una Giudite ch[e] talia la testa Aholofe', 'Nano',
'Per[?] un presepio'; on the verso: 'REMI pro 50 stampa a la
sua spesa 100 folli che sarano Carte 50'; in another hand:
'.P.N.o 44'; on the verso: 'Paulo Veronese'
PROVENANCE Anon. (Lugt 2103a; sometimes identified as the
Borghese collection);[1] Emile Wauters (Lugt 911), his sale
Amsterdam, Müller 15–16 June 1926, 32; Von Hirsch sale,
London, Sotheby 20 June 1978, 30
BIBLIOGRAPHY Borenius 1921 p54; Von Hadeln p27; Tietze and
Tietze-Conrat 2028; Cocke 1973 pp141–42

The drawing was made on a letter sent to Veronese from Treviso
by Marcantonio Gandini, which is dated 18 September 1582.[2]
The address on the recto reads: 'Al Molto Mag[nifi]co S[igno]r
Paulo Caliari Veronese comp[ar]e et S[igno]r mio Col[endissi]mo
Vinegia Con un rotolo di br[accia] 12½ rassa gottonata nera A
San Samuel presso la fabrica nova da ca mozenigo'. The letter on
the verso continues: 'Mag[nifi]co S[igno]r Comp[ar]e, Mando a
V[ostra] S[ignoria] li br[accia] 12½ rassa, la quale credo piacerà à
cui deve adoperarla; Se in altro posso servirla ella mi co[m]mandi;
et di core la saluto. Di Trivigi à 18 7bre 1582. D[i] V[ostra]
S[ignoria] Comp[are] aff[etuosissi]mo Marco Ant[oni]o Gandino'.
The drawing couples a *Judith and Holofernes* at the top with a
David and Goliath at the bottom, two of the subjects which,
according to Borghini in 1584,[3] Veronese painted for Charles
Emanuel I,[4] who had recently acceded to the dukedom of Savoy.
Neither work appears in the Savoy inventories in the 1630s
which does list the *Queen of Sheba before Solomon*, still in Turin[5]
in 1631,[6] and a copy of its companion the *Adoration of the Magi*
in 1635.[7] The *Judith* and *David* of the present drawing are
reflected in a pair of small panels at Hampton Court (Figs66,
67). These were acquired by Charles II in 1662[8] but the support,
size (30 by 69 cm excluding the strip at the top of the *Judith* as

against 344 by 545 cm of the *Queen of Sheba*) and handling show
that they are school versions as does the contrast with Veronese's
own small-scale paintings, such as the *Finding of Moses* in
Washington (Fig73). The formless figures, loose handling of the
white highlights and unusual profiles link with the smaller
paintings by Alvise dal Friso.[9]

The Hampton Court pictures are further from Veronese than
is Alvise's copy after the *Christ curing the daughter of Jairus* from
S. Bernardino, Verona.[10] The action of the *Judith* hovers un-
happily outside the tent, in contrast with the *Judith* in Caen
(Fig68) (from which it borrows the tasselled tent and Meleager-
like Holofernes), and is imperilled by the anachronistic cannon,
without precedent in a rendering of this subject. The rearing
horsemen of the *David* (a final tribute to Raphael's cartoon of the
Conversion of St Paul which Veronese had studied in the Grimani
collection nearly thirty years earlier)[11] are set in a schematic
landscape which lacks the coherence of an autograph Veronese.

This incoherence was presumably because the *Judith* and
David had been despatched to the court of Savoy some years
before but may reflect a change of plan. This is hinted at by their
absence from the later Savoy inventories and by the way in
which the present sheet anticipates the version in Caen (Fig68),
one of four paintings of heroic women acquired from the Bonaldi
family in Venice by Everard Jabach.[12] Although reversed, the
Caen picture retains the grouping of the three figures at the top
of the sheet, which Veronese reworked below by bringing Judith
closer to Holofernes. The servant in both these sketches holds
out her bag in a pose that recurs in reverse in the painting and in
the small sketch just over the cannon, which is in the same
direction as and closer to the painting.

Other motifs on the recto are connected with further commissions. The coach on the left reappears in the school *Finding of
Moses* in Liverpool.[13] The servant on the opposite side with one
arm upraised to the tree behind resembles the figure in a similar
pose at the top of the Fitzwilliam *Finding of Moses* (102), a
subject in which the dwarf (nano) played a prominent part. The
cannon recurs in the *Studies* at Kassel (91), made in preparation
for the *Conquest of Smyrna* (Fig 59). The horsemen, although
possibly intended for the *David*, develop the motif of the Oxford
Studies for the defence of Scutari (90) in a way that is closer to the
painting (Fig 58).

99   Studies for a Judith and Holofernes, David and Goliath and other compositions

Fig 66   Alvise dal Friso(?), *Judith and Holofernes*, H.M. the Queen, Hampton Court (reproduced by gracious permission of H.M. the Queen)

Fig 67   Alvise dal Friso(?), *David and Goliath*, H.M. the Queen, Hampton Court (reproduced by gracious permission of H.M. the Queen)

Fig 68   *Judith and Holofernes*, Musée des Beaux-Arts, Caen

The verso is more difficult to interpret, but the figure seated at the bottom right gesturing to companions anticipates the Lazarus in the Berlin *Studies for the Raising of Lazarus and the Consecration of St Nicholas* (100). The group at the opposite edge of a woman kneeling before a seated figure recalls the Christ with the Magdalen on the same sheet where, however, Christ stands.

NOTES

1   Monte Carlo 1966 intro. The mark was, however, only added in the late eighteenth century, *see* London, Sotheby 9 July 1981, 132

2   Gandini acted as Veronese's agent in Treviso in a number of property deals, *see* under (4) note 2

3   Borghini pp 561–63

4   Born 1562, he acceded in 1580, L. G. Michaud, *Biographie Universelle et Moderne* 40 (Paris, 1825), pp 547ff

5   Pignatti A313, wrongly, in my view, as school

6   G. Campori, *Raccolta di cataloghi e d'inventarii inediti* (Modena, 1870), esp. p 94

7   Rome, *Le Gallerie Nazionali Italiani* 3 (1897), no 501

8   Sir Oliver Millar, *The Queen's Pictures* (London, 1977), p 75 and Pignatti A159

9   Especially the *St Agatha* in the Uffizi, Pignatti 318, *see* further under (165)

10   Pignatti A238 and under (165)

11   *See* (6) note 8

12   Von Hadeln p 339 note 2 of Ridolfi; the others were the *Esther and Ahasuerus* in the Louvre, the *Rebecca and Eliezer* at Versailles (Fig 71) and the *Susanna and the Elders* also in the Louvre, Pignatti A237, A379 and A242, and (101) note 3

13   Pignatti A151

99v   Studies for a Raising of Lazarus (?)

100   Studies for the Raising of Lazarus and the Consecration of St Nicholas (actual size)

Fig 69   Workshop of Veronese (Benedetto Caliari?), *Consecration of St Nicholas* (detail), on deposit Palazzo Grassi, Venice

Fig 70   Workshop of Veronese (Benedetto Caliari?), *Raising of Lazarus* (detail), on deposit Palazzo Grassi, Venice

100   Studies for the Raising of Lazarus and the Consecration of St Nicholas

Pen and ink and wash
21.3 × 13.8 cm

LOCATION Berlin-Dahlem, Staatliche Museen KdZ 26361
PROVENANCE Marchese Jacopo Durazzo, Genoa
BIBLIOGRAPHY Von Hadeln pl 46; Tietze and Tietze-Conrat 2039;
   Oehler p 34; Pignatti A360 and A361

Von Hadeln recognised that the drawing was intended for the decoration of organ shutters which the Tietzes rightly identified as those from S. Nicolò dei Mendicoli now in Palazzo Grassi, Venice (Figs 69, 70). The scheme is not dated, but Veronese had provided Alvise dal Friso with a preparatory sketch for the *St Nicholas in glory* in 1578 (80) and the present designs must date from the end of 1582 because of their links with the verso of the ex-Von Hirsch drawing (99v). The sketch of Lazarus at the top left recalls the pose of the figure seated towards the bottom right of the Von Hirsch drawing. The sketches of the Magdalen kneeling to plead with Christ on behalf of her brother Lazarus are further connected with the sketches in the middle of the verso of the Von Hirsch drawing. The kneeling Magdalen is shown again lower down next to the two sketches of the *Consecration*, some of whose extraordinarily fluent details anticipate the paintings. The early sources attribute the shutters to Carletto but the connection with the Von Hirsch drawing, which is dated 18 September 1582, makes this unlikely, and the broad handling of the *Raising* suggests that it was executed by Benedetto.[1]

NOTE

1   *See* under (207) note 2

Fig 71 *Rebecca and Eliezer* (detail), Palais de Versailles

101   Studies of a pair of hands, camels and servants

Pen and ink and wash
15.2 × 16 cm

LOCATION England, private collection
INSCRIBED 'So potamia eal avendo admento molte m[?]olte di
  fare'
PROVENANCE Jonathan Richardson, Senior (Lugt 2184);
  Thomas Hudson (Lugt 2432); Sir Joshua Reynolds (Lugt
  2364); Earl of Harewood, his sale London, Christie 6 July
  1965, 147
BIBLIOGRAPHY Borenius 1921 p59; Von Hadeln pl27; Venice
  1939 p221 no9; Tietze and Tietze-Conrat 2102

The drawing, which has clearly been cut down, was linked by
the Venice catalogue with the *Queen of Sheba before Solomon* in
Turin.[1] This is reasonable since there are camels in the background of the canvas where the servant offering a casket at the
foot of the steps is not dissimilar to the standing figure in the
middle of the bottom line of the present sheet. The presents
offered to Solomon are, however, closed, while the five sketches
of a kneeling servant which end with him seen from behind,
show him opening a casket. Like the amiable camels this motif is
used in other works, most notably, as the Tietzes observed, the
Rebecca and Eliezer now at Versailles (Fig 71).[2] This painting,
which had already been enlarged to fit above a fireplace by
1709,[3] was one of four paintings from the Bonaldi collection.
Although undocumented, they must share the date of 1582 of
the *Judith and Holofernes* (Fig 68) which is established by its
connection with the Von Hirsch drawing (99).

The elegant pair of hands are not, apparently, related to any
surviving commission.

NOTES

1   Pignatti A313, *see also* under (99)
2   Pignatti A379
3   Its original dimensions *circa* 230 by 310 cm, were similar to those of the rest
of the series, *see* (99) note 12, the 1683 inventory of the French Royal collection
by Le Brun is cited by F. Engerand in N. Bailly, *Inventaire des tableaux du roy,
rédigé en 1709 et 1710* (Paris, 1899), p88, no5; it had been heightened by the
time of Bailly's inventory

101   Studies of a pair of hands, camels and servants (actual size)

102   Study for a Finding of Moses (*see also* colour plate)

102 Study for a Finding of Moses

Pen and ink and wash

30.5 × 21 cm

LOCATION Cambridge, Fitzwilliam Museum Inv. PD 21 1977
INSCRIBED 'denari' (?), 'strada'
PROVENANCE Sir Peter Lely (Lugt 2092); Jonathan Richardson,
  Senior (Lugt 2184); Sir Joshua Reynolds (Lugt 2364);
  Bellingham-Smith; Tancred Borenius
BIBLIOGRAPHY Borenius 1921 p 54; Von Hadeln pl 33; Venice
  1939 p 224 no 12; Tietze and Tietze-Conrat 2099; Cocke
  1973 p 142

Fig 72   Workshop of Veronese, *Finding of Moses*, Galleria Sabauda, Turin

The drawing, never doubted by Borenius and his successors, was first described as the preparatory sketch for the school painting in Turin[1] by Pallucchini in the 1939 Venice catalogue (Fig 72). Veronese worked out the composition in the upper part of the sheet with the distinctive motif of Pharaoh's daughter striding towards the servant who holds the infant Moses. When he framed this group for transfer to canvas the grid at the bottom of the sheet would have shown that the foreground needed filling out,[2] a process which he began lower down the sheet with the dwarf playing with a dog.

   The painting, which was probably that in the Mantua inventory of January 1627,[3] is undocumented but by common consent is placed in the 1580s. It is possible to be more precise and to suggest late 1582. The servant, who in the painting holds back a branch so that Pharaoh's daughter can see the infant Moses, is sketched to the right of the main group and on the upper left in a form which recurs on the right of the 1582 drawing formerly in the Von Hirsch collection (99). This date then applies to the Turin *Finding*, that in Liverpool[4] and possibly the Prado and Washington canvases (Fig 73). The sketch of a standing woman whose head is drawn just over the bottom framing line anticipates the left-hand sketch of Pharaoh's daughter in the Morgan Library drawing (103) for that painting.

NOTES

1   Pignatti A312 (337 by 510cm), wrongly citing Borghini, who does not mention this subject, and Ridolfi p 335 who refers the *Finding* to the Mantua collection (but *see* under note 3). The Turin picture, was not in the 1631 Turin inventory, G. Campori, *Raccolta di cataloghi e d'inventarii inediti* (Modena, 1870), p 94; it was no 434 in the 1635 inventory, *Le Gallerie Nazionali Italiani* 3 (1897), p 52

2   This must be because it is considerably larger than the prime version, which I believe to be that now in Dijon, Pignatti A63 (122 by 168cm); it was probably the picture that Bernini saw in Mignard's collection on 17 October 1665 where it was admired by M. de Créqui, P. Fréart de Chantelou, *Journal du voyage en France du Cavalier Bernin 1665*, ed. L. Lalanne (Paris, 1930), pp 260–61; M. de Créqui (presumably François Créqui de Blanchefort b. 1629 and d. 3 February 1687, rather than his unmarried brother the Marquis de Marines, Hoefer, *Nouvelle Biographie Generale* 12 (Paris, 1856), p 426) must have turned his admiration into action for it was acquired for the French Royal collection from his widow on his death in 1687, J. Guiffrey, *Comptes des bâtiments du Roi sous le règne de Louis XIV* 2 (Paris, 1882), col. 1094

3   Carlo D'Arco, *Delle Arti e degli Artifici di Mantova* 2 (Mantua, 1859), p 153, *cit*. Pignatti p 228 and emended by A. Luzio, *La Galleria dei Gonzaga venduta all' Inghilterra nel 1627–28* (Milan, 1913), p 92 no 10. It was no longer in the Mantuan collections by 1665, the date of the inventory of La Favorita, Pignatti 235 (D'Arco) and Luzio pp 315ff. That it was sold in the early 1630s is suggested by the sale of the rest of the collection at that time: Ridolfi never visited Turin and relied upon Borghini for his description of the collection (a point established by Von Hadeln in the preface to his edition of the *Maravaglie*), but had, as he says in his autobiography, been in Verona from 1628 to 1631, w ien he presumably saw the Mantuan collections including the *Finding* which could have been sold shortly after his return to Venice, Ridolfi II p 298

4   *See* under (99)

Fig 73 *Finding of Moses*, National Gallery of Art, Washington

103 Studies for a Finding of Moses

Pen and ink and wash
17.1 × 18.6 cm

LOCATION New York, Pierpont Morgan Library Inv. IV 81
PROVENANCE Thomas Hudson (Lugt 2432); Sir Joshua
   Reynolds (Lugt 2364); Earl of Aylesford (Lugt 58); Charles
   Fairfax Murray; J. Pierpont Morgan
BIBLIOGRAPHY Borenius 1921 p59; Von Hadeln p27; Tietze and
   Tietze-Conrat 2121; New York 1965 no126

Borenius linked the present drawing with the *Finding of Moses*
in the Prado and the autograph replica in Washington (Fig73).[1]
This was accepted by all subsequent writers even though the
Tietzes suggested, unconvincingly, that the architecture was
closer to that of the version in Dresden.[2] Veronese shows Pharaoh's
daughter on the right of the sheet leaning back as she extends her
right arm in a gesture that is repeated lower down but abandoned
to the left where she stands, her left leg raised on a block with one
arm on her hip, the other behind her. The pose resembles that
shown on the lower part of the Fitzwilliam *Study for a Finding of
Moses* (102) suggesting a date of 1582 for the present sheet.
Although the pointing gesture does not occur in any surviving
painting of this subject,[3] Veronese may well have used it since
Sebastiano Ricci adopted it for his version, engraved as a Veronese, which came to Hampton Court from Consul Smith's
collection.[4]

   The rest of the sheet shows a drapery study (not used in the
surviving versions of the *Finding*), studies of the servant presenting the infant Moses and a naked bather who, as Bean and
Stampfle noted, follows the account in Exodus and was used in a
version that Cochin engraved, as a Veronese, in 1691.[5]

NOTES

1   Pignatti 240 and 241; both may have been in the collection of Charles I;
one, curiously framed on the back of a *Nativity* by Bassano, was bought from
Daniel Nys in Venice and sold to Sir Peter Lely in 1650; it measured 38 by 38 cm
(close to the 50 by 43 cm of the Prado painting) and had been disposed of by the
time of his inventory in 1682 (*Burlington Magazine* 83 (1943), pp185ff); the
other, with small figures was sold to Gravenor in 1649/50, Sir Oliver Millar,
Walpole Society 37 (1958–60), p78 and 43 (1970–72), p262 no103. The
Madrid picture was probably no548 in the 1686 Alcázar inventory since the
dimensions fit although the artist is not mentioned, Y. Bottineau, *Bulletin
Hispanique, Bordeaux* 58 (1956), pp300ff
2   Pignatti 242
3   cf. Pignatti figs 560–69
4   F. Vivian, *Il Console Smith* (Vicenza, 1971), p183
5   C. C. Patin, *Pitture scelte e dichiarate* (Cologne, 1691)

103   Studies for a Finding of Moses (actual size)

104   Studies for a Baptism of Christ (actual size)

104 Studies for a Baptism of Christ

Pen and ink and wash over traces of grey chalk
17.3 × 18 cm

LOCATION Düsseldorf, Kunstmuseum Inv. FP 3550
PROVENANCE Lambert Krahe
BIBLIOGRAPHY Verona 1971 no 72; Ballarin *Arte Veneta* 1971
   p 118

The drawing, which had been classified as by Palma Giovane, was first attributed to Veronese by John Gere. His discovery was noted in the Verona catalogue although his article publishing the drawing has not appeared. Veronese first showed the whole composition on the left of the sheet, with a line indicating the frame underneath it. He then reworked the individual poses which formed the basis for the *Baptism* in the Courtauld Institute (Fig 74),[1] as Ballarin noted. The Baptist on the right kneels on his left leg only, his right leg being straight as in the painting and his left arm, with which he holds the staff, is shown on his chest in a *pentimento*. The kneeling Christ was not used in the painting but the angel on the bottom right, holding back a branch of the tree, recurs in a similar position in the canvas.

Stylistically, the drawing is close to the *Study for a Finding of Moses* in the Fitzwilliam Museum (102) from *circa* 1582, a date which corresponds with the execution of the painting, which, like the related *Baptism* in a private collection in London,[2] I believe to be by the workshop. In both, the figures are weaker and less coherent than those of the nearly contemporary *Baptism* from S. Nicolò ai Frari in the Brera.[3] They are not successfully related to the landscape whose handling differs from that of pictures of comparable scale, the *Finding of Moses* in Washington, (Fig 73) for instance.

Fig 74   Follower of Veronese, *Baptism of Christ*, Courtauld Institute of Art, London

NOTES

1   Pignatti 219
2   Pignatti 220 and *see* under (82)
3   Pignatti 292

105   Studies for a Birth and Death of Adonis

105 and 105v Studies for a Birth and Death of Adonis

Pen and ink and wash

30.5 × 21 cm

LOCATION London, Sotheby 27 March 1969, 7

INSCRIBED with a series of accounts and: 'di ditamo chi sta[n]a/
un arco in mano/co[n] saette'; in another hand: 'di Paolo
Veronese'

BIBLIOGRAPHY Cocke *Pantheon* 1977 p 124 note 27

In the lightly framed drawing on the recto, Venus kneels over
the dead Adonis watched by one of his dogs while Cupid flies
overhead. This is a study for the *Death of Adonis* from the
collection of the Emperor Rudolf II, now in Stockholm (Fig
75).[1] The painting was cut down in the eighteenth century[2] and
it is clear from the sketch that Veronese envisaged tall trees
behind the figures. The composition was clarified on the verso
where the main figures are reversed and a putto shooting two
dogs with the bow and arrow, to which the inscription refers, is
included in the background. In the painting, Venus's gesture is
similar to that of Cephalus in the *Death of Procris* in Strasbourg,[3]
and Cupid supports her dead lover's head in a scheme that takes
on the sombre overtones of a Lamentation.

Both here and on the recto the sketches of the *Death of Adonis*
merge with those of his Birth from his mother Myrrha, after she
had been turned into a tree.[4] This combination of subjects,
although there is no record of the Birth having been painted,
reflects the pessimisim of the combination of the *Venus and
Adonis* with the *Death of Procris*.[3] The Stockholm painting is
not dated, but unlike most of the mythologies from Rudolf II's
collection appears to be datable to the early 1580s. The free
handling with the skilful use of the *pentimenti* resembles that of
the *Studies for the Defence of Scutari* in Oxford from this period
(90).

A dating in the 1580s appears to be confirmed by the finished
variant of the design in a private collection, France, which has an
old and convincing attribution to Carletto (Fig 76).[5] Some of the
ways in which this version differs from the painting, the direction
and grouping of the lovers, the use of the expressive gesture of
Venus's right arm, were derived from the present drawing.
Carletto does not here appear to be looking back to an earlier
design, as was the case with the Windsor *Copy after a design for
the Venice enthroned* (Fig 53).[6]

Fig 75   *Death of Adonis*, Nationalmuseum, Stockholm

NOTES

1   Pignatti 252; no 1201 in the 1621 inventory of Rudolf's collection, ed. Zimmermann in *Jahrbuch des Kunsthistorischen Sammlungen des allerhöchsten Kaiserhauses* 25 (1905), p xivi

2   It now measures 140 by 169 cm; in the 1662 Palazzo Riario inventory it matched the *Hermes, Herse and Aglauros* in Cambridge (232 by 173 cm) as it still did in 1721 when in the Orléans collection; O. Granberg, *La Galerie de tableaux de la reine Christine de Suède* (Stockholm, 1897), p xcvi no 38. It was cut down by 1808 when engraved by Couché in the *Galerie du Palais Royal*, 2 no 2

3   Pignatti 251 failing to connect it with Borghini p 563 and with the companion *Venus and Adonis* now in Madrid both bought by Velazquez in Venice in 1650, M. Lorente Junquera, 'Sobre Veronés en el Prado', *Archivo Español de Arte* 42 (1969), pp 235–42

4   Ovid, *Metamorphoses* Book X pp 480 ff a subject shown in comparable guise in the illustrated editions of Ovid

5   Pen and ink and wash over traces of grey chalk on blue prepared paper, 21 by 18 cm. It clearly influenced the design of the Study for *Tancred and Erminia* in the Ambrosiana, Milan, *see* under (188) note 3

6   The attribution of the copy in the National Gallery, Prague to Carletto will have to be revised in the light of this discovery. Its dimensions fit with those of the Stockholm painting only after it was cut down sometime after 1721, A. Ballarin, 'Quadri Veneziani inediti nei musei di Varsavia e di Praga' *Paragone* 229 (1969), pp 52–65

Fig 76   Carletto Caliari, *Death of Adonis*, pen and ink and wash, private collection, France

105v   Studies for a Birth and Death of Adonis

Fig 77   *Mars and Venus*, National Gallery of Scotland, Edinburgh

106   Studies of Venus with Cupid

Pen and ink and wash, squared
17 × 12.5 cm

LOCATION London, British Musuem Inv. 1951–11–10–79
INSCRIBED 'spechio'
BIBLIOGRAPHY C. Thompson and H. Brigstocke, *National Gallery of Scotland, Shorter Catalogue* (Edinburgh, 1970), p 101; Cocke *Pantheon* 1977 p 122; H. Brigstocke, *Italian and Spanish Paintings in the National Gallery of Scotland* (Glasgow, 1978), p 182

The drawing is squared for transfer in grey chalk. It appears to be a preparatory study for the lost *Venus with a mirror* which, according to Borghini,[1] Veronese painted for the Emperor Rudolf II. The picture, however, was not mentioned in the earliest inventory of his collection,[2] and had been accompanied by a *Mars and Venus with a weeping Cupid*, also apparently lost.[3]

In the drawing Venus does not use the mirror. Veronese may therefore have rejected the design for one where she looks at it. He may also have wanted to establish a contrast between the *Venus with a mirror* and the *Mars and Venus* by showing her from behind in one of the pair. This is suggested by the similarities with the school *Venus with a mirror* in Omaha,[4] the pose of whose legs appears to reflect the drawing although the final composition owes a greater debt to Titian's erotic poesie for Philip II of Spain. After this change in plan, Veronese returned to the present drawing for a different version of *Mars and Venus*, that now in Edinburgh (Fig 77),[5] although he must have modified it in drawings now lost to add the rather ineffective Mars, who is related so awkwardly to the Venus.

NOTES

1   Borghini p 563
2   H. Zimmermann in *Jahrbuch der Kunsthistorischen Sammlungen des allerhöchsten Kaiserhauses* 25 (1905), pp xiiiff and Cocke 1977 p 124 notes 20 and 21
3   No 1151 in the 1621 inventory, ed. Zimmermann, was a *Mars and Venus* by Veronese which may be either the version in the Metropolitan Museum, Pignatti 248, or that now known through a fragment in a Roman private collection, Pignatti A266. The New York canvas fits with mythologies which I would date to the 1560s and in neither version does Cupid cry; I therefore believe them not to have been the painting referred to by Borghini. A *Venus with a weeping cupid* (although there is no mention of Mars) was in Paris in the latter half of the eighteenth century; it was no 5 in the Prince de Carignan sale, Poilly 1743; 106 in the Duc de Tallard sale, Rémy & Glomy 1756; and finally 1 in the sale Paillet 17 February 1777 in each case with dimensions of 54 in by 40 in, approx 140 by 100 cm
4   Pignatti 275
5   This was first noted by Miss Yonna Yapou as reported in the *Shorter Catalogue*

106   Studies of Venus with Cupid (actual size) (*see also* colour plate)

Fig 78   Carletto Caliari, *Rape of Europa*, Gemäldegalerie, Dresden

107   Study for a Rape of Europa

Pen and ink and wash
11.7 × 14.3 cm

LOCATION Paris, Musée du Louvre Inv. 4,708
BIBLIOGRAPHY Châtelet p 220 (for the Rasini *Rape*)

The drawing, which was rightly attributed to Veronese by
Châtelet, has the same almost abstract handling as the *Study of
Venus with Cupid* from the early 1580s, now in the British
Museum (106). When Châtelet published his discovery[1] he
related it to the cassone panel in the Rasini collection, Milan.[2]
Here Jupiter turns, as in the drawing, to kiss Europa's foot, and
the trees in the centre are similar to those on the left edge of the
drawing. In spite of these connections, I find it hard to believe
that the drawing was made for the Rasini version. The frame
shown on the drawing reveals a much smaller painting with the
abduction to the right of the main group, a servant preparing a
garland for Europa's head and flying putti with wreaths, an idea
that Veronese developed in the 1573 *Rape* now in the Palazzo
Ducale, Venice (Fig 33). The drawing's apparent date of the
1580s suggests that it was intended for a now lost version. This
in turn influenced Carletto's *Rape* in Dresden[3] (Fig 78) where
Europa's head is garlanded as she raises her arm to greet the
flying putto.

NOTES
1   His attribution was noted on the mount long before he published it
2   Pignatti 151
3   H. Posse, 'Die briefe des Grafen Francesco Algarotti an den sächsischen
Hof…', *Jahrbuch der preussischen Kunstsammlungen* (1931), Beiheft p 45

107   Study for a Rape of Europa (actual size)

108 Study for a Crucifixion

108   Study for a Crucifixion

Pen and ink and wash over grey chalk on blue prepared paper
heightened with white
37.4 × 24.1 cm

LOCATION Bayonne, Musée Bonnat Inv. 127
PROVENANCE G. Vallardi (Lugt 1223); Thibaudeau; Marquis de
Chennevières; L. Bonnat
BIBLIOGRAPHY Gombosi, *Magyar Müvészet* (1928), p 726;
Tietze and Tietze-Conrat 2031; Bayonne 1960 no 180

This magnificent drawing, which had always been accepted as a
Veronese, was first related to the *Crucifixion* in Budapest (Fig 79)[1]
by Gombosi. The picture is not documented but is clearly one of
the masterpieces of Veronese's late style. The drawing differs
from the painting in the omission of the background and in
details of the figure composition, most notably in the head of the
St John supporting the swooning Mary at the foot of the cross.
Although not squared for transfer like the *modelli*, the treatment
of the drapery and of the white heightening behind the figures at
the bottom left edge reveal that Veronese already knew precisely
the dimensions of the canvas for which the design was intended.
The painterly freedom with which the white heightening is
applied recalls that in the Harewood *Modello for the Venice
triumphant* (88), also from the beginning of the 1580s.

NOTE

1   Pignatti 266

Fig 79   *Crucifixion*, Museum of Fine Arts, Budapest

Fig 80   *Agony in the garden*, Brera, Milan

109   Studies for an Agony in the garden

Pen and ink and wash

13.1 × 17 cm

LOCATION Berlin-Dahlem, Staatliche Museen KdZ 18 457
INSCRIBED 'angonia'; in another hand: 'Al flor[issi]mo pitor M
  paulo/verones a suo oss. mo Venetia vicino a Sa Samuele'
BIBLIOGRAPHY K. Badt, *Paolo Veronese* (Cologne, 1981), p 47

Veronese used the letter addressed to him for a series of five
sketches for the *Agony in the garden*, from S. Maria Maggiore,
Venice, now in the Brera, Milan (Fig 80).[1] The composition of
the group on the left of the present sheet is furthest from the
painting while the other sketches, notably that at the bottom
right, are closer although in reverse. The iconography of the
badly abraded canvas differs from that of the older tradition of
Mantegna, Bellini and Titian, where the angel with the chalice
appears to Christ in the sky. The change to the 'angelic consolation',[2] suggested by Luke 22, 43: 'and there appeared an
angel unto him from heaven strengthening him' may well begin
with the S. Maria Maggiore painting, which, although difficult
to date in its present condition, must be late. Comparison of the
sketchy handling of the present drawing to that in the Berlin
Studies of horsemen of *circa* 1582 (89) confirms a dating to the
1580s.[3]

NOTES

1   Pignatti 431; the main altar from the church was the *Assumption of the
Virgin* of *circa* 1580 (Fig 64)
2   The phrase is that of P. Askew, 'The angelic consolation of St. Francis in
Post-Tridentine Italian Painting', *Journal of the Warburg and Courtauld Institutes*
32 (1969), p 293
3   Dr Askew, in her article *cit.* note 2 followed J. Goodison and G. Robertson,
*Fitzwilliam Museum, Cambridge: Catalogue of Paintings Volume II Italian
Schools* (Cambridge, 1967), p 118 in attributing the crucial role to the drawing
of this subject by Jacopo Palma, P. D. 3070, which is dated 1575 by an
inscription. Their suggestion of a connection with the panels from the tabernacle
of the Umiltà in the Museum must be ruled out by the discovery of the
provenance together with the dating of 1581 by S. Mason Rinaldi, *Catalogue of
Drawings by Jacopo Palma il Giovane*, London, Sotheby 4 July 1977, 5. This
was the original destination of the *Preaching of St John the Baptist* and the
Christ and the centurion in the Wengraf collection, Pignatti A153 and 154
rightly, in my opinion, as school. The Tietzes had already doubted the
inscription and dated the drawing later in Palma's career, Tietze and Tietze-
Conrat 859. Their doubts are shared by Julien Stock and Philip Pouncey as
well as by N. Ivanoff and P. Zampetti, 'Jacopo Negretti detto Palma il
Giovane' in *I Pittori Bergameschi: Il Cinquecento III* (Bologna, 1979), p 551
no 164 where they relate it to the canvas in Possagno Trevio, which they date
late

109   Studies for an Agony in the garden (actual size)

Ganimede rapito da Giove

di Paulo Veronese

110   Studies for a Last Supper and a Rape of Ganymede

Fig 81   Workshop of Veronese, *Last Supper*, Capella del Sacramento, San Giuliano, Venice

110   Studies for a Last Supper and a Rape of Ganymede

Pen and ink and wash
28.6 × 19 cm

LOCATION England, private collection
INSCRIBED 'Ganimede rapitto da Giove'; in another hand:
   'di Paolo Veronese'
PROVENANCE Anon. (Lugt 2103a; sometimes identified as the
   Borghese collection);[1] H. M. Calmann, his sale London,
   Christie 9 December 1982, 150

This magnificent drawing, which was brought to my attention
by Julien Stock, prepares three versions of an otherwise un-
recorded *Rape of Ganymede*, which may well have been based
upon a small wax model.[2]

   The rapidly executed sketch of the *Last Supper* at the top of
the sheet is a study for the school picture in the chapel of the
Sacrament in San Giuliano (Fig 81)[3]. The date of *circa* 1583[4]
suggests that it may be one of a group of paintings from the

1580s by Benedetto.[5] Veronese established the main elements of
the design, the balustrade on the left with the flight of steps in
front, Christ to the left of centre and a kneeling apostle on the
near side of the table just behind the balustrade. The composition
may have been elaborated in other studies since the *Study of the
head of an old man looking down* (112) shows that Veronese
prepared detailed sketches for Benedetto.

NOTES

1   Monte Carlo 1966 intro. The mark was, however, only added in the late
eighteenth century, *see* London, Sotheby 9 July 1981, 132
2   Ganymede's pose with his right arm raised behind his head recalls the St
Sebastian that Vittoria holds in his portrait in the Metropolitan Museum and
which inspired the St Sebastian flanking the *Doge Sebastian Venier's thanksgiving* in the Sala del Collegio (87)
3   Pignatti A341
4   This was the year that Vittoria's studio completed the ornate ceiling
decoration, R. Predelli, *Archivio Trentino* 23 (1908), pp 192ff had transcribed
the date as 1589, but was corrected by W. Timofiewitsch, *Girolamo Campagna:
Studien zur venezianischen Plastik um das Jahr 1600* (Munich, 1972), p 35
5   *See* under (207) note 2

111   Study of a decorative figure

111   Study of a decorative figure
111v   Studies for an Entombment of Christ

Pen and ink on blue prepared paper, on the recto with wash and
   heightened with white
19.5 × 14.7 cm
LOCATION France, private collection
INSCRIBED on the verso: 'andando ... contadi per certa ...
   inamorasim/ ben dato servigio/ resta vestita[?]'; some notes
   which are crossed out and a series of numbers: '4,1,2,1,2'
PROVENANCE Anon. (Lugt 2103a; sometimes described as the
   Borghese collection)[1]

In spite of the damage which the sheet has suffered, the highly
finished Parmigianesque figure on the recto shows a strikingly
sculptural use of the white heightening. This spandrel-figure,
sitting on what was clearly a triangular pediment with a large and
impressive tablet held in her right hand, was developed from the
rapid preliminary sketch on (117v). Here the initial scheme on
the left of the sheet showed the figure resting on a pointed arch,
with a companion to the (spectator's) right and another pair of
similar figures beneath. In the later version at the bottom of the
sheet the pediments were revised to triangular and the direction
of this figure's gaze was changed so that, as in (111), she looks
towards her companion. Such a decorative figure forms a standard

111v   Studies for an Entombment of Christ

part of Veronese's repertoire throughout his career in Venice, but was not made for any surviving painting.[2] Its highly finished character suggests that it might have been intended not for a painting but for a decorative ensemble. In his description of Ognissanti, the location of the *Coronation* prepared in (117), Boschini discusses the *portellina* of the tabernacle of the high altar as by Veronese.[3] He refers specifically to the long lost painting of the *Resurrection*, but it is tempting to suggest that the present drawing was intended for the sculptor responsible for that, or a comparable, tabernacle.

The *Studies for a Coronation of the Virgin* on the recto of (117) can be dated to before July 1586, and that date must extend to the present sheet and hence to the *Entombment of Christ* now in Geneva (Fig 82). The multiple *pentimenti* from which the figures on the verso emerge make the sheet difficult to read. In the upper and more crowded of the two sketches Christ is lowered into a rapidly indicated tomb. His pose, that of the figures holding his legs and head as well as the sepulchre anticipate those of the

Entombment of Christ in Geneva (Fig 82). The other mourners are not yet close to the painting, but two sketches at the very bottom of the sheet and again with the page turned upright through ninety degrees elaborate the mourning Mary on the right of the canvas. The handling here resembles that in the upper part of (117), before the application of the wash to clarify the design, a process which may well have been carried out in another now lost section of the present drawing.

NOTES

1   Monte Carlo 1966 intro. The mark was, however, only added in the late eighteenth century, *see* London, Sotheby 9 July 1981, 132

2   *See* the small grisaille canvases of *Fame* painted in the Palazzo Ducale and the decorative figures in the background of the *Queen of Sheba before Solomon* in Turin, Pignatti pls 53–56 and 987

3   M. Boschini, *Le Minere della Pittura Veneziana* (Venice, 1664), p 366

112   Study of the head of an old man looking down (actual size)

112 Study of the head of an old man looking down

Black and white chalk on blue paper

12.7 × 11.9 cm

LOCATION London, Sotheby 1 July 1971, 29

INSCRIBED 'Carletto C'; on the mount: 'C.C.nº: 53'

PROVENANCE Anon. (Lugt 2103a; sometimes identified as the
Borghese collection)[1]

This marvellous drawing was mis-attributed to Carletto by an
anonymous collector. It is a study for the head of the old man
(Joseph of Arimathaea or Nicodemus) who helps to lower Christ
into the tomb in the centre of the *Entombment of Christ* in
Geneva (Fig 82).[2] Its handling resembles that of the earlier *Study
of an apostle* (76) in its combination of realism of observation
with decoration in the treatment of the chalk on the blue
prepared paper. It is clearly superior to the *Study of the head of a
woman* in Stockholm (217), which is probably by Carletto, and
the *Study of a woman's head* in the Louvre (207), which may be
by Benedetto. Benedetto, though, was probably responsible for
the execution of the painting, which can be dated to before July
1586 through its connection with (111v). It has the incoherence
of a number of paintings attributable to Benedetto from this
decade which include the *Christ with the centurion* from the
church of the Umiltà of about 1581, whose handling recalls that
of the *Entombment of Christ* in Geneva.[3]

(111) and (112) are striking testimonies to the care with which
Veronese prepared designs for execution by members of the
studio and in this case the head was used more literally in the
canvas than were the *Study of an apostle* (76) or the *Study of a
Negro boy* (54) in their respective paintings.

Fig 82 Workshop of Veronese, *Entombment of Christ*, Collection Musée
d'Art et d'Histoire, Geneva

NOTES

1 Monte Carlo 1966 intro. The mark was, however, only added in the late
eighteenth century, *see* London, Sotheby 9 July 1981, 132

2 Pignatti cat 189. *See* the excellent catalogue by M. Natale, *Musée d'Art et
d'Histoire, Genève, Peintures Italiennes du XIV au XVIII siècles* (Geneva,
1979), pp25ff. It was presented to Louis XIV in 1696, probably by Daniello
Marco Delfino, the papal Nuncio in Paris

3 Formerly in the Wengraf collection, London, Pignatti A154. The date
depends upon the description of the newly built tabernacle by F. Sansovino,
Venetia città nobilissima et singolare (Venice, 1581) pp98 a and b, and the
provenance upon that by M. Boschini, *Le Ricche minere della pittura Veneziana*
(Venice, 1674), Sestier Dorsoduro p23 as S. Mason Rinaldi established in the
Catalogue of Drawings by Jacopo Palma il Giovane, London, Sotheby 4 July
1977, 5

113   Costume-studies for the Oedipus Tyrannus of Sophocles

113 and 113v   Costume-studies for the Oedipus Tyrannus of Sophocles

Pen and ink

26.3 × 20.6 cm

LOCATION Paris, Ecole des Beaux-Arts Inv. 415

INSCRIBED with a series of accounts:

> 'debito del m[on]ete e prima stara delo pasato 1583 poi del fitto che deve pagar questo anno 84 e del mo . . . L[ire] 18 s[oldi] 12 del porco da . . . per . . . lira con ragion de II per stara doe forme 20 che a m.le stara 30 sporte'; in another hand: '1584', jo ellema lasa asier gahome gugelmo li biaveri per consegna con le giave in su il biaver del cortivo che laso stava formeni numero nonanto una adi 5 di ottobre. in su il biaver di casa ch las stera vinti di formento e serre di schala'; in another hand, probably G. B. Maganza: 'figlio della Regina', 'servitore', 'Regina', 'Dona de governo', 'fate tutte quatro', 'un . . . vecchio'; on the verso: 'Pagg.o, fatto', 'homo della guardia fatto', 'consiliero fatto', 'Sacerdote fanciulio nobile della Regina, fatto', 'un cieco vechio', 'fatto fanciulio innob, fatto'

PROVENANCE His de la Salle (Lugt 1333)

BIBLIOGRAPHY Tietze and Tietze-Conrat 2141; D. Rosand, 'Theater and Structure in the Art of Paolo Veronese', *Art Bulletin* 55 (1973), pp 217ff

Comparison of the series of accounts with Veronese's autograph letter in the Fondation Custodia of 1578 (Fig 87) shows them to be by Veronese. The top five lines of the inscription are by another hand and the inscriptions on the individual figures are by the same hand as that on the costume-study formerly in the Rudolf collection (Fig 85), presumably G. B. Maganza. They show that the drawing has been cut since the inscription on the recto mentioning an old man refers to a missing figure.

The Tietzes suggested that this drawing, in which individual figures are studied in isolation, might be a costume-study for the stage. The argument was taken a step further by Janos Scholz who connected a drawing in his collection of a blind man, presumably Tiresias, with the sketch on the bottom right of the verso of the present sheet (Fig 83). He linked this drawing with another in his collection (Fig 84) and a further sheet in the Yacovleff collection attributing them to G. B. Maganza. The early sources identified Maganza as responsible for the costumes of the inaugural production of the *Oedipus Tyrannus* in the Teatro Olimpico, Vicenza on 3 March 1585.[1]

113v   Costume-studies for the Oedipus Tyrannus of Sophocles

Fig 83   G.B. Maganza, *Study for Tiresias*, pen and ink and wash, Janos Scholz, New York

114 and 114v   Costume–studies for the Oedipus Tyrannus of Sophocles

Pen and ink and wash

21.3 × 30.3 cm

LOCATION Buckinghamshire, private collection

INSCRIBED

'Citadino di riputation', 'fatta / Donzela Serve[n]te', 'Una fia dela Reg[in]a fanciuletta', 'Un no[n]cio del Citta / Fatto', 'un no[n]cio forestiero', 'Un no[n]cio dila Citta giovane', 'Un Patro[ne] Vechio / Fatto', 'Un uomo nobile / Fato', 'Ellipo vechio / Creonte'; on the verso: 'Chreo[n]te di meza eta'; addressed: 'Al Cl.mo Sig.or il Sig.or Vettor Sora[n]zo mio S.e Patro[ne] Oss.mo Venetia in frezzaria in Cale del Caro'

BIBLIOGRAPHY Venice 1980 no 31; S. Mason Rinaldi, 'Veronese e Palladio: Studi di costume per L'Edipo Tiranno', *Per A. E. Popham, Consigli Arte* (Parma, 1981), pp 75–81

The drawing, which is clearly related to the better known sheet in the Ecole des Beaux-Arts (113), confirms that both were made by Veronese for the inaugural performance of Sophocles's *Oedipus Tyrannus* in the Teatro Olimpico, Vicenza on 3 March 1585.[1] Few other performances in this period would have required a cast of this scale. Oedipus had a guard of twenty-four archers dressed like those of the Sultan of Turkey, as well as pages and nobles, Jocasta was accompanied by her ladies in waiting, Creon had a suite to match his rank and there was a chorus of fifteen.[2]

The decision to choose the *Oedipus Tyrannus* in the recent translation of the Venetian Orsatto Giustiniani was first recorded in the minutes of the Accademia Olimpica in May 1584, although it must have been made earlier. On 6 May 1584 a number of committees were set up under Leonardo Valmarana, elected prince of the academy in December 1582, to supervise the production. They included one responsible for the design and materials of the costumes which had authority to spend and incur travelling costs.[3]

The connection does not mean, as it is possible to argue, that this and the related sheet in a private collection in Buckinghamshire (114) are by Maganza. Their handling of the pen and ink resembles that of many drawings of the 1580s, the *Studies for a Finding of Moses* in the Morgan Library (103), for instance, but the absence of the wash with which Veronese usually corrects and clarifies the design betrays the haste with which they were made. This communicated itself to Maganza, if as seems likely, he annotated this sheet since he crossed out the words: 'della Regina' in the inscription on the verso referring to the noble youth, whose identity he misunderstood.

NOTE

1   His observation was reported by L. Puppi, 'La rappresentazione inaugurale dell'Olimpico', *Critica d' Arte* 51 (1962), p 64 and note 57

114 and 114v   Costume-studies for the Oedipus Tyrannus of Sophocles (*see also* colour plate)

Fig 84   G. B. Maganza, *Study for a noble*, pen and ink and wash, Janos Scholz, New York

Fig 85   G. B. Maganza, *Costume-studies for two councillors*, pen and ink and wash, formerly C. R. Rudolf, London

Contemporary accounts of the production refer the costumes to Maganza, who, in a drawing in the Scholz collection (Fig 84), combined[4] the noble at the bottom right of the present sheet with the noble youth of the queen's suite on the verso of the Ecole des Beaux-Arts drawing (113v). He further based his study of a citizen of repute in the Yacovleff collection[5] on the figure at the top left of the present drawing. Maganza's responsibility for the costumes is further documented in the study formerly in the Rudolf collection (Fig 85)[6] which is pricked for transfer and includes colour notes for the costumes of two councillors, based on those of the *patrone vecchio* and the *noncio* of the present sheet. Maganza, who in his paintings had been influenced by Veronese[7] must, presumably with the approval of the Accademia Olimpica, have contacted Veronese for initial designs[8] which he then worked out for the seamstresses.

NOTES

1   This is shown by the references to Creon and Oedipus on the present sheet, which were noted by S. Mason Rinaldi whose article formed the basis for Julien Stock's entry in the 1980 Venice catalogue; comparison with Veronese's autograph letter of 1578 (Fig 87) suggests that the inscriptions are not by him

2   They are mentioned by a contemporary spectator, Filippo Pigafetta, who also refers to Maganza as the designer, Leo Schrade, *La Représentation d'Edipo Tiranno au Teatro Olimpico* (Paris, 1960), pp 47–49

3   D. J. Gordon, 'Academicians build a theatre and give a play: the Accademia Olimpica' (first published in 1966) in *The Renaissance Imagination* (Berkeley, 1975), pp 247–65

4   *See* under note 2 and L. Puppi, 'La rappresentazione inaugurale dell' Olimpico', *Critica d'Arte* 51 (1962), pp 65 and 66 and figs 13–15

5   Puppi fig 15

6   London, Sotheby 4 July 1977, 38. It clearly fits with the other sheets by Maganza and cannot, as Rinaldi 1981 suggests, be by Veronese

7   A. Venturi, *Storia dell'arte Italiana, IX la pittura del Cinquecento VII* (Milan, 1934), pp 110ff

8   There must be at least one more sheet with studies of Oedipus and his suite

115   Study for a Noli me Tangere (actual size)

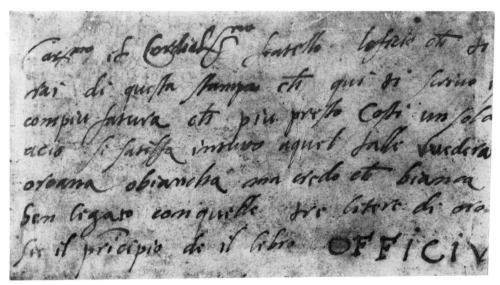

115v   Letter (actual size)

115   Study for a Noli me Tangere

Pen and ink
7.6 × 12.8cm

LOCATION Oxford, Ashmolean Museum Inv. P2 743
INSCRIBED 'P.C.V'; in another hand: 'Paolo Caliari Veronese';
   on the verso (115v) a fragmentary letter, probably by
   Benedetto Caliari
PROVENANCE Sir Joshua Reynolds (Lugt 2364); Douce
BIBLIOGRAPHY Tietze and Tietze-Conrat 2176 (school); Parker
   no743 (Veronese); Cocke 1973 p143

Like other drawings, notably that formerly in the Von Hirsch
collection (99), this was made on the back of a now fragmentary
letter:[1] 'Car.mo et Cordial.mo fratello loficio che si / rai di questa
stampa che qui si scrive / con pui fatura ch[e] piu presto costi un
sola / acio si sarissa insino a quel falle vedera / oroana o biancha
ma credo che bianca / ben ligato con quelle tre litere di oro / se il
pri[n]cipio di il libro OFFICIN'. It is concerned with having a
book printed and was probably sent to Veronese by his brother
Benedetto. Sir Karl Parker rightly returned the sheet to Veronese
since the rapid but sure handling is similar to that of the *Costume-
studies for the Oedipus Tyrannus* of 1584 (113, 114). This could
well be the date of the present sheet which was made in preparation for the *Noli me Tangere and Assumption of the Magdalen*
(Fig 86) executed by the workshop at the commission of Michele
Spavento for the main altar of S. Maria Maddalena, Treviso,
between 1576 and 1588.[2]

   The Christ in the drawing, striding forward with his right arm
upraised to greet the Magdalen,[3] anticipates the painting as does
the tombstone shown between him and the group which greets
him in poses far removed from those in the painting. Apparently
included in the group is St Jerome who witnesses the Magdalen's
Assumption in the upper part of the painting. This may also
have been shown on the present sheet before it was cut down.

Fig 86   Workshop of Veronese, *Noli me Tangere and Assumption of the
Magdalen*, S. M. Maddalena, Treviso

NOTES

1   Which Veronese turned upside down when he used it for the drawing

2   E. A. Cicogna, *Della Iscrizioni Veneziane. Raccolte ed illustrate* 4 (Venice,
1853), p231. Spavento had commissioned the *Virgin and the Child with an
unidentified saint and Michele Spavento* in S. Sebastiano from Veronese.
Pignatti 215 dates it 1578 when Spavento was first elected prior of S. Sebastiano.
The inscription around the border 'EMSME', referring to Spavento as a Frater,
would argue for a date before this, further borne out by the possibility, which I
originally doubted, that Spavento is shown on the right of the Treviso altar as
one of the two donors; the fuller beard, wrinkles, receding and greying hair of
the Treviso picture make him about twenty to twenty-five years older than in
the S. Sebastiano picture

3   The pose is deliberately differentiated from that of the smaller version in
Grenoble, which may be close in date to that in Treviso but is, I believe,
autograph, Pignatti A120

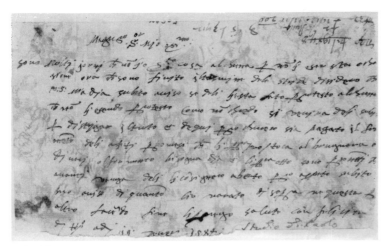

116v   Letter

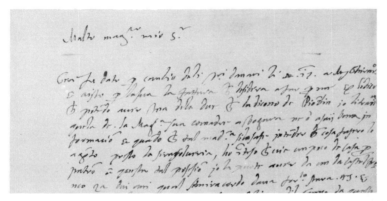

Fig 87   Detail of an autograph letter to Marcantonio Gandini, dated
28 March 1578, Fondation Custodia (Collection F. Lugt), Institut
Néerlandais, Paris

116   Studies for an Adoration of the shepherds

Pen and ink and wash

13.5 × 21.1 cm

LOCATION Berlin-Dahlem, Staatliche Museen KdZ 26 359

INSCRIBED The drawing is on the back of a letter dated 11 January
1584 (1585 Venetian style) which was sent, presumably to
Veronese, from Treviso (116v)[1]

PROVENANCE Marchese Jacopo Durazzo, Genoa

BIBLIOGRAPHY Von Hadeln pl 45; Tietze and Tietze-Conrat
2043; Oehler p 34; Pignatti 259 doc 65 (transcription of the
letter)

The letter on the verso (116v) reads: 'Magn.co S.or Mio Oss.mo /
sono molti jorni ch[e] no[n] ho s.to cosa alchuna p[er] non li esser
sta ocha / sione ora ch[e] sono finito il termine de li stride
disidero ch[e] / V.S. m' adia subito aviso se de la hasta fato p[er]
potesto alchuno / che no[n] li esendo p[er] potesto como no[n]
chredo si venira deli subi . . . / p[er] distrigar il tuto et de qui
prochurero sia pagato il for / me[n]to deli afiti p[r]omesi ch[e] li
stara venti toca al brugnora o / dinari o'l fornamento bisogna dia
et li sara otto sono prontti ch/avanti venga deli li co[n]segnero
a berto p[e]ro aspeto subito / suo aviso di quanto li o narato di
sopra ne questa per / altro face[n]do fine li prego saluti con
felicita di Treviso 19 Zener 1584', 'studi di Paolo' and a brief
series of sums at the top of the sheet, upside down, which
include 'f2 de Paulo 10/12 200'.

The fact that the letter came from Treviso argues against the
common view that it is by Veronese. Like the letter from
Marcantonio Gandini in Treviso of 1582 which Veronese used
for the sheet of studies formerly in the Von Hirsch collection
(99) the sketches on the recto seem to be on a letter that had been
sent him by one of his agents.

The drawing displays Veronese's magnificent sense of decoration in the positioning of the many *pentimenti* around the
central sketch of the *Adoration*. It cannot be related to any
surviving painting, although it may have been made to help the
workshop. The motif of the angels flying above the scene comes
from Veronese's own earlier *Adoration* now in SS. Giovanni e
Paolo.[2] The cow seen from behind but between the spectator
and the infant Christ, as well as Joseph's pose, derive from the
smaller version, also of the 1560s, from Mazarin's collection now
in a private collection in London.[3]

NOTES

1   It is by a different hand from that of the letter to Marcantonio Gandini
(Fig 87) of 20 March 1578 now in the Fondation Custodia, Paris J.5559 or of
that on the verso of the *Studies for a Baptism of Christ* in the Morgan Library
(125v)

2   Pignatti 158, *see* under (98) note 4

3   Pignatti 157; it was first mentioned as no 911 in the 1661 inventory of the
Mazarin collection, *Les Richesses du Palais Mazarin*, ed. G. J. de Cosnac (Paris,
1885), p 287 (with dimensions of 82 by 97 cm, as against those of 104 by 127 cm
of the canvas) and may have been no 18 in the De Conti sale, Paris, Boileau
15 March 1779 (dimensions of 82 by 92 cm)

116   Studies for an Adoration of the shepherds

117 Studies for a Coronation of the Virgin

Fig 88   *Coronation of the Virgin*, Gallerie dell'Accademia, Venice

117   Studies for a Coronation of the Virgin

117v   Studies for an Annunciation and decorative spandrel–figures

Pen and ink and wash

30.5 × 21 cm

LOCATION Oxford, Christ Church Inv.0341

INSCRIBED 'questo', 'basso', 'andrea', 'Pau', 'Dav';
in the centre a list:

	Giona	Giesue	
S.Jiopo	S.bastia	S.Lore[n]zo	S . . .
S.Franc.o	S.benedeto	S.antonio	
S.Paulo	S.andrea	S.Giacomo	
S.Giacobe	Davite	abra[hame]	moisse moise
stefan	bartol	agata	

'anton', 'F.m', 'S.agionto[?]', 'S.benedeto', 'S.Veronica[?]';
on the verso a series of numbers

PROVENANCE Sir Peter Lely (Lugt 2092); General Guise

BIBLIOGRAPHY Von Hadeln pls 38 and 39; Tietze and Tietze-
    Conrat 2128; Venice 1958 no41; London 1960 no565;
    Verona 1971 no64; Byam Shaw no793

The drawing, as Von Hadeln noted, is related to the great *Coronation* from the main altar of Ognissanti, now in the Accademia (Fig 88). This had presumably been completed by 21 July 1586, when the church was consecrated.[1] The list of saints shows how seriously Veronese set about combining the *Coronation* with an all-saints painting, an interest which must reflect that of the patrons. Even at this early stage in the design the saints are developed with a new freedom and sense of movement when compared with the *Allegory of Redemption* in the Metropolitan Museum (18), his first response to Titian's *Gloria*, the ultimate model for this treatment of an all-saints painting.

The first sketch of the Coronation, at the top of the sheet, is related to drawings for the *Coronation*, intended for the Sala del Maggior Consiglio (94, 95), where the Virgin is similarly shown from the side. In the next two sketches this changes and she is seen from the front with her hands crossed and God the Father and Christ behind in a grouping which, even when it is brought closer to the painting on the verso, shows a continued inventive response to Dürer.[2]

Fig 89   Follower of Veronese (Gabriele Caliari?), *Annunciation*, sold London, Sotheby 2 July 1958, 98

The rapid sketches at the top of the sheet are left without wash which is introduced from the middle onwards to clarify the central group, and is then worked out with greater precision on the verso. The wash is also used on many individual saints and whole groups lower down who recur in the painting. In the drawing they are not yet set on the triple band of clouds with the striking Tintorettesque play of light and shade which in the painting emphasises the New Testament figures in the foreground. The rapidly indicated *Annunciation* on the verso was made in preparation for the pair of organ shutters of that subject which reappeared recently (Fig 89). Although their early history is not recorded,[3] they may well be among the earliest works of Gabriele Caliari,[4] baptised 7 September 1568.[5] The two alternative decorative schemes involving superimposed pairs of spandrel-figures, one of which was developed in (111), could have been executed in preparation of a tabernacle, perhaps that mentioned by Boschini in Ognissanti.

NOTES

1   Pignatti A346; this view of it as a studio picture follows a long tradition among Italian scholars, but seems to me to seriously underestimate a great painting which had first been mentioned by F. Sansovino, ed. G. Stringa, *Venetia città nobilissima* (Venice, 1604), p190b with an account of the consecration of the church

2   The woodcut of the *Assumption and the Coronation of the Virgin*, Bartsch 7, no94

3   Pignatti A285 and 286; the curved tops shown on the drawing can just be made out in spite of the restoration

4   When sold London, Sotheby 2 July 1958, 98 they were attributed to Carletto; the attribution to Gabriele rests on the similarity in style and morphology of the Virgin's face with the *Virgin with St Anne and music-making angels* in the Capitoline Galleries (Fig91), although the *Annunciation* appears to be slightly less mature

5   Pignatti 255 doc35

117v   Studies for an Annunciation and decorative spandrel–figures

118   Study for St Herculanius visited by an angel

118   Study for St Herculanius visited by an angel

Wash on blue paper
29 × 12.8 cm

LOCATION Princeton, Art Museum Inv. 44–6
INSCRIBED 'paolo Veronese'; on the verso: 'P.n.o 35'
PROVENANCE Anon. (Lugt 2103a; sometimes identified as the Borghese collection);[1] Frank Jewett Mather, Junior (Lugt 1853a)
BIBLIOGRAPHY Rosand 1971 pp203–209; Gibbons no28

In spite of the old attribution, the drawing had remained among the anonymous sheets until Philip Pouncey suggested that it was by Veronese. David Rosand showed that it was made in preparation for the altar formerly in the church of Toscolano which was subsequently moved to the parish church of Maderno.[2] Although the altar was signed by Veronese, modern critics agree that it is by the workshop, perhaps Carletto, admitting, however, that Veronese may have been responsible for the initial design. That he was is, I believe, shown by a comparison with the *Study of St John the Evangelist* in Leningrad (43) drawn in a comparable technique over traces of grey chalk. The treatment of the saint's profile is similar to that of the angel in the present sheet as is the treatment of the hands in both drawings; the handling develops a new freedom comparable to that of the pen and ink sketches. This must be due to its late date. The parish priest of Toscolano, Giovanni Setti, had travelled to Venice in 1583 to sign contracts for three pictures for his church, but the *St Herculanius* was only ready by 10 May 1588, when the remains of the saint were moved to their new altar.[3] This drawing must then date from late 1586 or 1587.

NOTES

1   Monte Carlo 1966 intro. The mark was, however, only added in the late eighteenth century, *see* London, Sotheby, 9 July 1981, 132
2   Pignatti A169
3   G. Lonati, *Pieve e il Comune di Maderno* (Toscolano, 1933), pp18 and 14; most critics follow A. Morassi, 'Opere ignote o inedite di Paolo Veronese', *Bollettino d' Arte* 29 (1935–36), pp256–58 and refer the installation to 1587; Morassi, however, drew his documentation from Lonati

119   Study for Christ washing the apostles' feet

Fig 90   *Christ washing the apostles' feet*, Picture Gallery, Prague Castle

119   Study for Christ washing the apostles' feet

Pen and ink and wash
15.5 × 20.4 cm

LOCATION Berlin-Dahlem, Staatliche Museen KdZ 26 385
INSCRIBED 'il Sabelico e la instoria'
PROVENANCE Marchese Jacopo Durazzo, Genoa
BIBLIOGRAPHY Von Hadeln pl 43; Tietze and Tietze-Conrat
    2037; Oehler p 34; Neuman pp 290 ff

120   Studies for the Virgin with St Anne and angels, and an Adoration of the Magi

120v   Studies for a Christ washing the apostles' feet

Pen and ink and wash
15.7 × 21.7 cm

LOCATION Kassel, Staatliche Kunstsammlung Inv. 1123
INSCRIBED on the verso: 'studi di Paolo'
PROVENANCE acquired from a private collection in 1939
BIBLIOGRAPHY Oehler p 36; Neuman pp 290 ff; Cocke 1973 p 144

Both the Berlin sheet, which had been long known, and the verso
of that in Kassel were shown by Neuman to have been made
in preparation for the *Christ washing* (Fig 90) from the Duke of

Buckingham's collection in the Picture Gallery of Prague Castle.[1]
The sketches on the verso of the Kassel drawing are furthest
from the painting. Christ and Peter are to the right and the
remainder of the apostles are seated by the diagonal table in front
of the rich display of the family's crockery on the left. This is
elaborated in the Berlin drawing where one of the reclining
figures in the centre of the Kassel drawing is repeated and the
remaining apostles are now shown under the windows on the
right. Although the Berlin drawing has a scale at the bottom, no
doubt for transfer, it is still some way from the canvas. It also
includes another version of Peter preparing to have his feet
washed at the top next to the inscription, which is discussed
under (97).

The series of ten paintings, first mentioned in the Duke of
Buckingham's collection in 1635[2] is not documented. The conventional date of the 1580s is supported by the strong break in
quality between the autograph[3] and school paintings,[4] and by
the difference between the view-points. The autograph paintings
and the *Adoration of the shepherds*, which Veronese may have
supervised, were intended for a conventional height, while the
remaining five school paintings were intended to be hung high.
This suggests a change of plan, perhaps after Veronese's death.
The five school canvases appear to have been designed by the
workshop (as can be seen in the *Study of a woman's head* in the
Louvre (207)) which reworked and weakened earlier versions of
the same subjects.[5]

Fig 91   Gabriele Caliari, *Virgin with St Anne and music-making angels*,
Capitoline Galleries, Rome

The very free style of the drawings is close to that of the Fogg
Baptism of 1588 (125). The inclusion of a study for Gabriele
Caliari's *Virgin with St Anne and music-making angels* now in the
Capitoline Galleries (Fig 91)[6] confirms a late date for these
drawings. Gabriele, baptised in September 1568,[7] may have
begun painting with the *Annunciation* (Fig 89) which Paolo had
designed in 1586. The Rome painting, although perhaps cut down
at the top where the burst of light at which St Anne looks is missing,[8] is slightly bolder and more assured than the *Annunciation*.

The sketches for an Adoration of the Magi at the bottom of
the recto rework motifs that are common in Veronese's treatment
of this theme. The group of the magi kneeling to kiss Christ's
feet with a horse and squire behind recalls, in reverse, the
Adoration of the Magi by the workshop from the collection of the
Comte de Morville, now in a private collection, Switzerland.[9]

NOTES

1   Pignatti 306

2   R. Davies, 'An inventory of the Duke of Buckingham's pictures etc. at
York House in 1635', *Burlington Magazine* 10 (1906–1907), p 380

3   The division of hands is still an open question, but I follow Neuman's
position that, in addition to the *Christ washing*, the *Rebecca* in Washington, the
Christ with the woman of Samaria and the *Angel appears to Hagar* in Vienna,
are autograph, Pignatti 305, 302 and 303

4   The *Susanna and the Elders*, the *Flight of Loth*, the *Adoration of the
shepherds*, the *Christ and the centurion*, the *Christ with the woman taken in
adultery* and the *Esther before Ahasuerus* in Vienna, Pignatti 301, 304, 307 and
A383, A384, A388

5   *Compare* the Vienna and Louvre versions of the *Flight of Loth*, Pignatti
pls 661 and 662, although I consider the Louvre painting the late autograph
original, and the Vienna version the studio replica; the Louvre picture was first
mentioned by L. F. Dubois de Saint-Gelais, *Description des tableaux du Palais
Royal* (Paris, 1727), p 381; as W. Buchanan, *Memoirs of painting* 1 (London,
1824), p 136 noted it did not come to England with the rest of the collection but
remained in France to pass to the Louvre

6   *See* Cocke 1973 p 144 and note 46; the attribution rests on its similarity to
the signed version in Liettoli published by Dr L. Crosato-Larcher, 'Per
Gabriele Caliari', *Arte Veneta* 18 (1964), pp 174–75

7   Pignatti 255 doc 35 of 7 September 1568

8   The drawing suggests that the Capitoline Galleries version came first and
was followed by the larger Liettoli version where God the Father was added at
the top

9   Pignatti A299

120   Studies for the Virgin with St Anne and angels, and an Adoration of the Magi

120v   Studies for a Christ washing the apostles' feet

121   Study for a Crucifixion

121v   Study for a Circumcision of Christ

121 Study for a Crucifixion

121v Study for a Circumcision of Christ

Pen and ink and wash

29.5 × 20 cm

LOCATION Cambridge, Mass., Fogg Art Museum Inv. 1936.64
INSCRIBED on the verso: '381 Aqueta'
PROVENANCE Zaccaria Sagredo;[1] Philip Hofer, by whom
presented in 1936
BIBLIOGRAPHY Venice 1939 p 218 no 6; Mongan and Sachs
no 203; Tietze and Tietze-Conrat 2162 (workshop);
Birmingham, Alabama 1972 p 43 (citing the views of the
Tietzes); Pignatti 186 (citing the views of the Tietzes)

The drawing has always been viewed as the preparatory sketch
for the *Crucifixion* in the Louvre (Fig 92).[2] The doubts about its
attribution first voiced by the Tietzes have persisted even though
most critics regard the picture as autograph. The Tietzes noted
the painting's connection with that in the Accademia, from
S. Nicolò dei Frari,[3] which had probably been completed by
1582 when the church was consecrated.[4] They argued that the
arrangement of the crosses in the Louvre version was unsatisfac-
tory and that it was therefore a replica executed by the workshop
who prepared their design in the present drawing.

The demand for Veronese's work certainly led to the production of reduced replicas, often by the workshop, but sometimes
by Veronese himself.[5] Like most modern critics, I find the
Louvre picture an autograph version of the larger canvas whose
passionate drama is reduced to fit the smaller scale. The present
drawing, although it differs from the painting in many details,
has the clarity associated with the transfer of the design to the
canvas.

The *Circumcision* on the verso (121v) must have been for a
painting which no longer survives, although it may also have
been developed, in now lost drawings, by a member of the
workshop (perhaps Benedetto), into the *Presentation* in a private
collection in England.[6] The grand frame behind the figures in
the upper sketch recalls that of the *Consecration of St Nicholas*
from S. Nicolò dei Mendicoli (Fig 69).

The Tietzes' doubts about the recto, which I do not share,
may be a response to the looseness of the handling caused in part
by Veronese's desire to clarify his design. The extreme freedom
also fits with the *Studies for a Baptism* in the Fogg Museum,
dated February 1588 (125).

Fig 92   *Crucifixion*, Musée du Louvre, Paris

NOTES

1   Ballarin *Studi* (1971) pp 144ff
2   Pignatti 186; it was first mentioned as no 36 in the LeBrun inventory of
1683, *see* F. Engerand in N. Bailly, *Inventaire des tableaux du roy, rédigé en
1709 et 1710* (Paris, 1899), p 93 no 10
3   Pignatti 293
4   F. Cornaro, *Notizie storiche delle chiese e monasteri di Venezia* (Padua, 1758),
p 368
5   Another notable example is the small *Pietà* in Boston, Pignatti A31
6   Cocke 1974 pp 24ff. *See also* under (207) note 2

Fig 93   P. Monaco, *Engraving of the Christ healing at the pool of Bethesda*, then in the Grassi collection, Venice, from *Raccolta di 112 stampe di pitture* (Venice, 1763), no 67

122   Study for a Christ healing at the pool of Bethesda

Pen and ink and wash

15 × 20.2 cm

LOCATION formerly London, Mond

INSCRIBED 'Piedi n.ro 8'

PROVENANCE London 1953 no 6

BIBLIOGRAPHY Borenius 1930 p 106; Tietze and Tietze-Conrat 2103; T. Borenius and R. Wittkower, *Catalogue of the Collection of Drawings by the Old Masters formed by Sir Robert Mond* (London, n.d.), p 66

When Borenius published this fine drawing, which I know only from a reproduction, he connected it with the *Christ healing* on the organ shutters of S. Sebastiano completed in 1560.[1] The Tietzes rightly objected that it was for a smaller picture without the foreshortening of the shutters. Their suggestion that this drawing, which fits in style with the Fogg *Baptism* (125) at the end of Veronese's career, might have been used by the workshop is supported by the apparent connection with the group of figures around Christ and with the colonnade in the painting of this subject, which Pietro Monaco engraved in the Grassi collection, Venice (Fig 93).[2] The version from the Grassi collection has not survived. Its fanciful architecture, with a round temple behind Christ to replace the colonnade which was lengthened and switched to the opposite side, suggests an elaboration of the ex-Mond sheet by the workshop, which lost the logic of the initial design.

NOTES

1   Pignatti 252 doc 18

2   Here reproduced in reverse from *Raccolta di 112 stampe di pitture* (Venice, 1763), no 67. It may well be the version formerly in the Caliari collection described by Ridolfi p 357 giving its length as ten feet (*circa* 300 cm) and attributing it to Carletto and Gabriele. Another (?) smaller version was no 24 in the 1682 inventory, Gattinoni p 2, with dimensions of 7 by 11 quarte, about 120 by 187 cm

122   Study for a Christ healing at the pool of Bethesda (actual size)

123   Studies of figures and architecture

123   Studies of figures and architecture

Pen and ink and wash
25.1 × 19.4 cm

LOCATION Rotterdam, Museum Boymans-Van Beuningen
Inv. I 41
PROVENANCE Sir Joshua Reynolds (Lugt 2364); Thomas Bankes
(Lugt 2423); H. de Triqueti (Lugt 1304); F. Koenigs (Lugt
1023a); acquired by D. G. van Beuningen in 1940
BIBLIOGRAPHY Von Hadeln pl 34; Tietze and Tietze-Conrat
2074

The medieval buildings in the background suggest, as the Tietzes
noted, those that occur in the backgrounds of various Martyrdom
scenes[1] without, apparently, being connected with any surviving
painting. This is also true of the figures which recall those in the
Sheet of studies in Kassel (91) for the Sala del Maggior Consiglio
as well as those in the *Study for a Christ healing at the pool of
Bethesda* (122) and are hence datable to the 1580s.

NOTES

1   *See*, for example, the *Martyrdom of St Afra* from S. Afra, Brescia, Pignatti
A33; the saint's remains were moved to a new site in September 1580, and the
vault of the nave bore the date of 1583, suggesting a date in the 1580s for this
picture which, although signed, was executed by the workshop, P. Brognoli,
Nuova guida per la città di Brescia (Brescia, 1826), pp 93–105

124   Studies for a Rachel and Jacob at the well

124 Studies for a Rachel and Jacob at the well

Pen and ink and wash
26 × 17.5 cm

LOCATION Salzburg, Studienbibliothek Inv. VI 489
BIBLIOGRAPHY J. Meder, 'Weitere Venezianische Zeichnungen
der Salzburger Studienbibliothek, Paolo Veronese Studien
zu Rachel am Brunnen', *Die Graphischen Künste* (1933),
pp 25–26; Venice 1939 p 220 no 8; Tietze and Tietze-Conrat
2144; T. Crombie, 'Jacob and Rachel at the Well by
Veronese', *Apollo* 1 (1972), pp 11–115

Meder related the drawing to the painting of the same subject
recently on the London market (Fig 94).[1] This he rightly identified as that formerly in the Muselli collection (where it was
attributed to Tintoretto), although he knew it only from engravings.[2] This elegant drawing, the breadth of whose handling
reveals Veronese's late style,[3] shows that this attribution is
wrong. The painting is badly damaged which makes judgement
difficult, but I believe that it is unlikely to be autograph. This
can be seen by a comparison of Rachel bending forward (for no
apparent reason) with Loth's daughter in the *Flight of Loth*[4] in
the Louvre where the same pose fits into the composition and is
realised with an incomparable flow in the costume.

The Tietzes suggested that Veronese may have used a small
model to enable him to see the Rachel from front and back, but
the fluency with which the pose has been worked out makes this
unlikely.

Fig 94   Workshop of Veronese, *Rachel and Jacob at the well*, sold London,
Sotheby 12 December 1973, 111

NOTES

1   Pignatti 309; that it was the version mentioned by Ridolfi p 320 is confirmed
by its appearance in the 1662 Muselli inventory where its length is 2½ braccia,
about 150 cm (the canvas measures 150 by 170 cm), G. Campori, *Raccolta di
cataloghi e d'inventarii inediti* (Modena, 1870), p 184
2   By Claude Mellan and Peter Schenk
3   It is close to the Fogg *Baptism* of 1588 (125)
4   Pignatti 304, as a copy, *see also* under (119) note 5

125   Studies for a Baptism of Christ (actual size)

125v Letter

125 Studies for a Baptism of Christ

Pen and ink and wash
20 × 18 cm

LOCATION Cambridge, Mass., Fogg Art Museum
Inv. 1924.101

INSCRIBED on the draft of a letter on the verso (125v) which is
dated 4 (?) February 1588 (1587 Venetian style):[1]
'Io come homo c[he] mai manca della sua parolla / no[n] mi
ama[n]to p[er] fare qual ch[e] o' pottuto p[er] darli / satisfacio[n]e e
tralascio op[e]re da importanza / ch[e] mi collia farli meno e percio
de cio ch[e] co[n] . . . / mia tirato a farli no[n] vollio i p[er] che
senza / stima[n]do li omini p[er] il suo pezzo ma li vido con / p[er]
qua[n]to digno e posso. E li tuto cio che altre [ebbi?] p[er] elli
p . . . / cupato un pezzo de te[m]po e ch[e] . . . di questo [?] / no[n]
sia Patroni ch[e] li acertavo [acetero?] vole[n]tieri. P[er]ch[e] i . . . /
il te[m]po no[n] li ama[n]cava ricapitto e co[n] magior / Cosa prima
la mi avese ma[n]dato senzaltro da me r . . . / li avria ogni paze e
tra[n]quilita di animo m . . . / hora ch[e] altri li piacia cussi, io no[n]
posso di . . . / sento ch[e] facio piasti ma da leser suo ch[e] de
5 du[cati] / ma il si te[n]ga p[er] sicuro ch[e] no[n] avro un p[er]do
no / che la li avera a lui altri tanti come atri si gr . . . / qual pri.mo la
date p[er] d[ucati] 15, nel Junia p . . . / mil cento la mil charita ese
la [?] mia criava o . . . / me servira ad altro, con ch[e] con nostro
cuore all . . . / me racoma[nd]o di Venezia li 4 Fevraio 1587'

PROVENANCE Denman W. Ross, by whom presented in 1924

BIBLIOGRAPHY Mongan and Sachs no 205; Tietze and Tietze-
Conrat 2052; Birmingham, Alabama 1972 p 46; Pignatti cat 4
and p 295 doc 68

126 and 126v Studies for a Baptism of Christ

Pen and ink and wash
21.9 × 9.4 cm

LOCATION Edinburgh, National Galleries of Scotland
Inv. D4945

INSCRIBED in another hand on the verso: 'B.AB n.o 123',
'P.Ver.so 3.1'[2]

PROVENANCE Sir Joshua Reynolds (Lugt 2364), his sales
London, Christie 11 March 1795, 57 and H. Phillips
5 March 1798, 1461 (one of four);[3] sold London, Sotheby
26 June 1969, 8

BIBLIOGRAPHY Verona 1971 no 73

The drawing now in Edinburgh was rightly linked with that in
the Fogg Museum on its reappearance in 1969. The purpose for
which they were produced remains a more open question. Agnes
Mongan initially suggested a link between the Fogg drawing and
the *Baptism* in the sacristy in the Redentore.[4] She withdrew this
argument after Portogruaro had established that it dated from
1561[5] and replaced it with the suggestion that it was for the
Baptism in the second chapel in the right nave of the Redentore,
executed and signed by Veronese's heirs.[6] Here too the facts
tend to weaken the connection with the present drawings. Although Ridolfi said that the commission was given to Veronese,
the frames were only finished by 16 May 1588, a month after his
death, when the paintings were probably commissioned to be
ready with the church on 24 May 1590.[7] The heirs elaborated
upon the present drawing in the *Baptism* where they were also
influenced by Tintoretto in the landscape background and in the
reflections through which Christ's feet can be seen in the water.

The *Baptism* in Raleigh, North Carolina (Fig 96) is, as Pignatti
noted (although he included it among the early works),[8] close to
the group on the top right of the Fogg drawing. Here Christ
half-kneels with his hands crossed on his chest while the Baptist
stands frontally to pour the water over him from the right. The
Edinburgh sheet is rather more distantly related to the *Baptism*
in Brunswick[9] where the Baptist, on the left of the canvas, bends
to scoop water out of the Jordan in a pose suggested on the
bottom of the recto. The pronounced *contrapposto* of Christ,
although not his stork-like pose, recalls the verso.

The crude rather mechanical quality of the surfaces of the Brunswick painting excludes the possibility that it could have been painted by Veronese at any stage of his career. Although I only know the Raleigh painting from a photograph, I believe that it too is by a member of the workshop.[10] This can be seen by comparing it to the *Baptism* from S. Giovanni in Malta, Padua,[11] now in Palazzo Pitti (Fig 95).[12] Here the figures are realised with a splendid certainty not found in the Raleigh canvas and are set off by the screen of trees which have none of the irrelevant detail of the Raleigh and Brunswick *Baptisms*.

The Pitti *Baptism* has not been considered in the context of the Fogg and Edinburgh drawings because it was related, wrongly in my view, to the sketch of a Baptism on the recto of the *Studies for a Venice enthroned*, from the late 1570s, in a New York private collection (82).[13] It combines the Christ kneeling with his arms crossed in front of his chest from the upper right of the Fogg sketch with the half-crouching Baptist underneath. The painting thus sums up the variations which begin with both the Baptist and Christ standing on the left of the Fogg sheet and continue first with the Baptist standing and Christ half-kneeling and then with Christ standing in the water and the Baptist half-kneeling on the bank of the river. This theme predominates on the recto of the Edinburgh drawing, but is once again reversed on the verso.

Fig 96   Workshop of Veronese, *Baptism of Christ*, North Carolina Museum of Art, Raleigh

NOTES

1   The transcription was made by Mongan and Sachs and corrected in minor details in Pignatti

2   Ballarin *Arte Veneta* 1971 p92 suggests that this may be the mark of William Gibson

3   This was noted in the 1969 Sotheby sale catalogue

4   Pignatti 114

5   'Il tempio . . . del Redentore', *Rivista di Venezia* (1930), p 198

6   Ridolfi 354

7   Portogruaro pp 164 and 185

8   Pignatti 4

9   Pignatti 3

10   It could be Alvise dal Friso, *compare* it especially with the earlier *St Nicholas in glory* from S. Nicolò dei Mendicoli (Fig 51)

11   Ridolfi p 318, moved to S. Maria Iconia, P. Brandolese, *Pitture sculture architetture ed altri cose notabili di Padova* (Padua, 1795), p 230. It was removed to Venice whence it was sent to Florence on 28 April 1816, G. Ludwig, 'Dokumente über bildersendungen von Venedig nach Wien in den Jahren 1816 und 1838', *Jahrbuch der Künsthistorischen Sammlungen des allerhöchsten Kaiserhauses* 22 (1901), Beiheft p 11 and XX

12   Pignatti 221

13   This was suggested by J. Byam Shaw, *Old Master Drawings* (1934), pp 22–24; under (82) it was proposed that it might prepare the *Baptism* in a private collection in London, Pignatti 220

Fig 95   *Baptism of Christ*, Palazzo Pitti, Florence

126 and 126v   Studies for a Baptism of Christ (actual size)

127   Studies for St Pantaleon heals a sick boy

Fig 97   *St Pantaleon heals a sick boy*, S. Pantaleone, Venice

127   Studies for St Pantaleon heals a sick boy

Pen and ink and wash
21.4 × 24.5 cm

LOCATION Paris, Musée du Louvre Inv. RF 38 928

INSCRIBED '1587 / 1159 / 428'; on the verso, which is laid down,
is a letter, and in a later hand: 'Carletto Caliari', 'C.C.n.o 7'
and on the mount: 'C.C. n.o 30'

PROVENANCE Anon. (Lugt 2103a; sometimes described as the
Borghese collection);[1] private collection, France; acquired in
1982

BIBLIOGRAPHY Bacou 10

This splendid series of sketches reveals the first plan for the fully
autograph *St Pantaleon heals a sick boy* in S. Pantaleone (Fig 97).
It was commissioned as the main altarpiece by Bartolommeo
Borghi, the parish priest, in 1587,[2] a date which is included in
the inscription. That all the sketches were made in preparation
for the same scheme is underlined by a detail in the group of the
saint with Borghi at his feet supporting the boy possessed by the
devil. St Pantaleon holds the martyr's palm in his right hand and
looks up. That his gaze was fixed on the apparition of the Virgin
and Child is shown by the earlier sketch on the left of the sheet
with the setting lightly indicated by the background. In the
painting the martyr's palm is borne aloft by an angel to symbolise
the triumph of Christian medicine. In the initial scheme shown
in the drawing, this was to have been emphasised by the heavenly
appearance of the Virgin and Child, crowned by angels. The
main altar in the church, from which it was removed in 1732,
must have been too small to accommodate the vertical emphasis
implicit in this design. The marvellous certainty with which
Veronese clarified his design with the wash continues a mode
that he had used earlier in the *Studies for a Last Supper and a
Rape of Ganymede* (110).

NOTES

1   Monte Carlo 1966 intro. The mark was, however, only added in the late
eighteenth century, *see* London, Sotheby's 9 July 1981, 132

2   Pignatti 168

Attributed Drawings

This section includes twenty-six drawings which have a reasonable claim to be by Veronese, although their attribution cannot be demonstrated with absolute certainty. They include a large group of chalk studies, by their nature the most elusive and difficult of all drawings to classify. Even where they can be related to paintings, as with (149), (150) and (151), there is always the possibility of studio intervention. Some, presumably earlier, chalk studies continue the interest in life-studies of the *Study of legs* (2v) and the *Study of a seated nude* (55). These include the *Study of the head and right arm of a man* (139), the *Study of a head and hands* (142) and the *Study of a standing woman* (137). The precision with which the figure is rendered in this latter drawing resembles the *Study of a seated woman seen from behind* (131), which is generally given to Benedetto, but which appears to be beyond him, *see* (207).

This sense of observation is shared by three portrait-like studies which had old attributions to Veronese's son Carletto (128, 136, 143). Their directness of vision finds a parallel with the portraits which Veronese included in his canvases and is very different from the *Study of the head of a woman* (217), which has a better claim to be by Carletto. This same interest is underlined by the *Study of a seated Negro eating* (135) whose genre-like realism has raised doubts about its attribution. Comparison with two other studies of Negroes, which were made with paintings in mind (54, 67), justifies the view that (135) is by Veronese.

Other drawings of heads (130, 146) share the more generalised approach of the remaining studies in this group, where invention replaces observation (132, 140, 141, 146, 147, 152, 153). This is true even where, as with the *Study of a lady with a fan* (147), they were clearly made in preparation of a now lost painting.

None of the preparatory drawings included in this section (129, 134, 144, 148) relate to any surviving paintings, although one (148) may have been made in preparation for the long lost façade frescoes of Casa Cappello. All the sheets in this group have their closest stylistic parallels with early drawings (3, 4, 5, 6, 8). Their presence in this section underlines our comparative ignorance about Veronese's drawings from the first two decades of his career, before the mid-1560s.

128   Study of a monk looking upwards (actual size)

128   Study of a monk looking upwards

Black, red and white chalk on blue paper
13.5 × 12.3 cm

LOCATION Berlin-Dahlem, Staatliche Museen KdZ 26377
INSCRIBED 'Carletto C'; on the verso: 'C.C. no. 52'; on the
   mount: 'C.C. no. 50'
PROVENANCE Anon. (Lugt 2103a; sometimes identified as the
   Borghese collection);[1] sold London, Sotheby 1 July 1971, 30

As with other drawings with the same provenance, I believe that
the old attribution to Carletto undervalues the present sheet.
This can be seen by a comparison with the *Study of the head of
a woman* in Stockholm (217), probably by Carletto. Although
clearly a portrait, similar in type to that of Fra Bernardo Torlioni
as St Francis in the main altar of S. Sebastiano,[2] the fluent
graphic handling recalls the more generalised *Study of an apostle*
of 1575 (76), the *Study of young man* (136) and *Study of a bearded
man* (143).

NOTES

1   Monte Carlo 1966 intro. The mark was, however, only added in the late
eighteenth century, *see* London, Sotheby 9 July 1981, 132
2   Pignatti 132

129   Studies for the Martyrdom of a saint

129   Studies for the Martyrdom of a saint

Pen and ink and wash over traces of grey chalk on blue
   prepared paper
28 × 19.3 cm

LOCATION Budapest, Museum of Fine Arts Inv. 1995
INSCRIBED in chalk: 'R'
PROVENANCE Poggi (Lugt 617); Esterházy (Lugt 1965);
   O. Képtár (Lugt 2000)
BIBLIOGRAPHY Venice 1965 no 33

This magnificent drawing, which had an old attribution to
Veronese, was later catalogued as by an anonymous Venetian
artist. It was returned to Veronese by Philip Pouncey whose
attribution was followed in the 1965 exhibition. At the top of the
sheet a soldier gestures in horror as another lowers a dead saint
to the ground with a hooded priest standing behind. Although it
cannot be connected with any surviving *Martyrdom* the contrast
between the large figure in the foreground and the main group
further back, as well as the dramatic gestures, recall the *Martyrdom of Sts Primus and Felician*, painted for Santa Maria, Praglia
by 1562.[1] The firm handling of the pen is similar to drawings of
the 1550s, the *Study of Count Giuseppe da Porto with his son
Adriano* in the Louvre (4), for instance.

NOTE

1   Pignatti 126; the date derives from a manuscript of 1803 in the Museo
Civico, Padua. Placidus II da Marsistica was prior in 1552–54 and again from
1559 to 1562 when he commissioned Tintoretto's *Feast in the house of Simon*
also in Padua and dated 1562; *see* A. Ballarin in *Arte Veneta* 22 (1968), pp 39ff

130   Study of a woman's head

130   Study of a woman's head

Black and white chalk on blue-grey paper
26.6 × 18.7 cm

LOCATION Chicago, Art Institute Inv. 1962.809

PROVENANCE Sir Thomas Barlow, his sale London, Colnaghi
1936, 64; Springell, their sale London, Sotheby 28 June
1962, 21

BIBLIOGRAPHY Tietze and Tietze-Conrat 2097 (for the Pomona
in Cracow); Washington 1974 no 22; Pignatti under A55;
Joachim and McCullagh no 26

This fine drawing, which has long been associated with the
Study of a woman's head in the Uffizi (14), is close in its handling
to the *Study of a standing woman* in a private collection in
London (137). Like that drawing it may be early since the firm
bold contours contrast with the more fluent lines of the 1575
Study of an apostle (76). In spite of a general resemblance, the
drawing is not close enough to the *Pomona* in Cracow to have
been made for the painting, which Pignatti has attributed to
Benedetto, and in quality clearly contrasts with the *Studies*
attributed to Benedetto and Carletto in Stockholm (217) and
Paris (207).

131 Study of a seated woman seen from behind (*see also* colour plate)

131 Study of a seated woman seen from behind

Grey and white chalk on grey-blue paper
34.6 × 23 cm

LOCATION Florence, Galleria degli Uffizi Inv. 1715 F
INSCRIBED 'Ti 2'
BIBLIOGRAPHY Von Hadeln pl 50 (Veronese); Venice 1939 p 229
no 17 (Veronese); Tietze and Tietze-Conrat A 2059 (not
Veronese); Venice 1957 under no 27 (Benedetto); Oberhuber
and Walker under no 106 (inferior to the Scholz *Lady with
a fan*)

The old attribution to Titian was rightly challenged by Von
Hadeln whose attribution to Veronese was followed by Pallucchini
in the 1939 Venice exhibition, where he suggested that it could
be late. This was rejected, together with the attribution, by the
Tietzes, who knew few independent chalk studies, and compared
it to the *Modello for the Venice triumphant* (88). The subsequent
appearance of the *Study for the Portrait of a member of the
Soranzo family* (77) and the *Study of a lady with a fan* (147)
strongly supports Von Hadeln's attribution of the present drawing
which seems to me to be by the same hand as the Scholz *Study of
a lady with a fan* (147). Any differences[1] are a function not of
quality but of date. The *Study of a seated woman seen from behind*
(131) is perhaps less free than the Scholz drawing and the
handling of the folds recalls that of the *Study of legs* of 1548 (2v).
A woman seen from behind cannot prepare a portrait in the
usual way and her pose anticipates the compositional scheme of
Fasolo's frescoes in the salone of Villa Caldogno which date from
1570 to 1572 (when Fasolo died).[2] Fasolo's work appears to
reflect the lost frescoes by Veronese and Zelotti in the Villa da
Porto-Colleoni at Thiene which were described by Ridolfi:[3]
'dipinse a fresco nella Sala in partimenti, divisi da figure a chiaro
scuro, huomini e donne, che giuocano ad una tavola; un convito
di Cavalieri e di Dame; una Caccia & una ballo; e nella cornice,
bambocci e festoni' and of which we may see an echo in the
present drawing.[4]

NOTES

1 They are exaggerated by the oblique lighting of the photograph which
emphasises the grain of the sheet
2 L. Crosato, *Gli Affreschi nelle ville Venete del Cinquecento* (Treviso, 1962),
pp 100 ff
3 Ridolfi p 299; the frescoes were mentioned by Vasari 6 p 370; for the surviving
decoration, *see* Crosato pp 194 ff
4 The use of contemporary costume contrasts with that in Zelotti's fragment
of a concert, now in the Museo di Castelvecchio, Verona, painted for Villa
Foscari in 1561, Crosato pp 137 ff and pl 59

132   Study of a cloak

132   Study of a cloak

Black and white chalk on blue paper
29 × 22 cm

LOCATION France, private collection

INSCRIBED in another hand: 'Paulo V.', 'P.n.o 65', 'Paolo'; on the
    verso; 'P n.o 84'

PROVENANCE Anon. (Lugt 2103a; sometimes identified as the
    Borghese collection)[1]

This magnificent study with its vivid exploitation of black and
white chalk on the blue paper reveals the creative freedom with
which Veronese worked in this medium. His first sketch showed
a man standing with his cloak wrapped around him, his right
arm at his side. This was transformed into a partial rear-view by
changing the top line of the cloak, the addition of the shoulder
and out-stretched right arm together with hatching in the main
part of the cloak to cover up the arm hanging down at his side.
The pose is similar to that of the man striding away from Vice in
the *Honor et Virtus post Mortem Floret*, now in the Frick collection, but probably painted for Albrecht V of Bavaria by 1567.[2]
In view of the differences, it cannot be treated as the preparatory
sketch for the painting, and no-one wears a comparable cloak in
any surviving painting. The drawing resembles other certain
costume-studies (60, 67).

NOTES
1   Monte Carlo 1966 intro. The mark was, however, only added in the late
eighteenth century, *see* London, Sotheby 9 July 1981, 132
2   Pignatti 245 and Cocke *Pantheon* 1977 pp 120–25

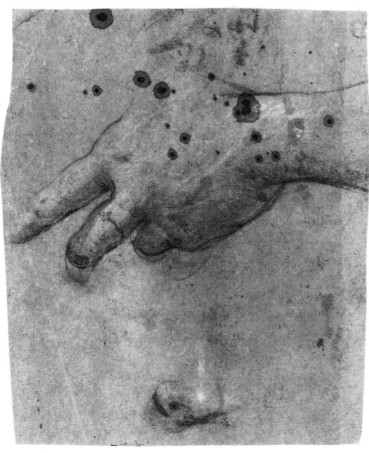

133 Study of a hand and a nose

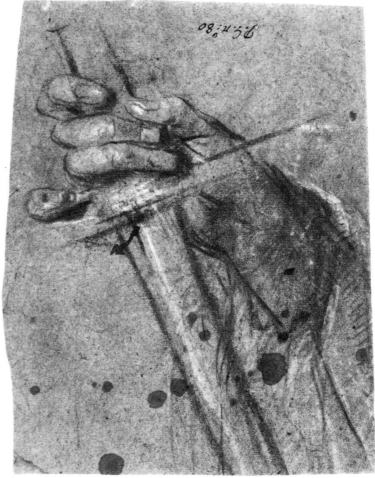

133v Study of a hand and a sword

133 Study of a hand and a nose

133v Study of a hand and a sword

Black and white chalk on blue prepared paper
22.4 × 17.5 cm

LOCATION France, private collection
INSCRIBED in a later hand on the verso: 'P.G.n.o 80'
PROVENANCE Anon. (Lugt 2103a; sometimes described as the Borghese collection)[1]

The traditional attribution to Veronese seems to be confirmed by its resemblance to other studies from life (2v, 143). On the verso, observation is combined with an inventive response to the drapery which falls from the wrist over part of the sword. Such detailed observation must have been made in preparation of a painting (but both recto and verso differ from any to survive)[2] and also in its firm use of contoured outlines from the *Study of hands* by Carletto Caliari now in Cleveland (168).

NOTES

1 Monte Carlo 1966 intro. The mark was, however, only added in the late eighteenth century, *see* London, Sotheby 9 July 1981, 132

2 *See*, for example, the sword held by the assassin in the *Martyrdom of St Mennas*, now in the Prado, Pignatti 280

134   Studies for an Ecce Homo (actual size)

134   Studies for an Ecce Homo

Pen and ink and wash

11.5 × 19.1 cm

LOCATION Frankfurt, Städelschen Kunstinstitut Inv. 4461

INSCRIBED with the remains of an old and probably autograph
   inscription on the top left where the drawing has clearly
   been cut

BIBLIOGRAPHY *Stift und Feder* 1926 pl 34 (Veronese); Tietze and
   Tietze-Conrat 2068 (perhaps Veronese)

The Tietzes were inclined to accept the present drawing, known
to me only from a photograph. They were uncertain about the
subject matter, which may well be an early attempt to fuse a
Christ crowned with thorns with an *Ecce Homo*.[1] The slumped
Christ with a figure kneeling in front of him together with the
architecture in the background recalls Titian's *Crowning of
thorns* from S. Maria delle Grazie in Milan.[2] The gesturing
figure in the background, who is repeated in the centre of the
sheet, is Pilate trying to persuade the Jews to release Christ.[3]
The kneeling figure is repeated next to the full-length study of
Pilate where Veronese introduces a bearded man whose gesture
shows that he recognises Christ as his saviour.

NOTES

1   *Compare* (3) and (6); according to Ridolfi, Veronese painted two versions of
the *Ecce Homo*, p 322 in the Lanzi collection, Bergamo, and p 335 in the Ruzini
collection, Venice; another single figure *Ecce Homo* was in the Vendramin
collection, T. Borenius, *The Picture Gallery of Andrea Vendramin* (London,
1923), pl 18 no 1

2   C. Hope, *Titian* (1980), pp 98–99 and pl 48

3   His costume is similar to that in Tintoretto's *Ecce Homo* in the Albergo of
the Scuola of San Rocco, De Vecchi no 167S

135   Study of a seated Negro eating (actual size)

135   Study of a seated Negro eating

Black and white chalk on brown prepared paper
15.5 × 19 cm, a strip has been added on the right

LOCATION formerly London, Russell

PROVENANCE A. G. B. Russell (Lugt 2770a), his sale London,
Sotheby 9 June 1959, 13

BIBLIOGRAPHY Von Hadeln, *Vasari Society* (1927), pl 4
(Veronese); Tietze and Tietze-Conrat A2109 (Bolognese
school)

The drawing, which I know only from a photograph, was
published by Von Hadeln who rightly described it as a study
from nature. He attributed it to Veronese on the basis of its
resemblance to the *Studies of Negroes* in the Lehman collection
(68) and the Louvre (54). The Tietzes argued that it did not
resemble those two drawings and that its realism was Bolognese.
Certainly the subject anticipates that of Annibale Carracci's
Bean-eater, but the handling is so very different from that of
Bolognese drawings and similar, as Von Hadeln argued, to the
two *Studies of Negroes* that the attribution to Veronese seems to
me plausible.

136   Study of a young man and of a right hand (actual size)

136   Study of a young man and of a right hand

Black, red and white chalk on blue prepared paper
14.6 × 11.6 cm

LOCATION London, private collection
INSCRIBED 'Carletto', 'C.C. n.o 48'
PROVENANCE Anon. (Lugt 2103a; sometimes identified as the
    Borghese collection);[1] sold London, Sotheby 1 July 1971,
    27 (Carletto)
BIBLIOGRAPHY Venice 1980 no 58 (Carletto)

The old attribution to Carletto is by the unreliable hand responsible for the attribution to Carletto of the *Studies for the four
Allegories of Love* now in the Metropolitan Museum (78). This
attribution has been supported by a comparison with the *Portrait
of Paolo Paruta* in the British Museum, which also has an old
attribution to Carletto[2] but which the Tietzes had attributed to
Leandro Bassano.[3] The artist responsible for the *Portrait of
Paolo Paruta* had a concern for textures and contrasts, of hair
and beard for example. This differs from the more pictorial
handling of the present sheet whose combination of strong
outline and fluid modelling are similar to that of the *Study of a
Negro* in the Lehman collection, New York (68).

NOTES

1   Monte Carlo 1966 intro. The mark was, however, only added in the late
eighteenth century, *see* London, Sotheby 9 July 1981, 132
2   Inv. 1946–17–13–23, *see* under (217) notes 1 and 2
3   No 210

137   Study of a standing woman

137   Study of a standing woman

Black chalk on greenish paper heightened with white
34.2 × 26.7 cm

LOCATION London, private collection

BIBLIOGRAPHY London 1952 no 15; Stockholm 1962–63
   no 237; Manchester 1965 no 393; London 1965 no 36;
   Venice 1980 no 32

The attribution of this study was suggested by J. Byam Shaw in
the Colnaghi catalogue. It is justified by a comparison with the
Study of a seated man of 1548 (2), which was not known when
this sheet was first discovered. The handling of the present study
is more fluent and graceful without approaching the boldness of
the later *Study for Liberality* (70),[1] suggesting a date in the 1550s.

The figure is not related to any surviving painting but the gesture
with which she places her right hand on her bosom occurs
throughout Veronese's work. Her appearance in a petticoat anticipates the Herse in the *Hermes, Herse and Aglauros* in the Fitzwilliam Museum, Cambridge,[2] which I believe to date from the
1560s.[3] There the *décolleté* is further emphasised to show her
left breast in a way that must have been impossible in a study of a
model.

NOTES

1   This must rule out the suggestion of a late date made in the Stockholm
catalogue before the discovery of the *Study for Liberality*
2   Pignatti 247
3   It fits with the Frick *Omnia Vanitas* which I believe to be mentioned in a
list drawn up by Jacopo Strada in the 1560s, Cocke *Pantheon* (1977) pp 120ff

138 Study of a woman with outstretched arms (actual size)

138 Study of a woman with outstretched arms

Grey chalk on greyish paper

20 × 20 cm

LOCATION London, private collection

PROVENANCE Colin Agnew, sold London, Christie 7 July 1981,
 30

The drawing has faded and the paper is foxed, especially on the lower right. The handling is unusual because of the absence of the white heightening used in the other chalk studies. Although weaker than other certain drawings, it is similar to the *Study of a seated man* of 1548 (2) in its dense but even cross-hatching and may be an early drawing. The pose, evidently studied from a model in the studio, may have been intended for a saint presenting a donor to the Holy Family,[1] although it cannot be connected with any surviving painting. In contrast with the comparatively undressed *Study of a standing woman* (137), which must be close in date, she wears a full costume of undercoat and ruff with a waistcoat on top.

NOTE

1 *See*, for example, the St Justina in *The Holy Family with Sts George, Justina and a donor (Girolamo Scrocchetto?)* in the Louvre, Pignatti 130. Probably of 1551–54, *see* (34) note 3

Fig 98   *Transfiguration of Christ* (detail), Duomo, Montagnana

139   Study of the head and right arm of a man

Black chalk on blue paper heightened with white
17.5 × 26.5 cm

LOCATION London, Sotheby 25 June 1970, 4
INSCRIBED on the verso: '85'
PROVENANCE Anon. (Lugt 2103a; sometimes identified as the
Borghese collection)[1]

Although the drawing is unusual among Veronese's chalk studies
in its concentration upon the sleeve and arm, the drapery recalls
that of the *Study of a seated man* (2) and the firm contour with
which the arm is drawn brings to mind the *Study of legs* on the
verso of that drawing of 1548 (2v). This suggests a dating in the
1550s, which is strongly supported by the fact that it appears to
have formed the starting-point for the gesture of the upper of the
three apostles in the *Transfiguration* of 1556 in Montagnana
(Fig 98).[2] In the painting the apostle is bearded, his head is
thrown back further and his arm is lower. In spite of these
differences the present drawing may well be the life-study in
which Veronese established the apostle's upward gaze and outstretched right arm with his sleeve rolled back. This view of its
possible function gains weight from the appearance of the *Study
of a seated woman* in the Louvre (65), which is a chalk study of a
comparable detail in the later *Rape of Europa*. The rather
abstract handling of the head which is treated as an oval formula
by contrast with the attention paid to the arm and the sleeve fits
with that of the head in the *Study of a seated nude* (55).

NOTES

1   Monte Carlo 1966 intro. The mark was, however, only added in the late
eighteenth century, *see* London, Sotheby 9 July 1981, 132
2   Pignatti 45, *see also* (1) note 5

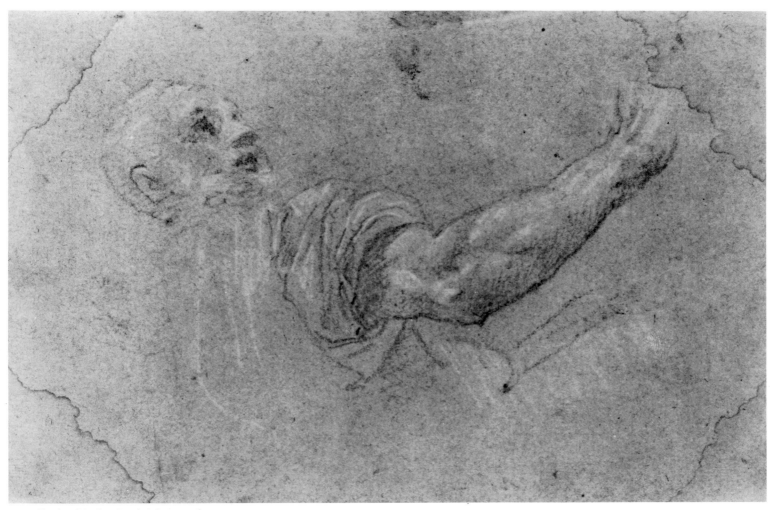

139   Study of the head and right arm of a man

140   Study of drapery

140   Study of drapery

Black and white chalk on blue paper
31.1 × 19.5 cm

LOCATION London, Sotheby 25 June 1970, 3
INSCRIBED in another hand: 'di Paolo Veronese'

The drawing was in the same sale as the *Study for the Portrait of
a member of the Soranzo family* (77). It appears to be by the same
hand as that *Study* but cannot be related to any painting. There
is a distant relationship to the Christ in the *Christ with the sons of*
Zebedee from the main altar of S. Giacomo, Murano at the end of
the 1570s. In the altar, now in the Burghley collection at Stamford,[1]
Christ is reversed and the drapery of his garments is more
complex with a cloak over his tunic-like robe. The connection
with the *Study for the Portrait* (77) makes a dating in the 1570s
possible, although the present drawing is very different from the
Study for Liberality now in the British Museum (70).

NOTE

1   Pignatti A289, wrongly as school

141 Study of a standing man

141 Study of a standing man

Black and white chalk

20.3 × 30.5 cm

LOCATION London, Sotheby 25 June 1970, 5

INSCRIBED in another hand: 'di Paulo Veronese'; on the
   verso: '404'

There are enough similarities between the handling of the
present sheet and of the *Study of a kneeling magus* of 1573 (67), to
support the old attribution to Veronese. The function for which
it was made is unclear since the pose recalls, in reverse, that of
Agostino Barbarigo in the portrait in Cleveland.[1] The half-
length format of the present drawing is not found in Veronese's
portraits and it may, as Sotheby's suggested, have been done in
preparation for a figure behind a parapet, like those in the
background of the *Peter of Amiens exhorts Doge Vitale Michele*
(Fig 63).

NOTE

1   Pignatti 172, establishing through the copy in Washington that it has been
cut down

142   Study of a head and hands

142   Study of a head and hands

Black chalk heightened with white

13.5 × 21.2 cm

LOCATION London, Sotheby 25 June 1970, 6

The first drawing on the sheet was the lightly indicated head, the lower part of which has been cut off. The sheet was then turned ninety degrees for the study of the hands, the right hand appears to hold a book while the left hand holds a stick or baton. Sotheby's were understandably tentative about the attribution to Veronese. Comparison to the *Study of legs* (2v) on the verso of the 1548 *Study of a seated man* (2) and the contrast with the

bolder hatching of the *Study of hands* in Cleveland (168), which has an old and apparently reliable attribution to Carletto Caliari, suggest that it is autograph.

The drawing is not related to any painting but the right hand is not dissimilar to that which God the Father rests on his leg in the 1555 *Coronation of the Virgin* in the sacristy of S. Sebastiano.[1]

NOTE

1   Pignatti 39; the right hand is less similar but comparable to that of the executioner with a staff in the *Martyrdom of Sts Primus and Felician* from Praglia, now at the Museo Civico Padua, probably of 1562, Pignatti 126 and (129) note 1

143   Study of a bearded man (actual size)

143   Study of a bearded man

Black, red and white chalk
14.2 × 12.6 cm

LOCATION London, Sotheby 1 July 1971, 31
INSCRIBED 'Carletto C'; on the verso: 'C.C. no. 51'; on the
    mount: 'C.C. no 56'
PROVENANCE Anon. (Lugt 2103a; sometimes identified as the
    Borghese collection)[1]

As with the *Study of a young man* (136) in the same sale, the old
attribution to Carletto appears misleading. It is not by the same
hand as the *Portrait of Paruta* in the British Museum[2] nor the
Study of the head of a woman in Stockholm (217) but it is similar
to the *Study of a Negro* in the Lehman collection (68) and the
Study of a monk looking upwards now in Berlin (128).

   Although not related to any painting, it corresponds to the
portrait heads that Veronese included in his religious paintings,[3]
which must be based upon comparable but now lost drawings.

NOTES

1   Monte Carlo 1966 intro. The mark was, however, only added in the late
eighteenth century, *see* London, Sotheby 9 July 1981, 132
2   Inv. 1946–17–13–23, *see* under (217) notes 1 and 2
3   *Compare* it with the self-portrait in the *Marriage feast at Cana* in the
Louvre, Pignatti pl 376

144   Study of St George and the dragon (actual size)

144   Study of St George and the dragon

Pen and ink

8.8 × 5.4 cm

LOCATION London, Sotheby 26 June 1969, 9

INSCRIBED on the verso: '23', 'P. Veronese' and also with the
    indication of the Reynolds sale 1461/3 and another sale
    inscription: '2/22 the three I.I.O. no. 1716'

PROVENANCE Sir Joshua Reynolds (Lugt 2364), his sales
    London, Christie 11 March 1795, 52[1] and Phillips 21 March
    1798, 1461/3

In this slight but spirited drawing St George is lightly indicated
on his horse as he fights the dragon with his long spear. The
dragon who dies expressively with a splendidly curled tail was
the main concern of the drawing being shown in an earlier
version next to St George. Such a drawing is difficult to date but
the handling has much in common with that of the *Study for the
Triumph of Mordechai* in Berlin of 1556 (6), and the design which
is here shown in an early stage, may have formed part of the
inspiration for the artists of the drawings, wrongly attributed to
Veronese, in the Louvre (210) and the Uffizi (172).

NOTE

1   As: 'St George with the Holy Dragon'

145   Study of a kneeling priest (actual size)

145   Study of a kneeling priest

Black and white chalk
19.5 × 14 cm

LOCATION formerly London, Springell .
PROVENANCE sold London, Sotheby 28 June 1962, 22

Although this study cannot be related to any surviving painting its style is developed from the *Study of a seated man* of 1548 (2) and therefore appears to be attributable to Veronese.

146   Study of a man's head

146   Study of a man's head

Black and white chalk on grey-blue paper
26.5 × 19.8 cm

LOCATION New York, Janos Scholz
BIBLIOGRAPHY Scholz 1976 no 62

The handling of this boldly modelled study conforms with that of the *Study of a woman's head* in Chicago (130) and like that sheet may well date from the 1550s, especially since Veronese's chalk studies become more portrait-like with the *Study of a Negro boy* in the 1560s (54) and more painterly with the *Study of an apostle* in the 1570s (76).

147   Study of a lady with a fan

147   Study of a lady with a fan

Black and white chalk on blue paper
26.2 × 17.6 cm

LOCATION New York, Janos Scholz
INSCRIBED on the verso:[1] 'La Cremesa-Ver-Tin', 'Acqueta 487',
   'I.T.N. 30'
PROVENANCE Zaccaria Sagredo; Anon. (Lugt 2103a; sometimes
   identified as the Borghese collection);[2] Michon
BIBLIOGRAPHY Venice 1957 no 27; Oberhuber and Walker
   no 106

This drawing, which is related to the earlier *Study of a seated woman seen from behind* in the Uffizi (131), is similar to the *Study for the Portrait of a member of the Soranzo family* of the mid-1570s (77). Like that sheet it is a costume-study for a now lost portrait comparable to the *Portrait of a woman with a handkerchief* in Munich.[3]

NOTES

1   There is a *Study of a woman's head* on the verso of which, unfortunately, no photograph is available at present
2   Monte Carlo 1966 intro. The mark was, however, only added in the late eighteenth century, *see* London, Sotheby 9 July 1981, 132
3   Pignatti 451

148   Studies of Diana and of decorative figures

148   Studies of Diana and of decorative figures

Pen and ink and wash over traces of red chalk (at the top of the sheet)

23 × 20.4 cm

LOCATION Paris, Musée du Louvre Inv. 1,105

INSCRIBED '33' and '35'; on the mount by P.J. Mariette: 'Domenico Passignano, Ecole Florentine'

PROVENANCE P.J. Mariette (Lugt 2097, his mount); Thomas Hudson (Lugt 2432)

The correct attribution to Veronese was first pointed out by J.Q. van Regteren-Altena, although it is at present classified with Veronese's studio drawings. This hesitation must reflect the restrained quality of the penmanship, which, however, resembles that of the drawings from the 1550s (9, 12). At the top left of the sheet is a vigorous sketch of Diana who is studied with her right arm raised above her head in four further sketches, one of which shows a niche. The remaining three sketches of decorative over-door figures recall those at Villa Barbaro, Maser.[1]

This combination of decorative elements recalls Ridolfi's description of the façade decoration of Palazzo Erizzo, quoted under (12), where Diana with her dog is said to embody spring and there are two slaves above the doorway.[2] Roseline Bacou has noted a connection between the present drawing and the small canvas of *Diana* now in Leningrad.[3] This is true but not as close as with Veronese's preparatory drawings for his own painting. The Leningrad canvas is one of a group by Alvise dal Friso,[4] which must derive from the earlier fresco prepared in the present drawing.

NOTES

1   *See* Pignatti pls 275, 306, 307 and 324
2   A *Diana* was also described on the façade of Casa Cappello, Venice by M. Boschini, *Le Ricche Minere della pittura Veneziana* (Venice, 1674), Sestier S. Polo, p4. The frescoes were first described by Vasari 6 p369 with a fuller account by Ridolfi 322 and 367 who attributes the lower figures to Veronese, the upper to Zelotti
3   Pignatti 155
4   *See* (165)

149   Studies of a man and a woman

149   Studies of a man and a woman

Black and white chalk on blue prepared paper
30.4 × 18.4 cm

LOCATION Paris, Musée du Louvre Inv. RF 38 930
INSCRIBED by a later collector: 'P.n.o 49'
PROVENANCE Anon. (Lugt 2103a; sometimes described as the
   Borghese collection);[1] private collection; acquired in 1982
BIBLIOGRAPHY Bacou 2

Bacou noted the relationship of the drawing with two figures on
the balcony in the background of the *Feast in the house of Simon*,
now in Turin, most probably of 1560.[2] I find this convincing but
comparison with the other autograph chalk studies (65, 71, 73)
reveals a decorative treatment of the white heightening not usual
in Veronese's drawings.

NOTES

1   Monte Carlo 1966 intro. The mark was, however, only added in the late
eighteenth century, *see* London, Sotheby 9 July 1981, 132
2   Pignatti 93

150 Studies of armour

150 Studies of armour

Black and white chalk on blue prepared paper
23 × 20.2 cm

LOCATION Paris, Musée du Louvre Inv. RF 38 934
INSCRIBED by a later collector on the verso: 'S.P.n.o 55'; on the
    mount: 'S.P.N.o 31'
PROVENANCE Anon. (Lugt 2103a; sometimes identified as the
    Borghese collection);[1] private collection; acquired 1982
BIBLIOGRAPHY Bacou 5

As with the *Studies of a suit of armour* in Berlin (51) no close
connection with any surviving painting can be established for
this sheet, although Roseline Bacou tentatively related it to that
at Mars's feet in the *Mars and Neptune* on the ceiling of the Sala
del Collegio.[2] The contrast with the Berlin study as well as with
the other chalk costume-studies (64, 67, 73) suggests that for
once the unidentified collector may have been correct in suggesting
that it was by the studio.[3]

NOTES

1 Monte Carlo 1966 intro. The mark was, however, only added in the late
eighteenth century, *see* London, Sotheby 9 July 1981, 132
2 Pignatti 192
3 The 'S' presumably refers to the scuola

151   Studies of a standing man

151   Studies of a standing man

Black and white chalk on blue paper
17.5 × 29.5 cm

LOCATION Paris, Musée du Louvre Inv. RF 38 932
INSCRIBED by a later collector on the mount: 'P.n.o 57'
PROVENANCE Anon. (Lugt 2103a; sometimes described as the
    Borghese collection);[1] private collection; acquired in 1982
BIBLIOGRAPHY Bacou 3

Bacou suggested that the three sketches on the left of the sheet
were made in preparation of Alexander, distinguished by his red
all'antica armour, in the *Family of Darius before Alexander* now
in the National Gallery.[2] He points to his companion who wears
contemporary parade armour. He must be Hephaestion who had
been greeted as Alexander by the defeated family of Darius, and
was in turn studied in the next of the five sketches (the second
from the right). This hypothesis is possible, but the absence of
any indication of costume in a preliminary drawing is unusual, as
is the execution of this stage of the design in chalk rather than
pen and ink and wash. The handling, most notably of the legs, is
also freer and looser than is usual with Veronese's chalk studies.

NOTES

1   Monte Carlo 1966 intro. The mark was, however, only added in the late
eighteenth century, *see* London, Sotheby 9 July 1981, 132
2   Pignatti 163

152   Study of drapery

152   Study of drapery

Black and white chalk on blue paper
30 × 18 cm

LOCATION Paris, Musée du Louvre Inv. RF 38 933
INSCRIBED by a later collector: 'P.V.'; on the verso: 'P.N.o 66'
PROVENANCE Anon. (Lugt 2103a; sometimes described as the
    Borghese collection);[1] private collection; acquired in 1982
BIBLIOGRAPHY Bacou 8

This fine study cannot be connected with any surviving painting.
The certain combination of the black and white chalk on the blue
paper and the masterly handling of the drapery resemble other
drapery studies attributable to Veronese (140, 141).

NOTE

1   Monte Carlo 1966 intro. The mark was, however, only added in the late
eighteenth century, *see* London, Sotheby 9 July 1981, 132

153   Study of drapery and of a man wearing a hat (actual size)

153   Study of drapery and of a man wearing a hat

Black and white chalk on brown paper
16.5 × 18 cm

LOCATION Paris, Musée du Louvre Inv. RF 39 034
INSCRIBED by a later collector on the verso: 'P.N.o 59'
PROVENANCE Anon. (Lugt 2103a; sometimes described as the
    Borghese collection);[1] private collection; acquired in 1983

This fine drawing resembles the *Study of a seated nude* (55) in its
use of brown rather than blue paper. The handling appears to be
autograph and to be similar to (139), although like (152) it cannot
be related to any surviving painting.

NOTE

1   Monte Carlo 1966 intro. The mark was, however, only added in the late
eighteenth century, *see* London, Sotheby 9 July 1981, 132

Rejected Drawings

No list of rejected attributions can ever be complete, but I believe that the present one includes the most important drawings which have been wrongly attributed to Veronese. Confusion may have started because Veronese followed traditional workshop practice in training his son, Carletto, who copied a number of his father's drawings (Figs 53 and 103). Carletto clearly benefited from the process, for after his father's death he provided drawings for a number of commissions which were carried out by Veronese's heirs (*see* under 188).

Carletto's active role in the workshop contrasts with the comparative obscurity of his uncle Benedetto, to whom only a small number of drawings can be tentatively attributed (185, 189, 207, 212). Benedetto contrasts with another prolific artist, who appears to have had access to Veronese's workshop and whose drawings, beginning with the *Study of the Virgin and Child with Sts John the Baptist and Louis of Toulouse* in Chatsworth (165) have often been confused with those of Veronese. They range from finished drawings like that at Chatsworth, to rapid brush sketches (205), but all share an awkwardness and flatness that contrasts with the certainty of the autograph drawings. They look back almost programmatically to Veronese's work in the 1550s, a taste which makes it all the more surprising that, as is argued under (165), they can be attributed to his nephew, Alvise dal Friso, who was born in Verona *circa* 1554.

The preliminary sketches attributed to Carletto, Alvise dal Friso and Benedetto reveal their study of Veronese's late drawings, without equalling his sure sense of decoration or ability to project forms in space. These failings are shared by other drawings in this section, many of which reveal a later generation of artists who were attracted to the greater freedom and more dynamic manner of Palma Giovane.

Although there will always be room for disagreement, the survival of so many rapid preliminary sketches makes it easier to separate the autograph drawings from the rejected attributions. This is also true of the chalk and *chiaroscuro* drawings, although the disappearance of so much of the material means that here one must be more cautious. In these cases, too, the criteria differ from that used for the preparatory drawings. Comparison, for instance, of the *Study of an apostle* (76), which has an old but misleading attribution to Carletto, with the *Study of the head of a woman* (217) underlines the painterly freedom of the former drawing, which I believe to be by Veronese, and the comparative stiffness of the latter sheet, which is probably by Carletto. The contrast holds good for other chalk studies and for a number of *chiaroscuro* drawings (157, 162, 210), lacking the marvellous spontaneity with which Veronese brushed in white heightening. The differences go beyond this, as in the pen and ink sketches, for the rejected drawings lack the sure sense of positioning figures in space that is found in the autograph drawings.

Some of the mistaken attributions in this section have a long critical history. This is understandable since most collectors would have known only a comparatively limited number of autograph drawings. Their enthusiasm, however, helped preserve Veronese's drawings and so have made this catalogue both possible and necessary.

154 Copy of the Martyrdom of St Lawrence

154v Study of a woman sewing

Pen and wash (recto); pen and wash over red chalk (verso)
15.5 × 9.5 cm

LOCATION Amsterdam, Rijksmuseum[1] Inv. 1981, K. 10
INSCRIBED on the verso: 'paolo Veronese'
PROVENANCE J. Schmidt-Degener
BIBLIOGRAPHY J. Schmidt-Degener, 'Portraits peints par
Rembrandt', *L'Art Flamand et Hollandais* 19 (1913),
esp. pp 180–81; Tietze and Tietze-Conrat A2158

Schmidt-Degener published the drawing, when in his collection, as an autograph Veronese. He argued that the *Woman sewing* on the verso influenced Rembrandt's *Study of Saskia van Uylenburch* of 1639 in Stockholm. This may well be correct, for although not by Veronese, it is an interesting preparatory sketch unlike the recto, which the Tietzes rightly recognised as a contemporary copy from the fresco of the *Martyrdom* in S. Sebastiano.

NOTE
1 On loan from the Rembrandthuis, Amsterdam, since 1971

155 Copy of the Victorious Horatius condemns his sister to death

Pen and ink and wash on blue paper heightened with white
34.2 × 25.9 cm

LOCATION Amsterdam, Rijksmuseum Inv. 1953; 322
INSCRIBED 'da Paolo'; on the verso a series of colour notes
PROVENANCE W. Argoutinsky-Dolgoroukoff (Lugt 2602d);
acquired in 1953
BIBLIOGRAPHY Paris 1962 no 118 (Veronese); Ballarin *Arte
Veneta* 1971 p 112 (Benedetto)

156 Copy of Mucius Scaevola before Porsenna

Pen and ink and wash on blue paper heightened with white
43.2 × 25.9 cm

LOCATION Amsterdam, Rijksmuseum Inv. 1953; 323
INSCRIBED 'da Paolo'; on the verso a series of colour notes
PROVENANCE W. Argoutinsky-Dolgoroukoff (Lugt 2602d);
acquired in 1953
BIBLIOGRAPHY Paris 1962 no 118 (Veronese); Ballarin *Arte
Veneta* 1971 p 112 (Benedetto)

The Rijksmuseum has now understandably abandoned the view that this pair of sheets is by Veronese in favour of the older opinion that they are copies. They record two of the subjects frescoed by Benedetto on the courtyard of Palazzo Mocenigo at San Samuele which were described by Ridolfi.[1] The victorious Horatius is about to condemn to death his sister for mourning her husband, one of the Curatii whom her brother had just slain in battle. Mucius Scaevola appears before King Porsenna, on the left edge of the sheet, and thrusts his hand into the fire, a scene also known through a copy by a different artist at Munich.[2]

Ridolfi explicitly referred to the frescoes as painted in grisaille, which conflicts with the detailed colour notes on the back of the Amsterdam sheets. Although Ridolfi may have been right it seems more likely that the copies record the original appearance of the frescoes which had faded by Ridolfi's day.

NOTES
1 Ridolfi p 359
2 Inv. 8723. A further scene, *The Roman hostages before Porsenna*, is recorded in a drawing in a private collection, France, by the artist responsible for (155) and (156). It measures 34.5 by 27 cm

157 Study of two palm trees

157 Study of two palm trees

157v Study of a ceiling

Black chalk on blue prepared paper heightened with white
25.7 × 18.8 cm

LOCATION Amsterdam, Rijksmuseum Inv. 1981:34
PROVENANCE J. Dupan (Lugt 1440); J. Q. van Regteren-Altena
BIBLIOGRAPHY Tietze and Tietze-Conrat 2026; Paris 1962
no 121

This has long been admired for the masterly study of the palm trees on the recto, while the weaker drawing on the verso has never been reproduced or identified. This is unfortunate for it raises serious questions about the recto since it relates to the window section of one of the vaults in S. Giovanni in Valletta on which Mattia Preti began work in 1661.[1] The drawing indicates the cornice in front of which sits the Knight Templar on the left who points to the *Ecce Agnus Dei* in the vaulting above. His companion is drawn in front of the window whose glazing is shown, rather than on the right of the bay as in the fresco, and

157v   Study of a ceiling

the angels are related to those who hover above the heavy cornice holding the shield of the Knights. It is not surprising that the drawing has never been connected with Preti, for this use of white heightening over chalk does not, as far as I can see, occur in his drawings. These are generally chalk studies of individual figures realised with great certainty and strength.[2] The differences from the finished window vault suggest that here, as in the related sheet in the Ashby collection in the Vatican,[3] an unknown artist had access to now lost drawings by Preti.

It is possible, although rather unlikely, that a later artist used the recto of a Veronese for a version of Preti's design, since there is a contrast between the masterly study of the palm trees and the more awkward handling of the verso. This, however, is due to the difference between a carefully worked out drawing and a freely sketched copy. The same artist may have been responsible for both sides of the sheet since the difference stems from the contrast between the finished chalk underdrawing of the recto and the much freer handling of the verso. In both, the white heightening is established with firm even strokes which are very different from the broken strokes of the autograph *chiaroscuro* drawings which resemble the uneven scumble in the highlights of Veronese's paintings.

NOTES

1   V. Mariani, *Mattia Preti a Malta* (Rome, 1929), pl 19
2   *See* the study for the right-hand saint in the Ashmolean Museum, Oxford, repr J. Anderson, *Arte Veneta* 27 (1963), p 293 fig 421
3   D. Bodart, *Dessins de la collection Thomas Ashby à la Bibliothèque Vaticane*, (Città del Vaticano, 1975), as Mehus. Bodart's identification of the artist as Mehus is not borne out by the comparison which he suggests to the Mehus drawings in the Uffizi. These differ in medium, handling and in being copies after sixteenth- rather than seventeenth-century decoration

158   Study for the Death of the Virgin

Fig 99   Carletto Caliari, *Study of Cupid and Psyche*, pen and wash, Staatliche Graphische Sammlung, Munich

Fig 100   Carletto Caliari letter to Paolo Veronese, verso of Fig 99

158   Study for the Death of the Virgin

Pen and ink and wash over grey chalk heightened with white
19.8 × 24.6 cm

LOCATION Amsterdam, J. Q. van Regteren-Altena
BIBLIOGRAPHY Amsterdam, Rijksprentenkabinet, *Italiaanse Tekeningen uit een Amsterdamse Collectie* (1970), no 55

This is the preparatory sketch for the grisaille of this subject, one of a set of five, which decorated the organ shutters in S. Antonio, Torcello.[1] The drawing, which is reversed, includes only eight apostles instead of the twelve shown in the canvas as well as differing in detail. Veronese's altar from the church, *St Anthony Abbot enthroned* (Fig 17) now in Milan,[2] was probably painted in 1570 when the altars were ready for gilding.[3] The organ shutters are later since the *Annunciation* derives from that sent to Philip II of Spain in 1583,[4] and modern critics agree that it is by the workshop.

The grisailles are the most attractive part of the later decoration but comparison of the, admittedly much earlier, autograph grisailles in the scrolls of the ceiling of the sacristy of S. Sebastiano and those in the rooms of the Consiglio dei Dieci in the Palazzo Ducale[5] suggest that they were executed by the workshop. The comparatively finished character of the present sheet suggests that it might be a copy after a lost drawing by Veronese who could have been responsible for their design. The graphic handling, with its characteristic treatment of the eyes, fits with Carletto's drawings as represented by the *Study for the Holy Family with Sts John the Baptist and Catherine* in the British Museum (Fig 101).[6] The schematic way in which the pen outlines the figures in the *Death* finds a precedent in the *Study of Cupid*

and Psyche in Munich (Fig 99) which is on the back of a letter by Carletto to his father identifying the recto as a preparatory sketch for his frescoes in Poisolo (Fig 100).[7]

Carletto certainly prepared the main altar from S. Antonio, the *Adoration of the Magi*, now in the Brera,[8] in a drawing in Besançon.[9] His responsibility for the main altar and possibly for the organ grisailles from S. Antonio, extend the date of the commission to after 1588, when Veronese died. Carletto is not identified by modern critics as one of those responsible for the execution of this scheme. This may well be right for a letter by Benedetto Caliari to Giacomo Contarini refers to a picture which he had drawn, Carletto laid in and Gabriele painted.[10]

NOTES

1   Pignatti A300–A306
2   Pignatti A186, wrongly, in my opinion, as school and overlooking the documentation published by Gallo
3   R. Gallo, 'Cinque Quadri Ignoti del Veronese alla Mostra di Venezia', *Ateneo Veneto* 125 (1939), p 200 notes the decision to 'dorare' the main altars on 5 February 1570: Gallo was responsible for the rediscovery of the grisailles from the altar
4   Pignatti A78, wrongly, in my opinion, as school
5   Pignatti pls 47–52 and cat 39
6   Discussed under (160) and (188)
7   Inv. 34850, pen and wash, 18.5 by 24 cm. There appears to be no justification for the doubts voiced by Tietze and Tietze-Conrat 2206. For the history of the destruction, *see* L. Crosato, *Gli Affreschi nelle ville Venete del Cinquecento* (Treviso, 1962), pp 168–69; that the letter is addressed to Veronese suggests a date in 1587 or 1588
8   Pignatti A183
9   Tietze and Tietze-Conrat 2160, wrongly connecting it with the version in Lyons (Fig 65)
10   P. Caliari, *Paolo Veronese, sua vita, sue opere* (Rome, 1888), pp 177–78

159   Study of Cephalus and Procris

Wash on blue prepared paper heightened with white
17.4 × 19.6 cm

LOCATION Berlin-Dahlem, Staatliche Museen KdZ 5072
BIBLIOGRAPHY Tietze and Tietze-Conrat 2033 (workshop)

Although the drawing differs from the painting of this subject
now in Strasbourg[1] in minor details, the introduction of a dog on
the right and the omission of the spear, it is, as the Tietzes noted,
not by Veronese. Their suggestion that it formed part of the
working material of the shop, although possible, is unlikely since
it is by an otherwise unidentified artist and appears to be a
variation on the painting. This had been produced shortly before
1584 together with the *Venus and Adonis* now in Madrid, and
remained in Venice with its companion until its purchase by
Velazquez in 1650.[2]

NOTES

1   Pignatti 251, with an erroneous provenance
2   The provenance was established by M. Lorente Junquera, 'Sobre Veronés
en el Prado', *Archivo Español de Arte* 42 (1969), pp 235–43

Fig 101   Carletto Caliari, *Study of the Holy Family with Sts John the Baptist
andfcatherine*, pen and wash over grey chalk, British Museum, London

160   Study of a Supper at Emmaus

Pen and ink over grey chalk on grey-blue paper
27.3 × 35.8 cm

LOCATION Berlin-Dahlem, Staatliche Museen KdZ 5127
INSCRIBED in another hand: 'Tintoretto'
BIBLIOGRAPHY Tietze and Tietze-Conrat A 2035; Ballarin
      Arte Veneta 1971 p 101

The Tietzes' view, that the figures were copied from the Chatsworth drawing (35), was challenged by Ballarin. He saw it as a
preparatory sketch, whose handling of the pen and ink he described
as similar to that of the Oxford *Study of a sacrifice* (Fig 106).

The drawing is, however, more complex than these views
suggest. The preliminary chalk study, which differs from that at
Chatsworth, although difficult to make out under the pen and
ink resembles drawings by Carletto, notably the *Study of the
Holy Family with Sts John the Baptist and Catherine* in the
British Museum (Fig 101).[1] This is an autograph variation of his
own *Study for the Holy Family with Sts John the Baptist and
Anne* (Fig 102)[2] for the painting in Dresden.[3] Carletto appears to
have used the Chatsworth drawing as the starting-point for a
drawing, which was completed by a second, and clumsier, artist
copying directly from the Veronese. Other drawings by Carletto
which confirm that he worked from his father's drawings include
the Windsor *Copy after a design for the Venice enthroned* (Fig 53)[4]
and the *Study of the Holy Family with Sts Barbara and John the
Baptist* in the Uffizi (Fig 103).[5] The latter relates with minor
differences to the painting of this subject which Cardinal Leopoldo
de' Medici finally acquired from Paolo del Sera in 1664.[6]

Fig 102   Carletto Caliari, *Study for the Holy Family with Sts John the Baptist
and Anne*, pen and wash, British Museum, London

160   Study of a Supper at Emmaus

Fig 103   Carletto Caliari, *Study of the Holy Family with Sts Barbara and John the Baptist*, wash over grey chalk, Galleria degli Uffizi, Florence

NOTES

1   From the Malcolm collection; Inv. 1895–9–15–848 pen and ink and wash over grey chalk on blue paper, 19 by 20.5 cm; Robinson 403

2   From the Malcolm collection, London, British Museum, Inv. 1895–9–15–847, pen and ink and wash on blue prepared paper, 22 by 20 cm; Robinson 402. Another closely related variation is in the Louvre Inv. 4,664, pen and ink and wash, 20.8 by 35 cm, squared; a related drawing at Windsor (Tietze and Tietze-Conrat 2212) was rightly regarded as too feeble to be by Carletto by Popham and Wilde no 1028. The design was further varied in a drawing in the Uffizi, 14955F, which is unlikely to be by Carletto (188 note 3)

3   The history of the painting and the old attribution to Carletto were noted by Von Hadeln p 357 note 6 of Ridolfi and by H. Posse, *Dresden Staatliche Gemäldegalerie: Die Romanischen Länder* (Dresden, 1929), no 241

4   Discussed under (82)

5   Uffizi 1857F, grey chalk and wash on green tinted paper heightened with touches of white, 26 by 30 cm, Tietze and Tietze-Conrat A2060

6   Pignatti 128; it was the most valuable of the pictures (1000 piastre) sold by del Sera to Cardinal Leopoldo de' Medici in 1654 and may well have been the version which Ridolfi described in the Widmann collection in 1648, Ridolfi p 340 and note 7, Florence, Archivio di Stato *Lettere Artistiche* V, 49. There were delays in despatching the purchase, partially because of trouble with the Venetian customs (Florence, Centro Di, *Tiziano nelle Gallerie Fiorentine* (1978), p 201). It was finally sent in May 1664 when it was mentioned by del Sera, *Lettere Artistiche* VI, 339 and by de Monconys who had just seen it in Florence, *Journal des Voyages* 2 (Lyons, 1665–66), p 478

161   Study of St Roch in glory

161   Study of St Roch in glory

Pen and ink and wash on green paper heightened with white
26.7 × 27.8 cm

LOCATION Boston, Isabella Stewart Gardner Museum

PROVENANCE P. Crozat, his sale Paris, Mariette 1741, part of
684; P. J. Mariette (Lugt 2097),[1] his sale Paris, Basan 1775,
249; Lord Palmerston, his sale London, Christie 24 April
1891, 184; J. C. Robinson (Lugt 1433), his sale London,
Christie 12 May 1902, 50

BIBLIOGRAPHY Boston 1968 pp 26ff no 12 (attributed to
Veronese); Macandrew p 75

Mariette convincingly identified this drawing as *St Roch in
glory*. He suggested that it had been made in competition with
Tintoretto for the commission of the ceiling of the Albergo of the
Scuola di San Rocco in the early 1560s.[2] In spite of this and its

distinguished provenance the lingering doubts about the attribution seem to me justified. This can be seen by comparison to
the *Study of twelve apostles* at Chatsworth (16), which must be
close in date to the competition for San Rocco.

The rich wash and brilliant use of white heightening reveal an
artist who has seen, but not mastered, the style of Veronese's
later *modelli*, that for the *Martyrdom of St Justina* (75), for
instance. Like Bassetti in the early years of the seventeenth
century the unknown artist may well have copied Veronese's
now lost project for the Albergo of San Rocco.[3]

NOTES

1   Mariette's mount with full inscription

2   De Vecchi p 107

3   This was noted by Hadley in the Boston catalogue, the Bassetti in the
Scholz collection was no 157 fig 166 in Verona, *Cinquant' anni di pittura
veronese 1580–1630* (1971)

162   Copy of the Mystic marriage of St Catherine

162   Copy of the Mystic marriage of St Catherine

Pen and ink on grey-green paper heightened with white
45 × 30 cm

LOCATION Boston, Isabella Stewart Gardner Museum

PROVENANCE Sir Peter Lely (Lugt 2092); Sir J. C. Robinson
(Lugt 1433), his sale London, Christie 12–14 May 1902, 49,
acquired for Mrs Gardner by Agnew's

BIBLIOGRAPHY Tietze and Tietze-Conrat 2045 (Veronese);
Boston 1968 no 11 (Veronese); Cocke *Master Drawings* 1977
p 267 (a copy)

The Tietzes suggested that this drawing, which differs in many
details from the altar of this subject now in the Accademia,[1] was a
modello. The empty heads, mechanical wash and dull appearance
of the sheet when compared to the Chatsworth *Modello for the
Martyrdom of St Justina* (75) reveal a copyist who must have had
access to a now lost preparatory drawing by Veronese.[2]

NOTES

1   Pignatti 183

2   It inspired another similar copy in the Louvre, Inv. 4,690 from the Jabach
collection, no 69 in the Venetian section of his manuscript catalogue, Paris
1978, as well as the free variation by the workshop Inv. I 92, Museum
Boymans-van Beuningen, Rotterdam, Tietze and Tietze-Conrat 2169.
Although badly faded I believe that this sheet is by Carletto

163 Study for a tomb

Pen and ink and wash
47.4 × 33.9 cm
LOCATION Budapest, Museum of Fine Arts Inv. 1989
INSCRIBED on the mount: 'ANDREA PALLADIO ARCHITETTORE VICE,
le figure son di Paolo Veronese', 'fuit Georgii Vasari nunc
P. J. Mariette'
PROVENANCE Vasari; P. J. Mariette (Lugt 1852), his sale Paris,
Basan, 1775, 551; Esterházy (Lugt 1965); O. Képtár (Lugt
2000)
BIBLIOGRAPHY O. Kurz, 'Giorgio Vasari's *Libro de' Disegni'*, *Old
Master Drawings* 12 (1937–38), p 42; Tietze and Tietze-
Conrat 2050; Venice 1965 no 31; L. Ragghianti Collobi, *Il
Libro de' Disegni del Vasari* (Florence, 1974), p 124 and pl 384

Vasari's attribution of the wall monument to Palladio has won
universal acceptance, and the figures were accepted as Veronese's by the Tietzes and Fenyö in the 1965 catalogue. It seems
much more likely, however, that if Palladio had needed help
with the figures he would have turned to a sculptor rather than a
painter. I share the doubts of Philip Pouncey, as noted in the
1965 exhibition catalogue, about the attribution of the figures to
Veronese.[1]

NOTE

1   These doubts are shared by Sergio Marinelli in the exhibition *Palladio e
Verona*, Palazzo del Gran Guardia (Verona, 1980), p 166, where he suggests
that the figures are by Battista del Moro

164 Study for a Feast in the house of Simon

Pen and ink and wash over traces of grey chalk heightened with
white
20.2 × 26.8 cm
LOCATION Budapest, Museum of Fine Arts Inv. 2409
PROVENANCE Sir Joshua Reynolds (Lugt 2364); Poggi (Lugt
617); Esterházy (Lugt 1965); O. Képtár (Lugt 2000)
BIBLIOGRAPHY Von Hadeln 1911 p 397; J. Meder, *Die Hand-
zeichnung* (Vienna, 1923), p 614 and fig 301; Tietze and
Tietze-Conrat A2048 (not Veronese); Venice 1965 no 34
(autograph)

In spite of Fenyö's defence of the attribution to Veronese, its
rejection by the Tietzes and Philip Pouncey seems to me to be
correct. The laboured construction of the space is both very
different from that used by Veronese and is incorrect in the
foreshortening of the barrel-vaulting. The formula for the heads
is unlike that of the drawing for the *Feast in the house of Simon*
(57) and the loose handling, as the Tietzes argued, points to a
later artist working in a style that looks back to Veronese.

165 Study of the Virgin and Child with Sts John the Baptist and Louis of Toulouse with unidentified donors

Pen and ink and wash heightened with white
31.3 × 23.1 cm

LOCATION Chatsworth, Devonshire collection Inv. 937
PROVENANCE Sir Peter Lely (Lugt 2092); Nicolaes Flinck (Lugt 959); 2nd Duke of Devonshire (Lugt 718)
BIBLIOGRAPHY D. F. von Hadeln, 'Veronese und Zelotti', *Jahrbuch der Königlich preussischen Kunstsammlungen* 35 (1914), pp 200–203 (a copy after the reduced version in the Uffizi); Tietze and Tietze-Conrat 2255 (Zelotti); Ballarin *Arte Veneta* 1971 p 98 (Veronese); Cocke 1971 pp 730–33 (Carletto)[1]

The drawing has long been connected with the Bevilacqua-Lazise altarpiece from the family chapel in S. Fermo in the Museo di Castelvecchio, Verona. One influential school of thought see this altarpiece as Veronese's first work of 1548, a date that is extended to the present drawing.[2] Although the Tietzes were wrong in their attribution to Zelotti their view (first put forward by Von Hadeln) that the drawing was not by Veronese was right. The Virgin can be compared to that in the *Virgin and Child with St Anne and angels* in the Mooney collection (20) where the wash and the white heightening are rendered with a skill lacking in the present sheet. The handling, when compared to that of *The supper at Emmaus* also at Chatsworth (35), is flat and fails to create volume.

While there should be little doubt about the rejection of the attribution to Veronese, the connection with the Bevilacqua-Lazise altar is complicated by the existence of the reduced replica in the Uffizi, which no-one since del Sera in 1669 has claimed as a Veronese (Fig 104).[3] Von Hadeln, although wrong to call the drawing a copy after the replica, since it differs in the omission of one music-making angel and the fluting of the column, was right to connect the two. Some of the details by which the Uffizi version differs from the larger altar (the donors, the pose and costume of St John the Baptist) are anticipated in the present sheet which must be an intermediary stage between the two, although the artist probably also turned to the original altar.

The altar may have been commissioned by Giovanni Bevilacqua and his wife between 1544, when they established the family chapel, and 1558, when the wife died, or by his brother Giovanni Battista Bevilacqua and his wife between 1571, when they were married, and 1580, when Giovanni Battista died.[4] Most critics favour the earlier date, but I believe that the contrast with the *Christ preaching* in the Prado of 1548 (Fig 1) and the *Sacra Conversazione* in the Giustiniani chapel of S. Francesco alla Vigna probably of 1551, the date of the dedication of the chapel, excludes this possibility. The artist was inspired by Veronese's later work, most notably in the complex twisting St Louis.[5]

Although badly damaged, the Bevilacqua altar appears to resemble other pictures also wrongly attributed to Veronese as early works. The thin pinched features of the Virgin and the drapery of St Louis, failing to suggest a body underneath, are similar to the Magdalen and the attendant who holds her hand in the *Magdalen laying aside her jewels* in the National Gallery, London.[6] The contrast between the Bevilacqua-Lazise altar and the reduced replica in the Uffizi where the white heightening takes on a new freedom suggests a justification to extend the group to include the *Christ curing the daughter of Jairus* in the Louvre. This is based upon a lost Veronese formerly in S. Berna-dino, Verona.[7] The weakly foreshortened head of the servant bending over the daughter resembles that of the woman who holds the Magdalen's hand in the National Gallery painting, just as the Christ is similar in both. The *Christ curing* forms the basis for the attribution of a number of other paintings which include the *Minerva* in the Pushkin Museum, Moscow, the *Diana* in the Hermitage and the *St Agatha* in the Uffizi,[8] which is similar to the *David and Goliath* (Fig 67) and the *Judith and Holofernes* (Fig 66) now at Hampton Court which must date from after 1582.[9]

The key to the attribution of this group of paintings lies in the connection of the Bevilacqua-Lazise altar with the *St Nicholas in glory* (Fig 51) from S. Nicolò dei Mendicoli for which Veronese provided the preparatory drawing in *circa* 1578 (79). When I originally drew attention to the parallels between the handling of the Bevilacqua-Lazise altar and the *St Nicholas in glory*, I followed the old attribution to Carletto for the *St Nicholas*, a view that is ruled out by Carletto's baptism in July 1570. The alternative view, that it is by Veronese's nephew Alvise dal Friso born in Verona *circa* 1554,[10] fits better with the facts and explains why some of these pictures were commissioned in Verona.

The Bevilacqua-Lazise altar is less assured than the *St Nicholas in glory* and may date from slightly earlier, when Alvise was about twenty-two or twenty-three years old. This would explain the immaturity because of which it is seen as Veronese's first work. The attribution of the Chatsworth drawing to Alvise also goes some way to provide a basis for the discussion of his work as a draughtsman.[11]

Fig 104   Alvise dal Friso(?), *The Virgin and Child with Sts John the Baptist and Louis of Toulouse with unidentified donors*, Galleria degli Uffizi, Florence

NOTES

1   A possibility that is excluded by his baptism on 20 July 1570, Pignatti doc 26

2   Pignatti 1; this is the view of Ballarin and Rearick in Florence 1976 p 158

3   Inv. 1316; it was sent from Poggio a Caiano in 1773 and was the picture acquired by Cardinal Leopoldo de' Medici from Paolo del Sera in May 1669 (Florence, Archivio di Stato *Lettere Artistiche* VII, 603). The attribution to Veronese is defended *ad nauseam* by D. G. Pechukas, 'Two oil-sketches and the youth of Veronese', *Art Bulletin* 64 (1982), pp 388–413

4   Cocke 1971 p 730 citing A. Bevilacqua-Lazise, 'Un quadro di Autore Controverso al Museo Civico di Verona', *Madonna Verona* 5 (1811), pp 106–111

5   Cocke 1971 p 733 comparing it with the St Paul from the Trevisan altar in S. Pietro in Castello

6   Pignatti 47; Mrs Newton has drawn attention to the inconsistencies in the costume not found in other Veronese's in C. Gould, *National Gallery Catalogues: The Sixteenth Century Venetian School* (London, 1959), pp 145 ff

7   Pignatti A 238 and Ridolfi p 298

8   Pignatti 155, 156 and 318; to these may be added the *Holy Family with St John the Baptist* in Amsterdam, the *Virgin and Child return the hands of the daughter of France* in Kassel and the *Madonna in glory appears to Sts John the Baptist and Anthony Abbot* in Chicago, Pignatti 53, A 131 and A 47

9   *See* under (99)

10   *See* under (80)

11   *Compare* Tietze and Tietze-Conrat 165–66 nos 695 and 696 with Verona 1971 cats 118–22 a group whose attribution was questioned by Ballarin *Arte Veneta* 1971 pp 113 ff. The Tietzes drew attention to Ridolfi's description of the paintings in Sant Aponal, one of which, the *Study for St Helen discovers the cross*, may relate to Florence, Uffizi 7409S, although there are significant differences, Ridolfi II, p 143. The style is more mature than the Chatsworth drawing, as in the *Study of the Virgin and Child enthroned with St George and other saints*, no 126108 in the Gabinetto Nazionale di Roma, attributed by Tietze and Tietze-Conrat to Porta Salviati, no 1391 and Ballarin *Arte Veneta* 1971 p 112 and note 27 to Zelotti. The drawing in the Uffizi, Ballarin *Arte Veneta* 1971 p 112 and note 27, seems to me to be the 'half finished copy' which the Tietzes cited in Turin, but about whose status they were accurate. The small, approx 20 by 15 cm, unpublished *Study of a kneeling woman* (pen and ink and wash) in a private collection, New York (Fig 108), fits closely with the St Louis in the Chatsworth drawing

165   Study of the Virgin and Child with Sts John the Baptist and Louis of Toulouse with unidentified donors

166 Studies of a Descent from the cross

166v Study of spandrel-figures

Pen and ink and wash
28.8 × 21.6 cm

LOCATION Chicago, Art Institute Inv. 1943.1060
INSCRIBED on the verso: '24'
PROVENANCE Leopold I Fürst von Anhalt–Dessau (Lugt 1708a); Philip Hofer; acquired in 1943
BIBLIOGRAPHY Tietze 1948 (not Veronese); Washington 1974 no 23 (Veronese); Joachim and McCullagh no 27 (attributed to Veronese)

The attribution of the present sheet, first suggested by Philip Hofer and C.O. Schniewind, was queried by Hans Tietze. He felt that the pedantic way in which the figures were placed on the sheet and the morphology of the handling were not typical of Veronese. Pignatti, in the Washington catalogue, accepted the attribution on the basis of a comparison with the *Studies of Mercury* in a private collection, England (11). Such a view fails to convince me of the identity of hands and I believe that Tietze was right to reject it, although I would not agree with Joachim and McCullagh that it was a sheet from the same sketchbook as the *Study for a Crucifixion* now in the Fogg Art Gallery (121), a sheet which had also been in the Hofer collection in the 1930s. The Fogg drawing is an autograph sketch for the painting in the Louvre while the Chicago drawing not only is not related to any surviving painting, but is extremely unlikely to be by Veronese.

167 Study of a Judgement of Paris

Pen and ink and wash heightened with white
39.3 × 51.4 cm

LOCATION Cleveland Museum of Art, Dudley P. Allen Fund Inv. 46.216
PROVENANCE Italico Brass
BIBLIOGRAPHY Cocke 1971 p 733 note 34 (Carletto); Birmingham, Alabama 1972 p 52 (Carletto)

Ridolfi attributed a fresco of this subject formerly on the Fondaco dei Tedeschi to Carletto.[1] This drawing, which may have been made in preparation for one of the many replicas,[2] is perhaps too weak to be by Carletto. The landscape is typical of him as is the line around the shoulders of the striding goddess seen from behind, which flattens the figure, like that in Carletto's *Study of Cupid and Psyche* in Munich (Fig 99). The schematic white heightening, which contrasts with Veronese's painterly freedom, is similar to that of the *Study of Mars, Venus and Cupid* in the Louvre (204).

NOTES

1 Ridolfi p 357; it was engraved by C. Patina, *Pitture Scelte e Dichiarata da Carla Patina* (Cologna, 1691), p 187 with no indication of the location which was confirmed by V. Zanetti, *Della Pittura Veneziana e delle Opere Publiche de' Veneziani Maestri Libri 5* 2 (Venice, 1792), p 709
2 Pignatti A144 refers to the Kress version in Lewisburg; another is in the collection of the Earl of Wemyss (photographed by the National Galleries of Scotland). Another version also attributed to Carletto was in the Pierre Crozat collection in 1740 no 221 with dimensions of 20.3 by 37.9 cm, probably no 63 in the 1751 sale catalogue, M. Stuffman, 'Les tableaux de la collection de Pierre Crozat', *Gazette des Beaux-Arts* 72 (1968), p 78 no 169

168   Study of hands

168   Study of hands

Black chalk on blue–grey paper heightened with white
27.3 × 17.9 cm

LOCATION Cleveland Museum of Art, Dudley P. Allen Fund
   Inv. 29.549

INSCRIBED 'Di Carlo Caliari figlio di Paulo Veronese'; on the
   verso: 'Amor di meritrice [repeated twice] Carletto Calliari e
   morto',[1] 'A questa 163', 'A a b c d e f g'

BIBLIOGRAPHY Birmingham, Alabama 1972 p 54

The energetic hatching of the shoulder and hands derives from
that of Veronese's late chalk studies, the *Study for Liberality* (70)
for the Sala del Collegio of *circa* 1576, for instance. This and the
contrast with the finer handling of the *Study of hands*, sold at
Sotheby's (142), which appears to be by Veronese, suggests that
the attribution to Carletto is reliable.[2] There is a faint sketch of a
hand on the verso.

NOTES

1   This seems to be preferable to the reading: 'e matto' suggested by the
Birmingham catalogue

2   The reference to Carletto's death dates this to *circa* 1596, *see* Von Hadeln
p 353 note 1 of Ridolfi

169   Study for Christ preaching in the temple

Pen and ink
19 × 22.7 cm

LOCATION Cornwall, Colville
BIBLIOGRAPHY Verona 1971 no 66 (Veronese)

The 1971 Verona catalogue related the drawing to the Prado *Christ preaching in the temple* (Fig 1). Comparison with the Schwarz drawing for the painting (1) reveals a very different hand which has nothing to do with Veronese. The subject was common: Zelotti included it among his wall paintings in the refectory of the monastery at Praglia at the end of the 1550s and the present sheet might have been made for that project.

170   Study of a dog

Oil on brown prepared paper
25.3 × 32.1 cm

LOCATION Edinburgh, National Gallery of Scotland
    Inv. D. 1674
INSCRIBED 'Passarota in Verona feci'
BIBLIOGRAPHY H. Coutts, 'A Veronese drawing in Edinburgh', *Master Drawings* 18 (1980), pp 142–44

This attractive sheet was discovered and published by Howard Coutts who rightly related it to the *Susanna and the Elders* in Vienna. The inscription suggests that it is a copy rather than a preliminary drawing. This is borne out by a comparison with certain brush drawings, such as the *Study of a dead Christ and a skeleton* in the British Museum (72).

171   Study for an Adoration of the shepherds (actual size)

171   Study for an Adoration of the shepherds

Pen and ink

8.1 × 16.3 cm

LOCATION Florence, Galleria degli Uffizi Inv. 1852F

INSCRIBED 'Paolo Veronese F'

PROVENANCE Lorenzo de' Medici (?)

BIBLIOGRAPHY Von Hadeln pl 47; Venice 1939 p 222 no 10;
   Tietze and Tietze-Conrat 2168 (a pupil); Florence 1976
   no 117 (autograph)

Both the attribution and reading of the action have been controversial since the drawing was first published by Von Hadeln as a
study for the *Feast in the house of Levi* (Fig 35). This view was
rightly rejected by the Tietzes who also doubted the attribution
to Veronese. They understandably saw the central action as
figures around a chest with the figures at the side related to the
Rape of Europa (Fig 32). This was corrected by Rearick who
realised that the central action was the Virgin lifting a cloth
which must have held the infant Christ who is adored by the
shepherds with their cattle at the side. His view that it was made
in preparation for the *Adoration of the shepherds* in SS. Giovanni
e Paolo,[1] which he dated to the mid-1550s, is difficult to follow
especially since I am convinced that the Tietzes were correct to
see here a freedom of stroke alien to Veronese himself, *compare
the drawing for the Dresden *Marriage feast at Cana* (58), for
instance.

NOTE

1   Pignatti 158 and (98) note 4

172 Study of St George and the Dragon

Pen and ink over traces of grey chalk heightened with white
41 × 50.5 cm

LOCATION Florence, Gallerie degli Uffizi Inv. 12845F
PROVENANCE Lorenzo de' Medici (?)
BIBLIOGRAPHY Florence 1976 no 114; Pignatti pl 11

Roger Rearick attributed this drawing, which had previously been kept with those by Zelotti, to Veronese. He related it to the Louvre copy of a lost altar dedicated to St George, published by Ballarin as being after a Veronese of 1552 and to which he related the *Study of the Virgin and Child with Sts Peter and Paul* in the Louvre (210).[1] The laboured, awkward handling of the Louvre drawing is not by Veronese, nor is the present sheet with its more vehement handling and weaknesses in the dragon's wings to which Rearick drew attention. The differences in handling between this sheet and the Louvre *Temptation of St Anthony* (36) and the Chatsworth *Supper at Emmaus* (35), with which it was compared by Rearick, do not, in my view, need underlining. The insistent but clumsy draughtsmanship cannot be reconciled with that of the Chatsworth drawing for the Bevilacqua-Lazise altar (165), also cited as an example of Veronese's early drawings, and the present drawing is close to Farinati.[2]

Rearick believed that this drawing formed the lower section of a larger sheet, of which the Louvre drawing (210) was the upper part. This view, however, overlooks the enormous stylistic gulf that separates the two. Farinati, if he was responsible for the Uffizi drawing, may have elaborated the curving, sprung forms on the basis of a lost Veronese for which the small pen and ink *Study of St George and the dragon* recently on the London market may have been the preparatory sketch (144).

NOTES
1 Ballarin *Arte Veneta* 1971 p 98. The Louvre copy is Inv. 4,839
2 *See* Verona 1971 cats 37–51

173 Copy of St Matthew and the angel

Black chalk and wash on green prepared paper heightened with white
14.5 × 31.4 cm

LOCATION Florence, Galleria degli Uffizi Inv. 1851F
PROVENANCE Lorenzo de' Medici (?)
BIBLIOGRAPHY Florence 1976 p 159 no 115

The drawing was first mentioned by Rearick in the 1976 catalogue. He argued that it was not, as had been suggested by Giglioli in the manuscript catalogue, a copy after, but rather a preparatory sketch for the *St Matthew* on the ceiling of the sacristy of S. Sebastiano.[1] Rearick emphasised the differences from the painting, most notable in the tree on the right. It is much more finished and closer to the painting than the other chalk studies, the *Study of a seated man* (2), the *Study for the Portrait of a member of the Soranzo family* (77), the *Study of a kneeling magus* (67), the *Study for St Lawrence* (73) and the *Study for the Liberality* (70).

The workshop is conspicuous in the tondi from the sacristy but not in the main figures and this sheet is unlikely to have played any part in the preparation of the ceiling of which it is a copy.

NOTE
1 Finished by 23 November 1555, the date displayed on one of the books supported by angels, Pignatti pl 90

174 Study for an Adoration of the Magi

Pen and ink
8.3 × 29.5 cm

LOCATION Geneva, Martin Bodmer Library
PROVENANCE Prince Castelbarco, Pesaro; H. M. Calmann, his sale London 1958, 12

175 Study for Christ washing the apostles' feet

Pen and ink
11.5 × 30 cm

LOCATION Geneva, Martin Bodmer Library
PROVENANCE Prince Castelbarco, Pesaro; H. M. Calmann, his sale London 1958, 12

These two drawings although clearly by the same hand are not by Veronese. The freedom of the handling and the energy of the movement reveal an artist influenced by Palma Giovane's free pen and ink sketches.[1]

NOTE
1 *See*, for example, his drawing for an *Entombment* in the British Museum, reproduced by S. Mason Rinaldi, 'Il libro dei disegni di Palma Giovane del British Museum', *Arte Veneta* 27 (1973), p 125 and fig 152

176 Study of a seated lady

Black chalk on grey paper heightened with white
39.5 × 20.9 cm

LOCATION formerly Haarlem, Franz Koenigs Inv. I91
INSCRIBED on the verso: 'I. T. n.o 28', 'Aque'ta 38'
PROVENANCE Zaccaria Sagredo;[1] Anon. (Lugt 2103a; sometimes
    identified as the Borghese collection)[2]
BIBLIOGRAPHY Tietze and Tietze-Conrat 2077 (Veronese?)

The doubts expressed by the Tietzes seem justified, although I only know the drawing from a reproduction. It shares the loose handling of the *Study of a man seen from behind* (214) from the same collection which appears to be by a later artist, perhaps trained in Veronese's workshop.

NOTES

1 Ballarin *Studi* 1971 pp 144ff
2 Monte Carlo 1966 intro, obviously at that time attributed to Jacopo Tintoretto (I. T.). The mark was, however, only added in the late eighteenth century, *see* London, Sotheby 9 July 1981, 132

177 Study of the head of an old man

Black chalk on blue paper heightened with white
36.3 × 31.3 cm

LOCATION Haarlem, Teyler Museum Inv. I24
PROVENANCE Queen Christina of Sweden; Cardinal Azzolino;
    Prince L. Odescalchi
BIBLIOGRAPHY Paris 1962 no 120

This splendid drawing could not be by Veronese as can be seen by a comparison with his certain chalk studies, the *Study of an apostle* of 1575 (76), for instance. The modelling seems more fully worked than is usual with Venetian drawings and in a letter to the Museum, Catherine Johnson has attributed it to Domenichino, and related it to his frescoes in S. Andrea della Valle.

178 Copy of Christ in Limbo

Pen and ink and wash heightened with white
26 × 35 cm

LOCATION Lille, Musée des Beaux-Arts
PROVENANCE J. B. Wicar
BIBLIOGRAPHY Pluchart 127; Tietze and Tietze-Conrat 2195
    (Benedetto); Cocke *Master Drawings* 1977 p 267

The Tietzes' attribution of this sheet to Benedetto rests upon two errors. Benedetto was not responsible for the design, as they believed, and the drawing is a copy. Ridolfi saw a version of this subject in the Caliari collection in 1648 which he attributed to Benedetto[1] and which was subsequently no 179 in the 1682 inventory of the collection with dimensions of 9 by 10 quarte (about 153 by 170 cm).[2] The Tietzes tentatively suggested that this was the canvas now in El Escorial. This version, however, was in the monastery's Aula de Escritura by 1657[3] and its size, 236 by 328 cm, is nearly double that of the lost version by Benedetto.

Both the faithfulness with which the Lille drawing follows the Escorial canvas and the poor quality of the execution with the scratchy penmanship and limited wash betrays its status as a copy which is extremely unlikely to be by Benedetto.

NOTES

1 Ridolfi p 360
2 Gattinoni pp 10–11
3 When it was mentioned by Francisco de los Santos, *Descripción breve del monasterio de S. Lorenzo el Real del Escorial*, ed. F. J. Sánchez Cantón, *Fuentes Literarias para la Historia del Arte Español* 2 (Madrid 1933), p 255ff

179 Studies of a Martyrdom and Crucifixion

Pen and ink and wash
12 × 22 cm

LOCATION formerly London, Bellingham-Smith
PROVENANCE P. H. Lankrink (Lugt 2090); Bellingham-Smith,
    their sale, Amsterdam, Müller 5–6 July 1927, 6

The central group with the martyrdom of an unidentified saint clearly depends, in reverse, upon the St Sebastian in the main altar of S. Sebastiano.[1] The vehement cross-hatching and the Michelangelesque muscularity of the nude figure at the bottom right of the sheet, which I know from a reproduction, reveal a later artist looking back to Veronese, not the master himself.

NOTE

1 Pignatti 132

180   Study of Venus, Adonis and Cupid (actual size)

180 Study of Venus, Adonis and Cupid

Pen and ink and wash

10 × 13.5 cm

LOCATION formerly London, Bellingham-Smith[1]
PROVENANCE Bellingham-Smith, their sale, Amsterdam,
    Müller 5–6 July 1927, 7; J. E. Huxtable; Mrs Pape;
    London 1956
BIBLIOGRAPHY Borenius 1921 p 59 no 5 (Mars and Venus);
    Tietze and Tietze-Conrat A2098 (a later hand)

Although I only know this drawing from a photograph I share
the doubts of the Tietzes, as do Philip Pouncey and Julien Stock.
The insistence on the outline and the view-point contrast with
autograph drawings, including the New York *Studies for the
four Allegories of Love* (78).

Borenius identified the subject as Mars and Venus but rightly
contrasted it with the painting in the Metropolitan Museum.[2]
I believe that he was nearly right but that it prepares the now lost
Venus, Adonis and Cupid formerly in the Dupille collection, Paris
(Fig 105).[3] Here Venus lies back to look up to her standing lover
whose head she holds in her raised arm while Cupid sits at her
feet and plays with her dress. In the painting, Adonis was moved
to the spectator's right to support his mistress and his gestures
were altered to combine affection for Venus with concern for his
hounds. The drawing develops the interlocking of the two lovers
and the pose of Venus with her arm raised above her head from
the *Venus with a satyr* of 1571.[4] Its sculptural appearance (with
few *pentimenti*) may well reflect the small *modello* of this subject
which Mariette knew in the Crozat collection but which is
unlikely to be by Veronese, as he believed.[5]

NOTES

1   Borenius suggested that it came from the Woodburn collection; it is not
among the Veronese's in his sale, London, Christie 4–12 June 1860

2   Pignatti 248

3   The engraving by Ravenet is here reproduced in reverse; *Recueil d'Estampes
d'après les plus beaux Tableaux qui sont en France, dans le Cabinet du Roy, dans
celuy de Monseigneur le Duc d'Orléans, et dans d'autres cabinets* 2 (Paris, 1792–42),
p 69 no 38. It measured 98 by 71 cm and was therefore smaller than the versions
which have been published, unconvincingly, as autograph, Pignatti A421

4   Pignatti A107, wrongly, in my view, as school

5   P. Ticozzi, 'Le incisioni da opere del Veronese nel Museo Correr', *Bollettino
dei Musei Civici Veneziani* 20 (1975), pp 6–90 notes Mariette's reference in his
discussion of the engraving of 1742 and in a letter to Temanza of 28 July 1772,
Raccolta di lettere sul la pittura, scultura ed architettura 8, eds G. Bottari and
S. Ticozzi (Milan, 1825), p 433

Fig 105   Ravenet, *Engraving of the Venus, Adonis and Cupid* formerly in the
Dupille collection, Paris, from the *Recueil d'Estampes d'après les plus beaux
Tableaux* . . . 2 (Paris, 1729–42), p 69, no 38

181   Study of a Venus seen from behind

181   Study of a Venus seen from behind

Pen and wash over black chalk heightened with white
31.3 × 20.1 cm

LOCATION London, private collection
INSCRIBED '[Siri]nga, 8, fortuna, venera' and an illegible word
PROVENANCE Emile Wauters (Lugt 911), his sale, Amsterdam,
    Müller 15–16 June 1926, 31; P. Larue; sold London,
    Sotheby 13 December 1973, 9
BIBLIOGRAPHY Venice 1980 no 33

The plastic, slightly awkward handling reveals Veronese's work-shop in one of their rare surviving studies from a model. It seems possible to attribute the drawing to Carletto.[1] The schematic handling of the eyes and mouth link with other sketches by him, notably the Windsor *Copy after a design for the Venice enthroned* (Fig 53) and the outlining of the figure recalls that in his Munich *Study of Cupid and Psyche* (Fig 99). The notes on the sheet seem to be by the same hand as the letter on the verso of the Munich drawing (Fig 100).

NOTE

1   This was suggested tentatively in the Venice catalogue by Julien Stock who now attributes the drawing to Carletto

182   Study for a Flagellation of Christ

Pen and ink
10.6 × 16.5 cm

LOCATION formerly London, Rudolf
INSCRIBED 'Paolo Callari Veronese'
PROVENANCE Anon. Venetian (Lugt 3005a); C. R. Rudolf;
    sold London, Christie 8 July 1979, 21
BIBLIOGRAPHY Venice 1966 no 18

The old inscription appears to me to be misleading. The handling fails to achieve the sense of form of Veronese's autograph pen and ink sketches, and is very different from the *Studies for Pope Alexander III recognised by Doge Sebastiano Ziani* in the Albertina (92) with which it was compared by Bettagno in the 1966 exhibition catalogue. It may well be by the artist, possibly Alessandro Maganza,[1] responsible for the *Study of the Madonna enthroned* in Vienna (222) and the *Studies of figures with boatmen* formerly in the Matthiesen collection (184).

NOTE

1   *See* under (222) note 1

184   Studies of figures with boatmen

183   Study of the skirt of a seated woman

Black and white chalk on blue paper
30 × 20.6 cm

LOCATION formerly London, Skippe
INSCRIBED 'Da Paulo V'
PROVENANCE John Skippe (d. 1812), thence to the Martin family,
    sold London, Christie 21 November 1958, 228

The old attribution of this fine sheet must have seemed reasonable
at the time of the Skippe sale. It cannot be maintained when it is
compared to the *Study for the Portrait of a member of the Soranzo
family* (77) and the *Study of a lady with a fan* (147).

184   Studies of figures with boatmen

Pen and ink
11.2 × 20.6 cm

LOCATION London, Sotheby 21 October 1963, 89
PROVENANCE Francis Matthiesen[1]

The drawing combines four different sketches of music-making
figures with boatmen. It is freer and looser in its handling than
Veronese in his late drawings, with which it has been compared.[2]
It resembles drawings attributed to Alessandro Maganza,[3] who
may well have been responsible for the *Study of the Madonna
enthroned with four saints and a donor* in Vienna (222), and the
Study for a Flagellation of Christ from the Rudolf collection (182).

NOTES
1   Exhibited London 1963, Matthiesen Galleries, *Old Master Drawings*, no 63
2   By James Byam Shaw, quoted in the Sotheby sale catalogue
3   Notably the *Pope granting a monk an audience* from the Rudolf collection,
which was attributed to Alessandro Maganza by Stefania Mason Rinaldi,
*Catalogue of Drawings by Jacopo Palma, called il Giovane from the collection of
the late Mr C.R.Rudolf*, London, Sotheby 4 July 1977, 41

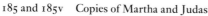
185 and 185v Copies of Martha and Judas

185 and 185v Copies of Martha and Judas

Grey chalk on blue paper heightened with white (recto);
   ink and wash (verso)
31.5 × 21 cm

LOCATION London, Sotheby 28 June 1979, 72
INSCRIBED 'da Paolo', 'D. P. no. 3'; on the verso: 'D. P. no. 55/
   de Paolo V./nella cena del Levita ch'hora e in Francia'
PROVENANCE Anon. (Lugt 2103a; sometimes identified as the
   Borghese collection);[1] sold London, Sotheby 1 July 1971, 15

The studies on both recto and verso relate to Martha and Judas
in the *Feast in the house of Simon*, painted for the Servites in 1573
and ceded to the French Royal collection in 1664.[2] That they are

copies is shown by the care with which they follow the figures,
the lack of *pentimenti* and the inclusion of the table cloth besides
Martha. The handling of the chalk is close to that of autograph
drawings, most notably the *Study for the Portrait of a member of
the Soranzo family* (77), but the insistence upon the outline and
the search for volume in the folds of Martha's costume reveal a
member of the workshop. The loose handling of the pen and
wash on the verso resembles the Rotterdam *Copy after a Rest on
the Flight into Egypt* (212), which may be by Benedetto.

NOTES

1 Monte Carlo 1966 intro. The mark was, however, only added in the late
eighteenth century, *see* London, Sotheby 9 July 1981, 132
2 Pignatti 176

186   Study of Christ and the centurion

Pen and ink
11.3 × 18.6 cm

LOCATION Madrid, Biblioteca Nacional Inv. 7254
INSCRIBED 'Verones'
PROVENANCE Carderera
BIBLIOGRAPHY De Barcia 7254 (for the Madrid painting);
A. G. B. Russell, 'Some drawings by Italian painters of
the sixteenth century', *Burlington Magazine* 45 (1924),
pp 120–25 (for the Madrid painting); Von Hadeln pl 26;
Tietze and Tietze-Conrat A2114 (derived from the painting);
Pignatti 165 (doubtful)

187   Study of a soldier and a page

Chalk and pen and ink
13.5 × 11.7 cm

LOCATION Madrid, Biblioteca Nacional Inv. 7255
INSCRIBED in chalk: 'Verones'
PROVENANCE José de Madrazo
BIBLIOGRAPHY De Barcia 7255 (for the Madrid painting); Tietze
and Tietze-Conrat A2115 (derived from the painting)

While there can be no doubt that both these drawings relate to
the *Christ and the centurion* now in the Prado[1] the older view that
saw them as preparatory sketches for the painting, albeit unique
in style, was rightly challenged by the Tietzes. They convincingly
argued that the handling has nothing to do with Veronese and
that the drawings derive from the painting.

NOTE

1   Pignatti 165. The early history is unclear; it was first mentioned in the large
cloister of El Escorial in 1698 (not having been there in 1657), Francisco de los
Santos, *Descripción breve del monasterio de S. Lorenzo el Real del Escorial*, ed.
F. J. Sánchez Cantón, *Fuentes Literarias para la Historia del Arte Español*
2 (Madrid, 1933), pp 296–97

188   Study of the Holy Family appearing to three saints

Pen and ink over chalk on grey prepared paper
30.6 × 17.6 cm

LOCATION Madrid, Biblioteca Nacional Inv. 7256
PROVENANCE Carderera
BIBLIOGRAPHY De Barcia 7256

The old attribution to Veronese has not won critical acceptance, understandably since it fits with Carletto's *Study of the Holy Family with Sts John the Baptist and Catherine* in the British Museum (Fig 101)[1] and also with Carletto's altar from San Nicolò del Lido, now in the Fondazione Giorgio Cini.[2] The connection is curious, since although they share the upright, round-headed, formula with the Virgin and Child in the sky and saints placed against architecture below, the drawing lacks Sts Lucy, Catherine, Agatha and Apollonia in the sky and reduces the male saints to three. It may have been submitted to the patrons who demanded the expansion shown in the painting or it might be a private variation based upon the altar.[3]

NOTES

1   Inv. 1895-9-15-848, *see* under (160) note 1

2   Both the provenance and the correct attribution were established by E. Tietze-Conrat, 'Not Paolo but Carletto Caliari', *Art Bulletin* 28 (1946), pp 53–54. It was Talbot sale, London, Christie 29 October 1941, 426 and Sotheby 7 December 1960, 119

3   Other drawings which can be linked with these and attributed to Carletto include: Besançon, *Study for an Adoration of the Magi* (for S. Antonio, Torcello) Tietzes 2160, *see* further under (158) notes 7 and 8. Cambridge, Mass., Fogg Art Museum Inv. 1918.29, *Study of Moses striking the rock*. Berlin-Dahlem, Staatliche Museen, *Study for the angel appears to St Catherine*, Tietzes 2197. London, British Museum Inv. 1890-415-172, *Study of an Ecce Homo*, Tietzes 2170; 1895-9-15-843, *Study of God the Father appears to three saints*, Robinson no 398; 1895-9-15-842, *Study of God the Father appears to five saints*, Robinson no 397. Lille Pluchart 128, *Study of the Fall of Manna* (for a companion picture to *Moses striking the rock* (?)). Milan, Ambrosiana, *Study of Tancred and Erminia*, Bora p 101 and the *Study for a Last Supper*, Bora p 102 (it prepares the painting signed by the Eredi in the Certosa di S. Martino, Naples). Paris, Louvre Inv. 4,662, *Study for the Marriage of the Virgin*, Tietze and Tietze-Conrat A2134 (the attribution to Carletto by K. Oberhuber is noted on the mount); 4,664, *Study of the Holy Family* (*see* under (160) note 2); 4,668, *Project for a tabernacle* (Tietze and Tietze-Conrat A2132), one of the unsuccessful designs for the high altar of S. Giorgio Maggiore which was commissioned from Girolamo Campagna from a design from Aliense on 20 January 1591, Sir J. Pope-Hennessy, *Italian High Renaissance and Baroque Sculpture* (London, 1970), pp 414–15; 4,686, *Study for an Adoration of the shepherds*, Tietze and Tietze-Conrat 2181 noting the connection with the painting, Pignatti A342. Stockholm, Nationalmuseum, NMH 1543/1863, *Study of the Virgin and Child visit St John the Baptist with his parents* and NMH 1544/1863 *Study of the Holy Family with saints*, Bjurström nos 9 and 10, clearly a variation on the *Study for the Holy Family with Sts John the Baptist and Anne* in the British Museum (*see* under (160) note 2). Vienna, Albertina, Inv. 1630, *Study for a Raising of Lazarus*, Tietzes A2210 (wrongly as a copy, *see* Cocke 1971 p 733). H.M. the Queen, Windsor Castle, Popham and Wilde 1035, *Study for an Adoration of the shepherds* for the picture in S. Afra, Brescia, *see* Dr L. Crosato-Larcher, 'Per Carletto Caliari', *Arte Veneta* 21 (1967), p 112 fig 124; 1022, *Study of the Birth of the Virgin*, a variation on Benedetto's *Birth of the Virgin* painted for the Scuola dei Mercanti in 1577, S. Moschini-Marconi, *Gallerie dell' Accademia, Opere d'arte del secolo XVI* (Rome, 1962), p 77; 1028, *Study of the Holy Family with St John the Baptist and unidentified saints*, Tietzes 2212. The *Study of the Holy Family with Sts Anne and Francis*, in the Uffizi, although attributed to Carletto appears weaker, 14955F. For other drawings by Carletto, *see* under (Fig 53) Amsterdam *Death* (158), Berlin *Supper at Emmaus* (160), Cleveland *Study* (168), London *Study for a Venus* (181), Milan *Adam and Eve* (190), Stockholm *Head of a woman* (217), and *Copy of the mystic marriage of St Catherine* (162) note 2

188 Study of the Holy Family appearing to three saints

189 Study of the Virgin and Child with two saints

189 Study of the Virgin and Child with two saints

Grey chalk on blue prepared paper heightened with white
24 × 37.5 cm

LOCATION Milan, Ambrosiana Cod.F.271 inf. no 67
BIBLIOGRAPHY Venice 1979 no 36

In his 1979 catalogue Ruggeri argued that the attribution to
Veronese, which had been tentatively suggested by Konrad
Oberhuber, should be accepted because it could not be related to
any member of the workshop. This is true, but the same argument
can be used against the attribution to Veronese. It differs from
the use of the chalk in the autograph drawings, the *Study for
St Lawrence* in Rotterdam (73), for instance. It is also very
different in handling from the *Copy of St Matthew and an angel*
in Florence (173), to which Ruggeri compared it, and may be by
a follower, possibly Benedetto, inspired by the *Madonna and
Child with saints* in Vicenza.[1]

NOTE
1 Pignatti 55

190   Study for Adam and Eve after the fall

190   Study for Adam and Eve after the fall

Pen and ink and wash over grey chalk
20 × 28 cm

LOCATION Milan, Ambrosiana 98/2 p 97
PROVENANCE Padre Resta
BIBLIOGRAPHY A. Morassi, 'Di due opere del Veronese',
Bollettino d' Arte 31 (1937–38), pp 241ff; W. E. Suida, 'Notes
sur Paul Véronèse', *Gazette des Beaux-Arts* 19 (1938), pp 169
fig 2; Tietze and Tietze-Conrat 2174 (school); Bora p 97
(school)

Morassi convincingly connected the drawing with the painting
of this subject, the prime version of which is now in Vienna.[1]
This presents a problem to those critics who follow the Tietzes
in recognising that the drawing is not autograph, but who wish
to maintain the attribution of the painting. Bora, for instance,
argued that the drawing derives from the painting, because
Adam's left hand, which in the canvas rests on the trunk of a
tree, is held up in the air. On the contrary, this proves that it is a
preparatory drawing since it alters the short post which had been
drawn in with grey chalk underneath. I believe that the solution
which the Tietzes proposed for the drawing, that it is by the
school, should be extended to the painting. The landscape is
simplified by comparison with that of Veronese's magnificent
Good Samaritan in Dresden.[2] The loose calligraphy of the
drawing fits with drawings by Carletto, most notably the *Study
of the Holy Family with Sts John the Baptist and Catherine* in the
British Museum (Fig 101),[3] and Carletto may be responsible for
the Vienna painting.[4]

NOTES
1   Pignatti 695
2   Pignatti 327; by 6 March 1649 it had passed from the Reinst collection and
was being offered for sale by N. Renier as del Sera noted in a letter to Cardinal
Leopoldo de' Medici, Florence, Archivio de Stato *Lettere Artistiche* V, 19; it
was first noted in Modena by Fr. Scanelli, *Il Microcosmo della Pittura* (Cesena,
1657), *ed. cit.* Milan 1966 p 247
3   *See* under (160) note 1
4   It is weaker than Veronese's treatment of the same subject, now in the
Prado, Pignatti 325 as *The family of Cain;* I see no reason to change the title of
Adam and Eve by which it was first cited as no 533 in the 1666 inventory of the
Alcázar, Y. Bottineau, *Bulletin Hispanique, Bordeaux* 60 (1958), p 165 no 325

193 Study of a prelate (actual size)

191 Copy of Neptune

Wash on blue prepared paper heightened with white
19 × 27 cm
LOCATION Milan, Castello Sforzesco Inv. 2021/6961
PROVENANCE Bolognini
BIBLIOGRAPHY E. Arslan, 'Note su Veronese e Zelotti', *Belle Arte*
5–6 (1948), p 230

192 Copy of Fame

Wash on blue prepared paper heightened with white
20.4 × 28.5 cm
LOCATION Milan, Castello Sforzesco Inv. 2372/6954
BIBLIOGRAPHY Tietze-Conrat 1940 pp 37–38: Tietze and
Tietze-Conrat 2171; E. Arslan, 'Note su Veronese e Zelotti',
Belle Arte 5–6 (1948), p 230

See under (3) for a discussion of these two sheets. They form
part of a group of fifteen, some of which were first discussed by
Mrs Tietze-Conrat. Her list was amplified by Arslan who argued
that the *Fame* and the *Neptune* were autograph. They are
however copies which are unlikely, as Mrs Tietze-Conrat suggested, to have formed part of the studio's working material.

193 Study of a prelate

Grey chalk on brown tinted paper heightened with white
21.6 × 18.1 cm
LOCATION Munich, Staatliche Graphische Sammlung
Inv. 12893
BIBLIOGRAPHY Von Hadeln pl 48; G. Fiocco, *Paolo Veronese*
(Rome, 1934), p 130; Tietze and Tietze-Conrat 2118

This fine portrait does not appear to have been retouched in the
white heightening as Von Hadeln suggested. It is very different
in handling from the *Study of an apostle* (76) and the *Study of the
head of an old man looking down* (112) recently on the London
art market, both of which have much better claims to be by

Veronese. Fiocco's identification of the sitter as Daniele Barbaro
(on the basis of the portrait in Amsterdam)[1] although attractive
is, I believe, to be rejected. In spite of a general similarity there
are significant differences, most notably the longer more aquiline
nose and the bushier beard of the figure in the painting, whose
hair has not receded as far as in the present sheet. The Tietzes
noted that the attribution of the present sheet had been much
discussed and I tend to agree with those critics who viewed it as
being by an older artist, perhaps Paris Bordone.[2]

NOTES
1   Pignatti 143
2   This is suggested by the Berlin drawing that was exhibited London 1930
no 276

194 Study of a kneeling woman with a man standing behind

Red chalk on blue coloured paper
29.5 × 21.1 cm
LOCATION New York, William H. Schab Gallery
PROVENANCE Skippe, thence to the Martin family; sold London,
Christie 20–21 November 1958, 229A
BIBLIOGRAPHY Birmingham, Alabama 1972 p 60

The catalogue of the Skippe sale rightly doubted whether the
present drawing had anything to do with Veronese and suggested
that it might be considerably later in date.

195 Study of a fur cape

Black and white chalk on grey-green paper
32.3 × 21.2 cm
LOCATION New York, Janos Scholz
BIBLIOGRAPHY Oberhuber and Walker no 107 (attributed to
Veronese); Scholz no 63 (Veronese)

This splendid study of a rich garment of a type often worn in
Veronese's paintings so differs in its handling from the *Study for
the Portrait of a member of the Soranzo family* (77) and the *Study
of a kneeling magus* (67) that it cannot be by Veronese.

196   Copy of the Omnia Vanitas

196   Copy of the Omnia Vanitas

Pen and ink over chalk on blue prepared paper heightened
with white

32.9 × 23.6 cm

LOCATION New York, Janos Scholz

INSCRIBED 'Paolo Veronese'

PROVENANCE Moscardo (Lugt 2990)

BIBLIOGRAPHY Venice 1957 no 26 (Veronese); Cocke
    Master Drawings 1977 p 267

Although the drawing differs from the painting of this subject in
the Frick collection (Fig 22),[1] the poor quality (when compared
to the Chatsworth *Modello for the Martyrdom of St Justina* (75))
reveals a copyist as in the Boston *Copy of the Mystic marriage of
St Catherine* (162).

NOTE

1   Pignatti 243 and Cocke *Pantheon* 1977 pp 120 ff for a dating before 1567

197   Study of a man on horseback (actual size)

197   Study of a man on horseback

Pen and ink and wash
8.5 × 5.5 cm

LOCATION New York, Janos Scholz
PROVENANCE Moscardo (Lugt 2990); Marquis de Calceolari
BIBLIOGRAPHY Oberhuber and Walker no 105

This charming small drawing reflects the style of Veronese's rapid pen and ink sketches without being by him. Oberhuber and Walker compared it to the Berlin *Studies for a Marriage feast at Cana* (58) and also noted that similar figures occur in the *Venice triumphant* (Fig 57). A comparison with the Berlin drawing for the *Triumph* (88) underlines that here the freedom of stroke takes on a decorative quality that militates against the creation of the three dimensional form found in the Berlin drawing and suggests that it might be by Palma Giovane.[1]

NOTE
1   This attribution is due to Julien Stock and Philip Pouncey

198   Study of God the Father

Black chalk on grey paper heightened with white
32 × 27.5 cm

LOCATION New York, Ian Woodner
PROVENANCE R. W. P. de Vries (Lugt 2496)
BIBLIOGRAPHY Birmingham, Alabama 1972 p 47;
     William H. Schab Gallery, New York *Woodner Collection 1
     A Selection of Old Master Drawings* (1972), no 33

The heavy forceful cross-hatching in the drapery and the forms of the head and hands have nothing to do with Veronese.

199   Study of a sacrifice (actual size)

Fig 106   Alvise dal Friso(?), *Study of a sacrifice*, pen and wash, British Museum, London

Fig 107   Battista Zelotti, *Study of an allegorical lady*, pen and ink and wash, British Museum, London

199   Study of a sacrifice

Pen and ink and wash over grey chalk
20.5 × 13.9 cm

LOCATION Oxford, Christ Church Inv. 1325
PROVENANCE General Guise
BIBLIOGRAPHY Ballarin *Arte Veneta* 1971 pp99–101 (Veronese);
   Byam Shaw 1976 no790 (Zelotti)

Ballarin attributed the drawing to Veronese as one of the projects for the now lost frescoes of Villa Soranza. The attribution was rightly doubted by Byam Shaw. He noted its connection with a drawing in the British Museum (Fig 106), which he attributed to Zelotti on the basis of its connection with the *Sacrifice to the golden calf* in the Scholz collection, which has an old attribution to Zelotti. While this is possible both the Scholz and British Museum drawings differ, as was noted under the *Studies of Fame* (3) in Hamburg, from the *Study of an allegorical lady* in the British Museum attributed to Zelotti with better reason (Fig 107),[1] and belong rather with the group of drawings attributed to Alvise dal Friso (165).

NOTE

1   Cocke *M.K.I.F.* 1977 pp214–16 and fig 5

200 Study of Hercules slays the Hydra and sacrifices to Athena (?)

Pen and ink and wash
16.2 × 29.9 cm

LOCATION Oxford, Ashmolean Museum Inv. 744A
PROVENANCE Sir Peter Lely (Lugt 2092); Jonathan Richardson, Senior (Lugt 2984); Anon. (Lugt 474)
BIBLIOGRAPHY Macandrew pp 74–76

In spite of Richardson's attribution to Veronese on the mount, Sir Karl Parker suggested at the time of the drawing's purchase in 1957 that it might be by Carletto Caliari. This view, is not substantiated by a comparison with Carletto's certain drawings (Figs 101, 102). It seems, however, to understand the quality of the sheet better than Macandrew's that it might be an early drawing by Veronese and that it is similar in style to the *Study of St Roch in glory* in Boston (161).

The absence of white heightening makes the connection difficult to assess but both here and in the superior version, to judge from a photograph, which was sold London, Sotheby 21 November 1974, 25, the absence of *pentimenti* suggests a copy, perhaps after a lost decorative scheme.[1]

NOTE
1 According to Ridolfi pp 359–60, Benedetto was responsible for frescoes of deeds of Hercules on the façade of Palazzo Nani on the Giudecca. They did not include this scene, which Macandrew identified as *Hercules slaying the lion and feasted by Molorchos*; the curling tail of the animal, which is clearer in the Sotheby version, makes it unlikely to be the Nemean lion. It could be a rejected design to go above the three small windows on the right of the now destroyed façade of Palazzo Nani, the engraving of which by Coronelli is reproduced by E. Bassi, *Palazzi di Venezia Admiranda Urbis Venetae* (Venice, 1976), p 515

201 Copy of a portrait of Paolo Veronese

Black chalk on faded blue paper
18.5 × 13.1 cm

LOCATION Paris, Ecole des Beaux-Arts Inv. 24290
INSCRIBED on the mount: 'Ritratto di Paolo Veronese'
PROVENANCE W. Esdaile (Lugt 2617), his sale London, Christie 18–25 June 1840, 435
BIBLIOGRAPHY Tietze and Tietze-Conrat 2140; P. Fehl, 'Questions of identity in Veronese's *Christ and the Centurion*', *Art Bulletin* 39 (1957), pp 301–302

The Tietzes were understandably sceptical about the attribution of the present drawing which is much weaker than the certain chalk studies by Veronese, notably the *Study of an apostle* of 1575 (76). They pointed out that the same man occurred on the right of the *Christ and the centurion* now in Kansas City, which Pignatti has convincingly attributed to Benedetto.[1] The differences in the hair, for instance, suggest that both refer back to a lost portrait, perhaps that of Veronese[2] in armour which Ridolfi described in the Contarini collection at San Samuele.[3]

NOTES
1 Pignatti A 130; it was probably no 20 in the Lauraguais sale, Paris 12 March 1772, as noted by C. Blanc, *Le Trésor de la curiosité* 2 (Paris, 1857), p 209 with dimensions of 52 by 77 ins and was in the Mildmay collection, exhibited London, Royal Academy 1883 no 184
2 The identity of the portrait was discussed by Fehl; by comparison with the certain portraits of Veronese, that in the *Marriage feast at Cana*, for instance, the head is idealised and the hair line restored
3 Ridolfi II p 225 and Pignatti 233

202 Study of Faith (actual size)

Fig 108 Alvise dal Friso(?), *Study of a kneeling woman*, pen and wash heightened with white, private collection, New York

202 Study of Faith

Pen and ink
11 × 8.8 cm

LOCATION Paris, Musée du Louvre Inv. 4,675
INSCRIBED presumably by Mariette: 'Paulo Verones';
   on the mount: 'Fuit Cardinalis Santa Croce, postea P. Crozat'
PROVENANCE Cardinal Santa Croce; P. Crozat, presumably his
   sale Paris, Mariette 1775; P. J. Mariette (Lugt 1852),
   probably his sale Paris, Basan 1775, part of 246[1]

In spite of the traditional attribution to Veronese, the drawing belongs with the group of sheets which I believe may be by Alvise dal Friso, including the *Study of a kneeling woman* in a private collection, New York (Fig 108) and the *Study of a decorative figure* also in the Louvre (206). As with other drawings in the group, the artist looks back to Veronese's early work, in this case the Parmigianinesque[2] St Catherine in the Giustiniani altar in S. Francesco alla Vigna, which is probably datable to 1551.[3] It, rather than the canvas of this subject in the O'Connor Lynch collection in New York,[4] formed the starting-point for the *Faith* by an unidentified member of the workshop, one of a set of four canvases now in Munich.[5]

NOTES

1   p 42, 'Trois petits sujets, dont le Martyre d'une sainte, Venus et l'amour etc'. *See* (209)

2   Here the inspiration was Schiavone's etching of the *Holy Family with Sts John the Baptist, Joseph and the Magdalen*, F. L. Richardson, *Andrea Schiavone* (Oxford, 1980), cat 64

3   Pignatti 5

4   Pignatti 141 no 208 dates it late. It was in the Countess Brownlow collection in 1893 as *St Barbara* but with dimensions of 96 by 70 cm which agree with those of the New York painting (93 by 77.5 cm), *see* A. Graves, *A century of loan exhibitions 1813–1912* (London, 1913–15), *ed. cit.* Bath, 1970, p 1577

5   Inv. 455. From Schleissheim since 1692, *see* Munich Bayerische Staatsgemäldesammlungen, Alte Pinakothek, *Venezianische Gemälde des 15. und 16. Jahrhunderts*, ed. R. Kultzen with P. Eikemeier (1971), pp 215ff

203   Studies for a Marriage feast at Cana

203 Studies for a Marriage feast at Cana

203v Studies of architecture

Pen and ink and wash (recto only)

18.5 × 32 cm

LOCATION Paris, Musée du Louvre Inv. RF 39,031
INSCRIBED by a later collector: 'S. P. N.o 10'
PROVENANCE Anon. (Lugt 2103a; sometimes described as the Borghese collection);[1] private collection; acquired in 1983

This striking sheet relates, as Roseline Bacou has noted, to the great *Marriage feast at Cana* painted for the refectory of S. Giorgio Maggiore by October 1563 and now in the Louvre.[2] Mlle Bacou has argued in conversation that the changes between the drawing and the canvas cannot be explained as derivations from the painting, but that, although unique, this represents Veronese's first idea for his great canvas. The round church in the background echoes that by a different hand on the verso and may be related to Palladio's initial project for the church, and the change in the position of the musicians to the left-hand side can only have been made by Veronese.

This is possible, but I share Mlle Bacou's initial doubts which led her to omit this drawing from the main group of acquisitions published in her article in *Master Drawings*. The freedom of handling goes beyond any certain Veronese to an almost Baroque formlessness. The church cannot, as Bacou has suggested, have been included in the background before being covered by the clouds on the left just above the architecture, for it is too large for such a position. The artist has similarly failed to appreciate the flow of the orders from the manly doric framing Christ in the foreground, through the composite to the ionic in the background. Here it is reduced to ionic.

The drawing has to be understood as part of the continued vogue for Veronese's *Feasts* on the part of both patrons and artists. Although by a different, unidentified hand, it can be compared with other variations on the theme of the Feast found in the *Study for a Feast in the house of Simon* (164) and the group of mainly, but not exclusively, classical subjects in grand settings attributable to Valentin Lefebre.[3] Its popularity is also shown by the large version over the nave entrance door in S. Trovaso, which after its recent cleaning has been attributed to Andrea Vicentino[4] and which must have been produced in the early 1590s.[5]

NOTES

1 Monte Carlo 1966 intro. The mark was, however, only added in the late eighteenth century, *see* London, Sotheby 9 July 1981, 132
2 Pignatti 131
3 *See* (212) note 2 and also Florence, Uffizi 1850 F, *A Marriage feast at Cana*, with the musicians behind Christ on the left
4 F. Valcanover, 'L'attivita nel 1978/79 della soprintendenza ai beni artistici e storici di Venezia', *Arte Veneta* 33 (1979), p 228
5 G. Lorenzetti, *Venice and its Lagoon* (Trieste, 1975), p 551 notes that the church was rebuilt after its collapse in 1583

204 Study of Mars, Venus and Cupid

Pen and ink and wash on grey prepared paper heightened with white

27.9 × 21 cm

LOCATION Paris, Musée du Louvre Inv. 4,676
PROVENANCE Everard Jabach (Lugt 2959), no 66 in the Venetian section of his manuscript catalogue; ceded to the French Royal collection in 1671
BIBLIOGRAPHY Tietze and Tietze-Conrat A2137 (a follower, possibly Farinati); Cocke *Master Drawings* 1977 p 267 (possibly Carletto); Paris 1978 (unpaginated)

The composition is a free variation on the now lost *Venus with a mirror* painted by Veronese for the Emperor Rudolph II in the early 1580s.[1] It was developed from the *Studies of Venus and Cupid* in the British Museum (106) and could be by the same hand as the Cleveland *Study of a Judgement of Paris* (167).

NOTE

1 There is another, weaker, version in the Teyler Museum, Haarlem, Inv. NB57

Fig 109   Follower of Veronese, *Martyrdom of St Justina*, Museo Civico, Padua

205   Study for the Martyrdom of St Justina

Pen and ink and wash over traces of grey chalk
19.6 × 15.5 cm

LOCATION Paris, Musée du Louvre Inv. 4,673
PROVENANCE P. J. Mariette (Lugt 1852), his sale Paris, Basan
1775, part of 246

The drawing, although reversed and upright in format, was
made in preparation for the *Martyrdom of St Justina* in the
Museo Civico, Padua (Fig 109). The picture has an old, but, in
my opinion, unreliable attribution to Veronese.[1] It came to the
Museum from the abbey of S. Giustina in Padua and may be the
modello for the altarpiece in S. Giustina to which Ridolfi referred,
since although not a drawing it is in Ridolfi's words 'in alcuni
parti variato'.[2] It can be related not to the altarpiece (Fig 42)
but to the reduced version now in the Uffizi. A comparison of the
saint in the Padua and Uffizi *Martyrdoms* reveals the Padua
picture as a weaker derivation, a point further confirmed by the
feeble handling of the executioners and by the failure to control
the lighting. The drawing differs from the painting so that it may
be the preparatory sketch whose fluid wash and dancing figures
recall the Chatsworth *Study of the Virgin and Child with Sts John
the Baptist and Louis of Toulouse* (165), and may well be by
Alvise dal Friso.

NOTES

1   Pignatti 60; the engraving by Menarola bears the date of 1556, but I believe
that the connections with the Uffizi painting make this unlikely and point to a
date in the late 1570s, *see* (75) note 5
2   Ridolfi p 317, *see also* the discussion under (75)

205 Study for the Martyrdom of St Justina (actual size)

206   Study of a decorative figure (actual size)

206   Study of a decorative figure

Pen and wash on blue paper heightened with white
17 × 11 cm

LOCATION Paris, Musée du Louvre Inv. 9,060

The drawing, which had previously been attributed to Pellegrino Tibaldi, was brought to my attention by Philip Pouncey. Although it has parallels with a number of autograph sheets, notably the *Studies of Fame* in Hamburg (3) and the *Study of Count Giuseppe da Porto with his son Adriano* (4), there are differences. The closest parallel for the insistent penmanship and bold use of *pentimenti* is in the *Study of a kneeling woman* in a private collection, New York (Fig 108),[1] which can in turn be connected with the twisting pose of St Louis on the right of the *Study of the Virgin and Child with Sts John the Baptist and Louis of Toulouse* at Chatsworth (165), very probably by Alvise dal Friso. If, as I believe this is right, the group of drawings which can be attributed to Alvise dal Friso includes the *Study of Faith* (202), the *Study for Venus disarms Cupid* (209), the *Study for the Martyrdom of St Justina* (205) all in the Louvre and the two *Studies of a sacrifice* at Christ Church, Oxford (199) and the British Museum (Fig 106). Alvise dal Friso looks back to earlier works by Veronese, in this case to the *Temperance* of 1551 in Castelfranco, from Villa Soranza.[2]

NOTES

1   It measures approx 20 by 16 cm and is in pen and wash heightened with white

2   Pignatti pl 13

Fig 110   Workshop of Veronese (Benedetto Caliari?), *Christ with the woman taken in adultery* (detail), Kunsthistorisches Museum, Vienna

207   Study of a woman's head

Grey and white chalk on buff coloured paper
33.3 × 24.5 cm

LOCATION Paris, Musée du Louvre Inv. 4,720
INSCRIBED 'Paulo Veronese'

The museum's attribution to Benedetto appears to be borne out by its connection with the *Christ with the woman taken in adultery* in Vienna (Fig 110). This is one of the series of paintings from the collection of the Duke of Buckingham[1] which was begun by Veronese (119), but completed by the workshop, presumably after his death in 1588. The division of hands in the series remains an open question but the *Christ with the woman taken in adultery* is a bolder reworking of the version now in Munich which had been presented to S. Maria Maggiore in 1584 and which may have been executed by Benedetto.[2] This large-scale chalk study is very different from the softer, more Titianesque, handling of the heads attributed to Veronese (14, 130). Its scale shows the care with which the remainder of the series in the Duke of Buckingham's collection was prepared by the workshop.

NOTES

1   Pignatti A384; it was first mentioned in the 1635 inventory of the Duke of Buckingham's picture at York House, ed. R. Davies, *Burlington Magazine* 10 (1906–1907), p 381

2   Pignatti A198 (the provenance is cited under A196). The attribution to Benedetto can be extended to the *Christ's farewell to his mother* and *Christ with the Maries* in Palazzo Pitti, the *Presentation of Christ* in a private collection, England, Pignatti A84, A85 and A128 as well as the pair of paintings in the Wengraf collection, London, Pignatti A153 and A154 (*see* (112) note 3), the *Entombment* in Geneva (Fig 82), and possibly the *Raising of Lazarus* (Fig 69) and the *Consecration of St Nicholas*, from S. Nicolò dei Mendicoli (Fig 70)

207   Study of a woman's head

208   Copy of Venus and Mercury before Jupiter

Pen and ink and wash on green tinted paper heightened with
white

31.1 × 42.5 cm

LOCATION Paris, Musée du Louvre Inv. 4,719
PROVENANCE Everard Jabach (Lugt 2959), no 53 in the Venetian
section of his manuscript catalogue; ceded to the French
Royal collection in 1671
BIBLIOGRAPHY Cocke *Master Drawings* 1977 p 268; Paris 1978
(unpaginated)

The mechanical handling reveals that in spite of minor changes
this is a copy after the painting of the same subject formerly in
the Contini-Bonacossi collection in Florence.[1] Here Veronese
rendered a myth invented by the fourth-century rhetorician
Themistius[2] which was printed by the Aldine Press in 1534 and
which was made available to a wider public by Lodovico Dolce's
1554 Italian translation (itself based on the work of Mario
Equicola who had noted the importance of the passage for a
discussion of the nature of Anteros). According to Themistius:
'When Aphrodite bore Eros the lad was fair and like his mother
in every way, save that he did not grow. This matter perplexed
his mother and the muses who nursed him, and presenting
themselves before Themis they begged a cure. So Themis spoke
"Why", she said "I will solve your difficulty, for you have not
yet learned the nature of the child. Your true Eros, Aphrodite,
might indeed be born by himself, but could not possibly grow by
himself; if you wish Eros to grow you need Anteros." So
Aphrodite gave birth to Anteros'.

Veronese has concentrated the action so that Anteros appears
behind Venus, already a healthy five- or six-year-old child. The
tiny Eros is held by Mercury and presented to Jupiter. This
indicates that the subject has been transposed from Greek to
Roman mythology. The presence of Mercury reflects the passage in Cicero's *De Natura Deorum* in which, in his second
incarnation, Cupid is the son of Venus and Mercury.[3]

NOTES
1   Pignatti 117
2   R. V. Merrill, 'Eros and Anteros', *Speculum* 19 (1944), pp 271–73
3   Noted by Merrill p 269

209   Study for Venus disarms Cupid (actual size)

Fig 111   Silvestrini, *Engraving of the Venus disarms Cupid*, from the *Choix de Gravures . . . de la Galerie de Lucien Bonaparte* (London, 1812), no 79

209   Study for Venus disarms Cupid

Pen and ink and wash over traces of grey chalk
8 × 7.7 cm

LOCATION Paris, Musée du Louvre Inv. 4,675 bis
INSCRIBED 'PAULO VERONENSIS'; on the mount: 'Fuit Cardinalis Santa Croce, postea P. Crozat'
PROVENANCE Cardinal Santa Croce; P. Crozat, presumably his sale Paris, Mariette 1775; P. J. Mariette (Lugt 1852), his sale Paris, Basan 1775, part of 246
BIBLIOGRAPHY Mariette 1, 1851–53, pp 243 ff

The modern neglect of this drawing contrasts with its earlier fame. Mariette noted apropos of an anonymous engraving after the sheet that it had inspired the painting by Watteau, now in the Musée Condé, Chantilly.[1] This estimate is not borne out by a comparison of the handling of the pen and wash over the grey chalk to the *Studies of Venus with Cupid* in the British Museum (106), which can be dated to the early 1580s. Like the *Study of*

Faith (202) on the same mount it belongs with a group of drawings probably by Alvise dal Friso which includes the Chatsworth *Study of the Virgin and Child with Sts John the Baptist and Louis of Toulouse* (165), the *Study of a kneeling woman* in a private collection, New York (Fig 109) and the *Study of a decorative figure* in the Louvre (206). The drawing formed the starting-point for the now lost *Venus disarms Cupid* from the collection of Lucien Bonaparte (Fig 111),[2] and that from the Colonna collection now in a private collection in Rome.[3] The action in the Rome version is set in a boudoir which, as in the drawing, reflects Titian's *Venus of Urbino*.

NOTES
1   E. Camesasca, *The complete paintings of Watteau* (London, 1971), p 124
2   Engraved by Silvestrini in the *Choix de Gravures à l'eau forte d'après les peintures originales et les marbres de la Galerie de Lucien Bonaparte* (London, 1812), no 79, sold London, Stanley 14–16 May 1816, 25 (21 by 21 ins), bt Buchan
3   Pignatti 255; how do Venus's legs connect with her body? The modelling has none of the subtlety of other certain mythologies

210 Study of the Virgin and Child with Sts Peter, Paul and angels

Pen and ink over grey chalk heightened with white
37.4 × 51.4 cm

LOCATION Paris, Musée du Louvre Inv. 4,816
PROVENANCE Everard Jabach (Lugt 2959), no 72 in the Venetian section of his manuscript catalogue (Veronese); ceded to the French Royal collection in 1671
BIBLIOGRAPHY Ballarin *Arte Veneta* 1971 p 98; Florence 1976 p 157; Paris 1978 (unpaginated)

Ballarin identified this drawing, which had been given to Farinati, as a preparatory sketch by Veronese for a lost altar dedicated to St George. He identified a copy after it in the Louvre, Inv. 4,839, and Rearick added the *Study of St George and the dragon* in the Uffizi (172). The style has been compared with that of the *Temptation of St Anthony* in the Louvre (36) and *The supper at Emmaus* at Chatsworth (35). The application of the white heightening has none of that sense of lightness which Mariette characterised so well:[1] 'ce blanc qui est merveilleusement bien mis, exprime différentes nuances de clair, qui conduisent par degrée depuis le demi-teinte jusqu'à la lumière la plus vive. Cette manière qui est pleine d'intelligence appartient à quelque façon en propre à Paul Veronésè'. The laboured awkward handling of the drawing, suggests a copyist inspired by Veronese's *chiaroscuro* drawings. It also contrasts with that of another drawing of this subject in the Fitzwilliam[2] which Ballarin classified as a copy, on the basis of its correspondence with the copy of the whole design in the Louvre, but whose status has been queried by Byam Shaw.[3]

NOTES
1 1741 pp 75–76
2 PD 132–1961, Tietze and Tietze-Conrat 2254 (Zelotti)
3 1976 p 213

211 Copy of the Virgin and Child appear to Sts Anthony Abbot, Paul the Hermit, Peter and Paul

Pen and ink and wash
65.7 × 42 cm

LOCATION Paris, Musée du Louvre Inv. 4,716
BIBLIOGRAPHY Dr L. Crosato-Larcher, 'Per Carletto Caliari', *Arte Veneta* 21 (1967), p 111; Cocke *Master Drawings* 1977 p 267

In quality the drawing is clearly a copy, probably after the picture, and not, as Dr Crosato-Larcher has argued, a preparatory drawing by Carletto.[1] It has been torn on the left where St Anthony's hat has been repaired by a later hand and this may account for the differences from the painting now in Dijon[2] which are confined to this area of the sheet.

NOTES
1 *Compare*, for instance, the *Study for the Death of the Virgin* by Carletto in Amsterdam (158)
2 Pignatti A62; I cannot follow his attribution of the picture to the workshop, Cocke *Veronese* 1981 p 104

212 Copy after a Rest on the Flight into Egypt

Pen and ink and wash
30.6 × 21 cm

LOCATION Rotterdam, Museum Boymans-van Beuningen
Inv. I408
INSCRIBED on the verso with a series of accounts by Veronese
which run from 4 June 1570 through 26 October 1571 to
18 October 1572
PROVENANCE F. Koenigs (Lugt 1023a); acquired by D. G. van
Beuningen in 1940
BIBLIOGRAPHY Cocke 1973 p 145

This drawing is rightly classified by the Museum as a school
sheet. The accounts on the verso (212v) are clearly by the same
hand as those on the verso of the sheet of *Studies* (53v) also in
Rotterdam, dating from 1560 to 1564 and which are by the same
hand, albeit rather neater, as Veronese's autograph letter to
Marcantonio Gandini of 1578 (Fig 87). The Rotterdam drawing
has the looseness of stroke of Veronese's mature drawings,
without however, his sense of form, and is similar to the *Rest*
now in Sarasota.[1] The differences are so slight that they reveal a
copyist, recording a painting about to leave the studio. The date
of *circa* 1572 suggests that it could well be by Benedetto Caliari,
Veronese's younger brother (b. *circa* 1538) who appears to have
made another copy after one of his brother's paintings in the
Copies of Martha and Judas (185) recently sold at Sotheby's. The
attribution to Benedetto of the Judas and of the present study
gains weight from their resemblance to the *Study for the Marriage
of the Virgin* in the Uffizi.[2] This was made in preparation for
the painting from the Othobon collection, Venice,[3] now in the
Wadsworth Atheneum, Hartford, which was shown with the
date of 1577 in an old engraving.[4]

NOTES
1   Pignatti 320
2   Inv. 17233p Cocke 1973 p 145; the drawing in Windsor (Popham and Wilde
no 1025) seems to me now to belong with the group that Julien Stock has
attributed to Valentin Lefebre, Venice 1980 nos 53 and 54 to which can be
added the *Study for a Purification of the Virgin* in Munich, Tietze and Tietze-
Conrat A2119

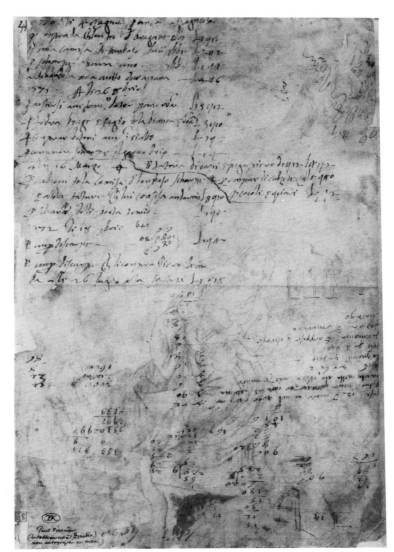

212v   Series of accounts

3   Mentioned by Ridolfi p 339 and as being a small canvas with eight to ten
figures by B. de Monconys, *Journal des Voyages* 2 (Lyons, 1666), p 425. Del Sera
wrote to Leopoldo de' Medici in September 1664 that it was one of the pictures
acquired by the Duke of Mantua (Florence, Archivio di Stato *Lettere Artistiche*
VI, 301), where it was in the 1665 and 1709 inventories of La Favorita with
dimensions of 6 by 5 quarte (it is not clear whether height precedes width) –
equivalent to 103 by 85 cm which are close to those of the Hartford canvas,
80.5 by 72 cm, A. Luzio, *La Galleria dei Gonzaga venduta all' Inghilterra nel
1627–28* (Milan, 1913), p 315. It subsequently passed to the Corsini Gallery in
Rome whence it came to London at the beginning of the nineteenth century to
be sold Ransom and Morland 6 January 1801, 37; London, Christie, Ottley
collection, 16 May 1801, 37 and Christie, Walsh Porter sale, 14 April 1810, 31.
The 1750 inventory of the Corsini collection confirms the provenance from
the Mantua collection and its gift to the pope, presumably Benedict XIV,
G. Magnanimi, 'Inventarii della collezione romana dei Principi Corsini',
Bollettino d'Arte 65 (1981), p 104

4   Bibliothèque Nationale, Bc folio II, pl 14 no 16, *cit.* Cocke 1973 note 56.
The *Study of Vigilance* in the Teyler Museum, Haarlem, which has an old
attribution to Battista Veronese, *see* Verona 1971 no 19, seems to be by
Benedetto rather than Battista del Moro to whom it is attributed; the imagery
reflects that of Veronese's work in the Sala del Collegio, completed after del
Moro's death in 1574

212   Copy after a Rest on the Flight into Egypt

213   Study of Hercules walking to the left

213   Study of Hercules walking to the left

Chalk on brown paper heightened with white
31 × 15.8 cm

LOCATION Rotterdam, Museum Boymans–Van Beuningen
    Inv. I45

INSCRIBED on the (renewed) verso: 'P: n.o 39'

PROVENANCE Anon. (Lugt 2103a; sometimes identified as the
    Borghese collection);[1] F. Koenigs (Lugt 1023a); acquired
    by D. G. van Beuningen in 1940

BIBLIOGRAPHY Cocke 1974 p 31 (Veronese); Pignatti 38
    (Veronese)

The drawing has a traditional attribution to Veronese which at
first I was prepared to accept. I now feel that the generalised
treatment of form, which is similar to that of the *Study of Venus
and Cupid* in the same collection (216), is very different from that
of Veronese's certain chalk studies;[2] the *Study of a seated man* (2)
the *Study of legs* on the verso (2v) and the later *Study for the
Portrait of a member of the Soranzo family* (77). The approach of
the unknown artist to his sculptural model, the Apollo Belvedere
seen from the side,[3] differs from that of Veronese himself in the
Studies of Mercury (11), where the pose is manipulated with
greater inventive freedom.

NOTES

1   Monte Carlo 1966 intro. The mark was, however, only added in the late
eighteenth century, *see* London, Sotheby 9 July 1981, 132

2   My doubts were prompted by the comments of Julien Stock and Philip
Pouncey

3   This view was often adopted in Renaissance prints. *See*, for example, the
engraving by Marcantonio Raimondi, Bartsch 14, p 249, nos 330–31, illustrated
by H. H. Brummer, *The Statue Court in the Vatican Belvedere* (Stockholm,
1970), pl 4

214 Study of a man seen from behind, study of a right arm with drapery   214v Study of a flag

214 Study of a man seen from behind, study of a right arm with drapery

214v Study of a flag

Black and white chalk on blue paper
29.5 × 18.7 cm

LOCATION Rotterdam, Museum Boymans-Van Beuningen
 Inv. I 94
INSCRIBED 'P. V'; on the verso: 'S. P.n.o 58', '582'
PROVENANCE Anon. (Lugt 2103a; sometimes identified as the
 Borghese collection);[1] F. Koenigs (Lugt 1023a); acquired by
 D.G. van Beuningen in 1940
BIBLIOGRAPHY Tietze and Tietze-Conrat 2079

Comparison of the present sheet with the *Study for the Portrait of a member of the Soranzo family* (77) from the 1570s underlines the heavier use of hatching and the failure to integrate the white heightening with the modelling, suggesting that, like the *Study of a seated man* in the same collection (215), this drawing is not by Veronese.

NOTE

1 Monte Carlo 1966 intro. The mark was, however, only added in the late eighteenth century, *see* London, Sotheby 9 July 1981, 132

215 Study of a seated man

Black and white chalk on blue prepared paper
27 × 21 cm

LOCATION Rotterdam, Museum Boymans-Van Beuningen
Inv. I95
INSCRIBED on the verso: 'P.n.o61'
PROVENANCE Anon. (Lugt 2103a; sometimes identified as the
Borghese collection);[1] F. Koenigs (Lugt 1023a); acquired by
D. G. van Beuningen in 1940
BIBLIOGRAPHY Tietze and Tietze-Conrat 2080

Like the closely related *Study of a man seen from behind* also in
Rotterdam (214), this interesting sheet is unlikely to be by
Veronese. This can be seen by a comparison with the *Study for
the Portrait of a member of the Soranzo family* (77) of the 1570s.

NOTE

1   Monte Carlo 1966 intro. The mark was, however, only added in the late
eighteenth century, *see* London, Sotheby 9 July 1981, 132

216 Study of Venus and Cupid

Black chalk heightened with white
29.2 × 16.4 cm

LOCATION Rotterdam, Museum Boymans-Van Beuningen
Inv. I44
INSCRIBED on the (renewed) verso: 'P:n.o 38'
PROVENANCE Anon. (Lugt 2103a; sometimes identified as the
Borghese collection);[1] F. Koenigs (Lugt 1023a); acquired by
D. G. van Beuningen in 1940
BIBLIOGRAPHY Cocke 1974 p 31 (Veronese); Pignatti 38
(Veronese)

The drawing has a traditional attribution to Veronese which I
once accepted but now feel cannot be sustained when it is
compared to other more certain chalk studies (2, 66, 73).[2] The
pose was developed from the *Venus Felix* in the Belvedere[3]
which formed the starting-point for the Venus and Cupid in the
centre of the *Studies of Mercury* in an English private collection
(11). In his rapid pen and ink sketch, Veronese projects the
forms in space and in the round, probably as a result of this use
of small-scale studio models, in a way beyond the skill of the
artist of the present sheet.

NOTES

1   Monte Carlo 1966 intro. The mark was, however, only added in the late
eighteenth century, *see* London, Sotheby 9 July 1981, 132
2   My doubts were confirmed by the views of Julien Stock and Philip
Pouncey
3   H. H. Brummer, *The Statue Court in the Vatican Belvedere* (Stockholm,
1970), pp 123–29

216   Study of Venus and Cupid

217   Study of the head of a woman (actual size)

217 Study of the head of a woman

Black and red chalk on bluish paper heightened with white
17.6 × 14.3 cm

LOCATION Stockholm, Nationalmuseum NMH 1463/1863
INSCRIBED 'P. Veron', '1279'; on the verso: '421 Aquito'
PROVENANCE Zaccaria Sagredo;[1] P. Crozat, perhaps his sale
　　Paris, Mariette 1741, part of 686; Count C. G. Tessin
BIBLIOGRAPHY Van Hadeln 1911 p 397; Tietze and Tietze-
　　Conrat 2265 (Zelotti); Verona 1971 no 55 (Zelotti); Ballarin
　　Arte Veneta 1971 pp 115 and 118 (Carletto); Bjurström no 8
　　(Carletto)

The Tietzes were right to doubt the old attribution to Veronese.
They rested their attribution to Zelotti on the drawing's supposed
resemblance to the *Virgin with St Anne and music-making angels*
in the Capitoline Galleries (Fig 91). This is implausible, but if
accepted would suggest an attribution to Gabriele Caliari, the
member of the workshop responsible for translating Veronese's
design (120) into the rather feeble painting in the Capitoline
Galleries.

Ballarin's attribution to Carletto is entirely convincing, although
the reason that he cites, the provenance from the Sagredo
collection, is utterly wrong.[2] The head is very close to that of the
Virgin in the *Adoration of the shepherds* from Ognissanti Treviso,
signed by the heirs[3] but prepared by Carletto in a drawing in the
Louvre.[4] It transposes the characteristics of Carletto's pen and
ink studies into a combination of chalks which reveals the
influence of the Bassani[5] and is very different from Veronese's
autograph chalk studies, that for an apostle (76), for instance.

NOTES

1　This was argued by Ballarin *Studi* 1971 esp. pp 138 ff on the basis of the
numbers which occur on the *Portrait of Paolo Paruta* now in the British
Museum Inv. 1946–17–13–23 which was established as coming from Sagredo
(1653–1729) by Jonathan Richardson, Junior

2　Sagredo's attribution of the *Portrait of Paruta* in the British Museum to
Carletto is much too late to carry conviction and was rightly ignored by the
Tietzes who gave it tentatively to Leandro Bassano, no 210

3　Pignatti A342

4　Inv. 4,686, Tietze and Tietze-Conrat 2181; in style it fits with the certain
drawings by Carletto notably the *Study of the Holy Family with Sts John the
Baptist and Catherine* (Fig 101), *see also* under (186) note 3

5　It is, though, very different in handling from both the *Portrait of Paolo
Paruta* in the British Museum and another group of heads formerly in the
Marignane collection attributed by Tietze and Tietze-Conrat to Leandro
Bassano, nos 233–42 but which Ballarin, *cit.* under note 1, and Rearick are now
inclined to give to Carletto, *see* most recently Christie 24 June 1980, 18

218 Study of a woman with a heron

Black chalk heightened with white
25 × 21 cm

LOCATION Stockholm, Nationalmuseum NMH 1382/1863
INSCRIBED 'Titien' (partly cut), '1200'
PROVENANCE P. Crozat, his sale Paris, Mariette 1741, 655
　　(Titian); Count C. G. Tessin
BIBLIOGRAPHY Tietze and Tietze-Conrat A2146; Pignatti A387;
　　Bjurström no 12 (attributed to Veronese)

The drawing has been related to the painting in Vienna whose
old attribution to Titian has been abandoned by some scholars in
favour of one to Veronese. The *pentimenti* in the heads, in the
angle of the head and in the lips suggest that it is a preparatory
sketch. The Tietzes, who recognised that the handling had
nothing to do with Veronese, argued that it would help with the
attribution of the painting. Pignatti attributed the canvas and
presumably the drawing (although he does not say so) to Fasolo,
and Bjurström attributed both to Veronese and suggested that
they could be early. Comparison of the drawing with the *Study
for the Portrait of a member of the Soranzo family* (77) shows that
it cannot be by Veronese and that it is unlikely to be a preparatory
sketch. The care with which the figure and the heron are
rendered, suggest that it is a copy. Even the curtain shown in the
background of the drawing can just be made out in the canvas,
an indication of the damage that it has suffered. The damage is,
I believe, one reason for the controversy about the attribution of
the painting.[1] Here the sitter is related to the canvas and her
head is characterised in the same way as in the *Portrait of a
woman with a handkerchief* in Munich, whose attribution to
Veronese has never been seriously doubted.[2]

NOTES

1　The picture has been cleaned since the publication of Pignatti's monograph.
This has revealed the details previously concealed by layers of varnish and
confirms the attribution to Veronese rather than to a follower or member of his
studio

2　Pignatti 173

220   Study of two men (actual size)

219   Studies of a Martyrdom of St Lawrence and of an Immaculate Conception of the Virgin

Pen and ink
19 × 27 cm

LOCATION Toronto, Heinrich
BIBLIOGRAPHY Birmingham, Alabama 1972 pl 42; Pignatti 114
cat 72

Pignatti related the drawing to the fresco of the *Martyrdom of St Sebastian* on the upper walls of S. Sebastiano, but the 1972 exhibition catalogue is closer to the mark in dating it *circa* 1585 or later. The elongation of the figures with no suggestion of plastic form, reveals a later artist perhaps influenced by Veronese's pen and ink sketches.

220   Study of two men

Pen and ink and wash
7.8 × 9.5 cm

LOCATION formerly Vermont, Wunder
PROVENANCE Emile Wolf; Richard Wunder, his sale London, Christie 7 July 1967, 176

The action of the present sheet is difficult to make out with the exaggerated torsion of the figures: one on the right appears to hold a club and to be placed on clouds while his companion flees (?) from the buildings behind. The freedom of handling is more extreme than that of late Veronese and suggests that this small sketch is by a follower.

221 Study of a landscape with shepherdess

Pen and ink
28 × 42.7 cm

LOCATION Vienna, Albertina Inv. 24365
BIBLIOGRAPHY Stix and Fröhlich-Bum no 42 (Titian); Paris
1975 no 60 (Veronese)

This fine drawing clearly fits with the type of landscape associated with Titian and Campagnola. If it is later it may well be by a Bolognese artist from the circle of the Carracci since it has nothing to do with Veronese's conception of landscape.

222 Study of the Madonna enthroned with four saints and a donor

Pen and wash
18.5 × 17 cm

LOCATION Vienna, Albertina Inv. 23161
PROVENANCE L. Zatzka (Lugt 2672); acquired in 1923
BIBLIOGRAPHY Stix and Fröhlich-Bum cat 107 (Veronese); Von
Hadeln pl 25 (Veronese); Tietze and Tietze-Conrat A2151 (a
follower); Venice 1961 cat 41 (Veronese)

In spite of the distinguished support for the attribution to Veronese since the drawing's acquisition in 1923, the doubts expressed by the Tietzes seem to me to be fully justified. Comparison with the *Studies of the Virgin and Child enthroned with saints* in London (7) reveals that the artist of the present sheet emulated the freedom of Veronese's drawings, without achieving his understanding of form. The standing saint on the very right of the sheet is similar to the standing man nearly in the centre of the *Studies* sold at Sotheby's (184), which is also by a follower of Veronese, influenced by Palma Giovane, possibly Alessandro Maganza.[1]

NOTE
1 It is similar to the *Pope granting a monk an audience* from the Rudolf collection, which was attributed to Alessandro Maganza by Stefania Mason Rinaldi, *Catalogue of Drawings by Jacopo Palma, called Il Giovane from the collection of the late Mr C. R. Rudolf*, London, Sotheby 4 July 1977, 41

223 Study of a kneeling saint and copy after Bocchi's Symbolicarum Quaestionum

Pen and ink and wash
14 × 14.7 cm

LOCATION Vienna, Albertina Inv. 27036
INSCRIBED 'KARDIA'
BIBLIOGRAPHY Stix and Fröhlich-Bum no 111; Tietze and
Tietze-Conrat A2155 (not Veronese); Cocke *Pantheon* 1977
p 122 and note 9 (Veronese)

Although there are analogies with Veronese's pen and ink sketches I now feel that the Tietzes were right to doubt the attribution to Veronese,[1] which had been suggested by Fiocco. The main sketch is a free adaptation of the 120th symbol of the *Symbolicarum Quaestionum de Universo Genere Libri Quinque* by Bocchi published in 1555. Hermocrates kneels in sacrifice before an altar decorated with a swan and heart, while an eagle, having snatched the heart from the dead ox, flies above the city which is being built in the background. In the drawing, Hermocrates has a more dynamic pose as he kneels in sacrifice, the decoration of the altar recurs in the sky above the flying eagle and part of the inscription is repeated under the architecture, all of which suggests a copy made from memory rather than from the book.

NOTE
1 These doubts are shared by Julien Stock and Philip Pouncey

224 Study of a bearded prophet

Black chalk and wash on blue paper
41 × 35.4 cm

LOCATION Windsor Castle, H.M. The Queen
INSCRIBED in another hand: 'Paulo Calliari VE'
BIBLIOGRAPHY Popham and Wilde no 1006

Popham rightly noted that the figure type was close to early Veronese, but was understandably cautious about the old attribution. The prophet is similar to the recently discovered *Astronomer*, now in Los Angeles.[1] The detail with which the shadow is built up and the insistence upon the silhouette achieve a powerful sculptural effect at odds with Veronese's painterly chalk studies and support the suggestion made in the Windsor catalogue that it is by a contemporary rather than Veronese.

NOTE
1 Pignatti 136; Pignatti is wrong to identify the cross held by his companion as a 'linear astrolabe'. He presumably means a cross-staff in which a transom ran to and fro along a five or six foot rod which was graduated to the degrees subtended, *see* the *Marriner's Mirrour* of 1588, reproduced as the frontispiece by E. G. R. Taylor, *The Haven-Finding Art* (London, 1956). This bears no relation to the object in the painting which is a cross with double arms that are turned up at the ends. Like the upward gaze this is intended to indicate the need for faith to supplement the astronomical skill of his companion with his astrolabe. A similar cross is held by the apostle in S. Sebastiano in one of the niches framing the organ, who looks towards the main altar, *see* Pignatti fig 181

Bibliography of frequently cited works

BACOU, R.
'Ten unpublished drawings by Veronese recently acquired by the Cabinet des Dessins du Louvre', *Master Drawings* 21 (1983), pp 255–63

BALLARIN, A.
'Considerazioni su una mostra di disegni Veronesi del Cinquecento', *Arte Veneta* 25 (1971), pp 92–118

'Introduzione a un catalogo dei disegni di Jacopo Bassano, II', *Studi di Storia dell' Arte in Onore di Antonio Morassi, Arte Veneta* (1971), pp 138–58

BARDI, G.
Dichiaratione di tutte le istorie, che si contengono ne i quadri posti nuovamente nelle Sale dello Scrutinio, e del Gran Consiglio (Venice, 1587)

BARTSCH, A.
Le Peintre Graveur 21 vols (Vienna, 1803–1821)

BAYONNE, MUSEE BONNAT
Les Dessins Italiens de la collection Bonnat, cat by J. Bean (Paris, 1960)

BIRMINGHAM, ALABAMA 1972
Veronese and his studio in North American collections (1972)

BJURSTRÖM, P.
Italian drawings, Venice, Brescia, Parma, Milan, Genoa, Nationalmuseum, Stockholm (Stockholm, 1979)

BORA, G.
I disegni del Codice Resta, Fontes Ambrosiani 56 (Milan, 1978)

BORENIUS, T.
Catalogue of the pictures and drawings at Harewood House and elsewhere in the collection of the Earl of Harewood (Oxford, 1936)

'A group of drawings by Paul Veronese', *Burlington Magazine* 38 (1921), pp 54–59

'Two Venetian Cinquecento drawings', *Burlington Magazine* 56 (1930), pp 104–107

BORGHINI, R.
Il Riposo (Florence, 1584; reprinted Hildesheim, 1969)

BOSTON 1968
Isabella Stewart Gardner Museum, *Drawings* ed R. van N. Hadley (Boston, 1968)

BYAM SHAW, J.
Drawings by Old Masters at Christ Church, Oxford (Oxford, 1976)

CHÂTELET, A.
'Deux dessins de Véronèse du Musée du Louvre', *Arte Veneta* 32 (1978), pp 220–22

COCKE, R.
'An early drawing by P. Veronese', *Burlington Magazine* 113 (1971), pp 726–33

'Veronese and Daniele Barbaro: the decoration of Villa Maser', *Journal of the Warburg and Courtauld Institutes* 35 (1972), pp 226–46

'A preparatory drawing for the "Triumph of Mordechai" in S. Sebastiano', *Burlington Magazine* 114 (1972), pp 322–25

'Observations on some drawings by Paolo Veronese', *Master Drawings* 11 (1973), pp 138–50

'New light on late Veronese', *Burlington Magazine* 116 (1974), pp 24–31

'Veronese's *Omnia Vanitas* and *Honor et Virtus post Mortem Floret*', *Pantheon* 35 (1977), pp 120–25

'Three fragments from Villa Soranza', *Mitteilungen des Kunsthistorischen Institutes in Florenz* 21 (1977), pp 211–18

'Veronese's independent Chiaroscuro drawings', *Master Drawings* 15 (1977), pp 259–68

COHEN, C.E.
  The Drawings of Giovanni Antonio da Pordenone (Florence, 1980)

DE BARCIA, A.M.
  Catalogo de la collección de Dibujos Originales de la Biblioteca Nacional (Madrid, 1906)

DEGENHART, B.
  'Eine Zeichnung des Paolo Veronese', *Münchner Jahrbuch der Bildenden Kunst* 6 (1955), pp 207–12

DEUSCH, W.R.
  'Ein unbekanntes skizzenblatt von Veronese', *Pantheon*, 26 (1968), pp 295–96

DE VECCHI, P.
  L'opera completa del Tintoretto (Milan, 1970)

DOBROKLONSKY, M.B.
  Drawings of the Italian school of the XV–XVI centuries. Catalogues of the collection of the Hermitage, I (Moscow, 1940)

DRESDEN, STAATLICHE KUNSTSAMMLUNGEN
  Zeichnungen alter meister aus der Ermitage (Dresden, 1972)

FLORENCE 1976
  Galleria degli Uffizi, *Tiziano e il Disegno Veneziano del suo Tempo* cat by W.R. Rearick (Florence, 1976)

GATTINONI, G. ed.
  Inventario di una casa Veneziana del Secolo XVII (La casa degli eccellenti Caliari eredi di Paolo il Veronese) (Mestre, 1914)

GIBBONS, F.
  Catalogue of Italian Drawings in the Art Museum, Princeton (Princeton, 1977)

HADELN, D.F. VON
  Venezianische Zeichnungen des Spätrenaissance (Berlin, 1926)

JOACHIM, H. and McCULLAGH, S.F.
  Italian drawing in the Art Institute of Chicago (Chicago, 1979)

KOENIGS, F.
  Meisterzeichnungen aus der Sammlung Franz Koenigs, ed. M.J. Friedlander, Vol II Venezianische Meister, cat by D.F. von Hadeln (Frankfurt, 1932)

LONDON 1965
  Agnews, *Art historians and critics as collectors* (London, 1965)

LONDON 1977
  Agnews, *Old Master Drawings from Holkham*, cat by C. Whitfield (London, 1977)

LONDON 1948
  Arts Council, *Old Master Drawings from the collection of the Earl of Leicester*, cat by A.E. Popham (London, 1948)

LONDON 1952
  Colnaghi, *Old Master Drawings* (London, 1952)

LONDON 1953
  Colnaghi, *Old Master Drawings* (London, 1953)

LONDON 1956
  Colnaghi, *Old Master Drawings* (London, 1956)

LONDON 1959
  Colnaghi, *Loan exhibition of drawings by Old Masters from the collection of Dr. and Mrs. Springell* (London, 1959)

LONDON 1962
  Colnaghi, *Old Master Drawings* (London, 1962)

LONDON 1931
  Royal Academy, *Italian drawings exhibited 1930*, cat by A.E. Popham (London, 1931)

LONDON 1958
  Royal Academy, *The Paul Oppé Collection* (London, 1958)

LONDON 1960
  Royal Academy, *Italian Art and Britain* (London, 1960)

LONDON 1969
  Royal Academy, *Old Master Drawings from Chatsworth* (London, 1969)

LONDON 1973
  Victoria and Albert Museum, *Old Master Drawings from Chatsworth*, cat by J. Byam Shaw (London, 1973)

LUGT, F.
  Les Marques des collections de dessins et d'estampes (Amsterdam, 1921), *Supplément* (The Hague, 1956)

MACANDREW, H.
  Catalogue of the Collection of Drawings, Ashmolean Museum, Oxford, Volume III Italian Schools: Supplement (Oxford, 1980)

MALKE, L.
  Italienische Zeichnungen des 15. und 16. Jahrhunderts, Städelsches Kunstinstitut (Frankfurt, 1980)

MANCHESTER 1965
  City Art Gallery, *Between Renaissance and Baroque*, cat by F.G. Grossmann (Manchester, 1965)

MARIETTE, P.J.
  Description sommaire des desseins des grands maistres d'Italie, des Pays-Bas et de France, du cabinet du feu M. Crozat (Paris, 1741)

  Abécédario . . . et autres notes inédites de cet amateur sur les arts et les artistes. Ouvrage publié par Ph. de Chennevières et A. de Montaiglon 6 vols (Paris, 1851–60)

MEDER, J.
  'Weitere Venezianische Zeichnungen der Salzburger Studienbibliothek', *Graphische Künste* 56 (1933), p 25

MONGAN, A. and SACHS, P.J.
  Drawings in the Fogg Museum of Art (Cambridge, Mass., 1940)

MONTE CARLO 1966
  Palais des Congrès, *Catalogue de l'exposition de dessins italiens de la collection H. de Marignane*, cat by G.A. Caviggiolo (Monte Carlo, 1966)

NEUMAN, J.
The Picture Gallery of Prague Castle (Prague, 1967)

NEW YORK 1965
Metropolitan Museum of Art, *Drawings from the New York collections I: The Italian Renaissance*, cat by J. Bean and F. Stampfle (New York, 1965)

OBERHUBER, K. and WALKER, D.
Sixteenth Century Italian drawings from the collection of Janos Scholz (National Gallery of Art, Washington and Pierpont Morgan Library, New York, 1973)

OEHLER, L.
'Eine Gruppe von Veronese Zeichnungen in Berlin und Kassel', *Berliner Museen* 3 (1953), pp 27–36

PARIS 1962
Institut Néerlandais, *Le Dessin Italien dans les collections Hollandaises* (Paris, 1962)

PARIS 1965
Musée du Louvre, *Le Seizième Siècle Européen; Dessins du Louvre* (Paris, 1965)

PARIS 1967
Musée du Louvre, *Le cabinet d'un grand amateur, P.-J. Mariette, 1694–1774* (Paris, 1967)

PARIS 1975
Musée du Louvre, *Dessins Italiens de l'Albertina de Vienne* (Paris, 1975)

PARIS 1978
Musée du Louvre, Cabinet des Dessins, *Collections I; Dessins de la collection Everard Jabach* (Paris, 1978)

PARIS 1977
Orangerie, *Collection de Louis XIV, dessins, albums, manuscrits* (Paris, 1977)

PARIS 1965–66
Petit Palais, *Le Seizième Siècle Européen. Peintures et dessins dans les collections publiques Françaises* (Paris, 1965–66)

PARKER, SIR K.T.
Catalogue of the Collection of Drawings, Ashmolean Museum, Oxford, Volume II Italian Schools (Oxford, 1956)

PIGNATTI, T.
Veronese, L'Opera Completa (Venice, 1976)

PLUCHART, H.
Musée Wicar; Notice des dessins (Lille, 1889)

POPHAM, A.E.
Catalogue of the drawings in the collection formed by Sir Thomas Phillipps Bart., F.R.S., now in the possession of his grandson T. Fitzroy Phillipps Fenwick of Thirlestaine House, Cheltenham (London, 1935)

POPHAM, A.E. and WILDE, J.
The Italian drawings of the XV and XVI centuries in the collection of His Majesty the King at Windsor Castle (London, 1949)

RIDOLFI, C.
Le Maravaglie dell' Arte (Venice, 1648), ed. D.F. von Hadeln, 2 vols (Berlin, 1914–24)

ROBINSON, J.C.
Descriptive catalogue of Drawings by Old Masters forming the collection of John Malcolm (London, 1876)

ROSAND, D.
'An early chiaroscuro drawing by Paolo Veronese', *Burlington Magazine* 108 (1966), p 421
'Three drawings by Veronese', *Pantheon* 30 (1971), pp 203–210

SCHOLZ, J.
Italian Master Drawings from the Janos Scholz collection (New York, 1976)

SCHWEIKHART, G.
'Paolo Veronese in der Villa Soranza; materialen zur rekonstruktion der ausmalung und zum verlieb der abgenommen fresken', *Mitteilungen der Kunsthistorischen Institutes in Florenz* 15 (1971), pp 187–207

SINDING-LARSEN, S.
Christ in the Council Hall, Studies in the Religious Iconography of the Venetian Republic, Institutum Romanum Norvegiae Acta ad Archaelogiam et Artium Historiam Pertinentia 5 (1974)

STIX, A. and FRÖHLICH-BUM, L.
Beschreibender Katalog der Handzeichnungen in der Graphischen Sammlung Albertina; Die Zeichnung der Venezianischen Schule (Vienna, 1926)

STOCKHOLM 1962–63
Nationalmuseum, *Konstens Venedig*, cat by P. Bjurström (Stockholm, 1962–63)

STOCKHOLM 1966
Nationalmuseum, *Christina Queen of Sweden* (Stockholm, 1966)

TIETZE–CONRAT, E.
'Decorative painting of the Venetian Renaissance reconstructed from Drawings', *Art Quarterly* 3 (1940), pp 15–39

TIETZE, H. and TIETZE–CONRAT, E.
The Drawings of the Venetian Painters in the 15th and 16th Centuries (New York, 1944)

TIETZE, H.
'Nuovi disegni veneti del Cinquecento in collezioni americani', *Arte Veneta* 1 (1948), pp 56–66

VASARI, G.
Le Vite de' piu eccelenti pittori, scultori ed architettori . . . (Florence, 1568), ed. G. Milanesi (Florence, 1878–1906) (*cit.* as Vasari) and Club del Libro (Milan, 1962) (*cit.* as Vasari 1962)

VENICE 1939
Ca' Giustiniani, *Mostra di Paolo Veronese*, cat by R. Pallucchini (Venice, 1939)

VENICE 1957
Fondazione Giorgio Cini, *Disegni Veneti della collezione Janos Scholz*, cat by M. Muraro (Venice, 1957)

VENICE 1958
Fondazione Giorgio Cini, *Disegni Veneti di Oxford* (Venice, 1958)

VENICE 1961
Fondazione Giorgio Cini, *Disegni Veneti dell' Albertina di Vienna*, cat by O. Benesch and K. Oberhuber (Venice, 1961)

VENICE 1964
Fondazione Giorgio Cini, *Disegni Veneti del Museo di Leningrado*, cat by L. Salmina (Venice, 1964)

VENICE 1965
Fondazione Giorgio Cini, *Disegni Veneti del Museo di Budapest*, cat by I. Fenyö (Venice, 1965)

VENICE 1966
Fondazione Giorgio Cini, *Disegni di una collezione Veneziana del Settecento*, cat by A. Bettagno (Venice, 1966)

VENICE 1976
Fondazione Giorgio Cini, *Disegni di Tiziano e della sua cerchia*, cat by K. Oberhuber (Venice, 1976)

VENICE 1979
Fondazione Giorgio Cini, *Disegni Veneti dell' Ambrosiana*, cat by U. Ruggeri (Venice, 1979)

VENICE 1980
Fondazione Giorgio Cini, *Disegni Veneti di Collezioni Inglesi*, cat by J. Stock (Venice, 1980)

VERONA 1971
Museo del Castelvecchio, *Disegni Veronesi del Cinquecento*, cat by T. Mullaly (Venice, 1971)

WASHINGTON 1974
National Gallery of Art, *Venetian Drawings from American Collections*, cat by T. Pignatti (Washington, 1974)

WOLTERS, W.
'Der Programmentwurf zur Dekoration des Dogenpalastes nach dem Brand von 20 Dezember 1577', *Mitteilungen des Kunsthistorischen Institutes in Florenz* 12 (1965/66), pp 271ff

Photograph acknowledgements

I am grateful to the owners, both public and private, both for supplying photographs and for granting permission to reproduce.

Reproduced by gracious permission of H.M. the Queen Figs 53, 66, 67

Reproduced by permission of the Trustees of the British Museum, London 7, 24, 28, 70, 72, 87, 106, Figs 26, 106, 107

Reproduced by permission of the Chatsworth Settlement Trust 15, 16, 35, 62, 75, 165

Reproduced by permission of the Governing Body, Christ Church, Oxford 117, 199

Reproduced by permission of the Trustees of the National Gallery, London Figs 34, 45, 46, 47, 48

Reproduced by permission of the Réunion des Musées Nationaux, Paris 4, 5, 12, 19, 23, 25, 31, 33, 36, 41, 42, 54, 63, 65, 71, 81, 84, 107, 108, 113, 127, 148, 149, 150, 151, 152, 153, 202, 203, 205, 206, 207, 209, 210, Figs 10, 18, 20, 25, 27, 68, 71, 92

Other photographs and transparencies were supplied by

Alinari Figs 2, 3, 13, 24, 29, 49, 63, 91

M. Brandon-Jones Figs 12, 26, 78, 89, 93, 111

Christie's 8, 138, 220

Sarah Cocke 3, 13, 57, 79, Fig 105

Colnaghi 30, 137, 180

A. C. Cooper 70, 75, 106

Courtauld Institute of Art 39

J. R. Freeman 122

Instituto di Storia dell' Arte, Fondazione Giorgio Cini 43, 44, 49, 50 (by kind permission of Larissa Haskell), Figs 40, 69, 70, 86

Knoedler Gallery 20

Kunsthistorisch Instituut der Universiteit van Amsterdam 157, 158 (by kind permission of the late Professor J. Q. van Regteren-Altena)

W. B. Pollard Fig 38

Professor David Rosand 1

Scala Istituto Fotografico Editoriale, Florence 14, 131

Soprintendenza alle Gallerie, Venice Figs 4, 5, 6, 7, 8, 11, 32, 35, 36, 39, 51, 64, 81, 88

Sotheby's 2, 52, 55, 61, 67, 76, 77, 96, 99, 105, 112, 114, 135, 139, 140, 141, 142, 143, 144, 145, 181, 184, 185, Fig 94

Staatgemäldesammlung, Stuttgart 64

Warburg Institute Fig 19

Indices

NOTE numbers refer to catalogue entry not to page;
page references to introduction are indicated in bold

Index of locations of drawings by, or attributed to, Veronese and his school, including rejected attributions

Subject index of drawings by, or attributed to, Veronese and his school including rejected attributions

Index of previous owners and of sales of drawings by,
or attributed to, Veronese and his school,
including rejected attributions

Index of paintings by, or attributed to, Veronese

General Index